UNDERSTANDING MASS MEDIA

UNDERS
MASS
MEDIA

ANDING

_____
Third Edition
_____

JEFFREY SCHRANK

 NATIONAL TEXTBOOK COMPANY • Lincolnwood, Illinois U.S.A.

Cover Acknowledgments

Top left: courtesy of the *Chicago Tribune; top center:* Brian Seed, Click/Chicago; *top right:* Milt & Joan Mann.

Middle left: Joan Liftin, ARCHIVE Pictures Inc.; *middle center:* National Textbook Company

Lower center: Milt & Joan Mann.

PREFACE

It's too bad this book wasn't written a few thousand years B.C. Back then an edition could last a thousand years before it would need revision. This edition revises one made only a few years ago.

To put communication into perspective, imagine that the history of human communication could be compressed into one 24-hour period. The day started at midnight; and there was language. Darkness gave way to dawn and around eight in the morning a crude painting appeared on a cave wall. The morning passed with no further communications revolutions; afternoon was equally uneventful. It is now sunset; speech and a few scratchings on caves are the sole means of communication.

Around 8:00 at night it happens. The year is 4000 B.C., the place is Sumeria, the event is the invention of writing. In other words, we humans have spent five-sixths of our history without the written word. Writing itself is a mere newcomer on the stage of history.

Night in human history shows signs of activity. Forty minutes after the Sumerians, the Egyptians devise hieroglyphics and the alphabet makes its debut around 9:30. Homer's *Iliad* is written at 10:00.

But what of the media revolution? Day's end is near.

Gutenberg's *Bible* appears with only 20 minutes left in the day. But what a 20 minutes! The telegraph appears at 11:53 and the telephone a mere two minutes later. Five minutes left! The phonograph sneaks in with the day well over 99 percent complete. Now every second counts.

11:55:47 Thomas Edison shows a movie in his Black Maria.

11:56:48 A few hundred people huddled around radios in Pittsburgh hear the first public radio broadcast.

11:57:04 A movie called *The Jazz Singer* startles audiences with the sound of a human voice.

11:57:52 An obscure device called a transistor is invented only 12 seconds after the first computer.

11:58 Color television is introduced.

This edition of *Understanding Mass Media* was printed at the stroke of midnight. It deals with the last two minutes of the day. Think of it as a history book covering 120 seconds. Since you began reading this Preface, a new technology was invented somewhere that will make its mark at 11:59:59.

CONTENTS

LIST OF MEDIALABS

LIST OF READINGS

INTRODUCTION

A medium is merely a channel or system of communication. Speech is the most widely used medium. Other media (*media* is the plural of medium—there are no ''mediums'') include painting, sign language, music, the printed word, or even smoke signals.

Some media have developed into systems that can reach masses of people in a very short time. Because of this ability, media such as television, radio, newspapers, and film are commonly called mass media. Today, one person with access to mass media can reach several hundred million people in a matter of hours.

But imagine that same person two thousand years ago. He or she might speak to a crowd the size of one that would attend a major league baseball game today. But how would the crowd hear the speech without electric amplification? The speaker depended on relays in the audience who would stand up and echo the message to a few hundred people further away. Each relay person would in turn be relayed by another echo, and so forth, until the back row finally heard the whole speech. In the days before electricity and printing presses, this system of human messengers was as close to a mass medium as existed. In medieval towns, a town crier would wander the streets announcing the latest rulings of the king.

In other words, truly MASS media did not exist until the Modern Age. As recently as 75 years ago, there was no truly mass medium. Although there were more newspapers then, few had large circulations. There was no network radio or television. In fact, 75 years ago a large percentage of Americans were illiterate in English. Mass media required almost universal literacy before it could exist.

When did mass media begin? There are no universally agreed upon answers, but certainly the development of network radio in the late 1920s qualifies as a major turning point in mass media.

How many people a mass medium has to be able to reach to deserve the label ''mass'' has never been determined. A telephone, for example, is not considered a mass medium even though a battery of phones could be used in a day to reach thousands of people. Amateur shortwave radios can reach large numbers of people at one time but are not a mass medium since they are normally used to enable people to talk to each other. Mass media all share the characteristic of one-way communication. Mass media enable a few people to communicate with the masses but do not allow the masses to communicate with the few. Mass media are one-way streets.

Yet to be perfected is a means of communication that would allow the president of a country, the mayor of a city, the manufacturer of a new car, or the artist to communicate with a vast number of people and quickly receive their reactions. Until such a medium is perfected we have to settle for our present one-way system of mass media. Because media do not allow us to talk back (with the very limited exception of letters to editors, radio phone-in shows, etc.), it is important to learn the special techniques of media persuasion. The absence of a real voice to talk back to those who speak through mass media makes the critical study of their messages essential.

In this book we will learn what mass media teaches and what language it uses to speak. We will consider all mass media to be educational and will examine them to determine what is being taught. The language of each medium will also be considered so that the ability of the media to deceive will be minimized.

Past ages are often known by some major force that dominated the lives of the people who lived then—the Ice Age, Feudal Age, Industrial Revolution, the Age of Discovery, and so forth. Historians of the future may look back on the 1980s and label it the Media Age. Time-use studies have shown that the average high school student has spent more time with mass media (TV, movies, radio, records, books, magazines) than with any other single activity except sleep.

Personal Media Inventory

We live in an environment partially shaped by the opinions, sights, sounds and values presented by mass media. To obtain some idea of the importance of media, analyze your own time and money use with the ''Personal Media Inventory'' on this page. Answer the questions on a separate sheet of paper and compare your answers with those of others. Compile all the answers to arrive at a class average: for example, ''the average student in this class spends x hours a week watching television.''

1. How much money do you spend in one year (estimate) on:

    Books
        (a) for school
        (b) for other reading
    Magazines and comic books
    Movies at theaters
    Records, tapes

    Videotapes, video discs
    Equipment (TV, radios, tape
       and record players, etc.)

2. How much time in a typical week (estimate) do you spend on these activities?

    Watching television
    Listening to radio
    Watching movies (not on TV)
    Reading comics and magazines
    Reading newspapers
    Reading books
    Listening to records
       or tapes (not on radio)

Multiply each of the time figures above by 52 to determine the amount of time you spend with mass media each year. Realize that your answer will be approximate. Take this approximate figure and use it to determine about how many years of your lifetime will be spent in the company of mass media.

Project Teams

Some of the projects in this book require a period of several weeks to gather information. These projects are best assigned to project teams early in the course. A project team consists of three students who are responsible for preparing a class presentation on some media-related topic. If the teams are formed now, they will have enough time to prepare the reports and present them during the course.

The presentations can be made near the end of this course or, if possible, scattered throughout the course at appropriate times. Each report should last at least 30 minutes and should include examples and demonstrations using the medium under study.

POSSIBLE TOPICS FOR PROJECT TEAMS

1. Any topic about mass media that a group of three students wishes to research and present to the class. Teacher and/or class approval might be required.

2. The role of women or men as portrayed on television, both in shows and in commercials.

3. The role of women or men as presented in advertisements.

4. Find, select, and order the short films for use in the chapter on film. This team should work with the teacher and/or school media director.

5. Arrange for various guest speakers and tours during the course.

6. Do a research project on one heavily advertised product category (e.g., mouthwash, headache remedies, toothpaste). Find out the main competing brands; write down the advertising claims for those products; find out who makes the products and what they contain. Run tests where possible to see if the products satisfy their advertised claims. Write to the manufacturers and ask them to back up their claims.

7. Explain and demonstrate videotape equipment.

8. Study the image of law enforcement officers on television. Analyze how they are presented on TV and compare this with reality.

9. Study the image of any of the following as presented on television: doctors, the elderly, teenagers, or criminals.

10. Design a Personal Media Inventory Questionnaire asking the same questions as the inventory on page x and give it to your parents. Compare the totals of the student inventory for the entire class with those of the parents.

11. Arrange for two local media experts (a TV or radio announcer, station manager, filmmaker, advertiser, etc.) to appear before the class to explain their work and answer questions.

12. Collect as many different magazines as possible for the class to use during the study of magazines in Chapter Seven. Use the local library to obtain the names and addresses of a variety of magazines. Obtain at least one copy of fifty or more different magazines. The magazines can be acquired by requesting a sample copy from the publisher or by buying copies through the mail or from a newsstand.

13. Conduct a detailed study of all the local news outlets (radio, newspaper, TV). Compare them by pointing out their strengths and weaknesses. Present your comparison to the class.

14. Present a history of popular music in the United States complete with taped excerpts from records. The presentation should take an entire class period and should point out how music has changed and some of the reasons for the changing tastes of the record-buying public.

15. Present a history of the comic book. Use the local library as an information source. Perhaps a local comic book collector will provide some examples of old comic books. The presentation should attempt to explain the changes in comics over the years and relate them to changing tastes and events in American history.

16. Present a report on television as a means of two-way communication. The report should explain how cable television is being used in some communities as a means of polling public opinion, shopping by video, and even paying bills.

17. Present a report on cable television in your area as it exists today. If it does not yet exist, report on plans in progress and what decisions must be made before your area can be wired for cable.

Chapter 1
TELEVISION

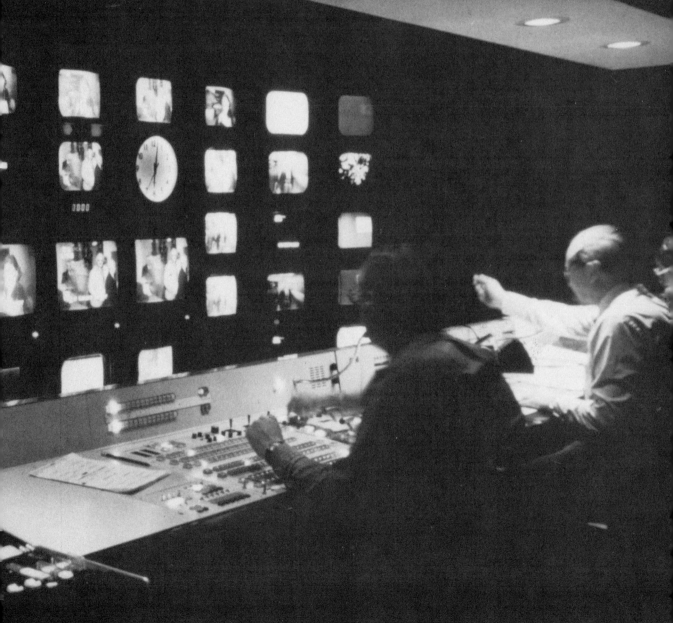

TV: Beneficial or Harmful?

Some people say that television is the greatest invention of the twentieth century. Others claim it is a drain on valuable time, an evil influence on the nation. There are those who blame television for teaching violence and inviting young viewers to imitate criminals and gun-slinging heroes. There are those who say that TV turns people into passive vegetables able to do little more than sit and watch the tube. Still others see television as history's most effective educator, bringing the wonders and knowledge of the world into the homes of even the poorest citizens. Such education, they point out, was once available only to the very wealthy who could afford travel and the best schools. Children today seem to know much more about the world than their parents and grandparents did at the same age. Many educators give television some of the credit for this increase in knowledge.

When asked for their opinion of television, some people answer that TV is a harmless pastime that provides an escape from the troubles of daily life; while others argue that it presents a dangerously unreal picture of the world. The arguments rage on, and for every convincing statement about the harmfulness of TV there is an equally compelling

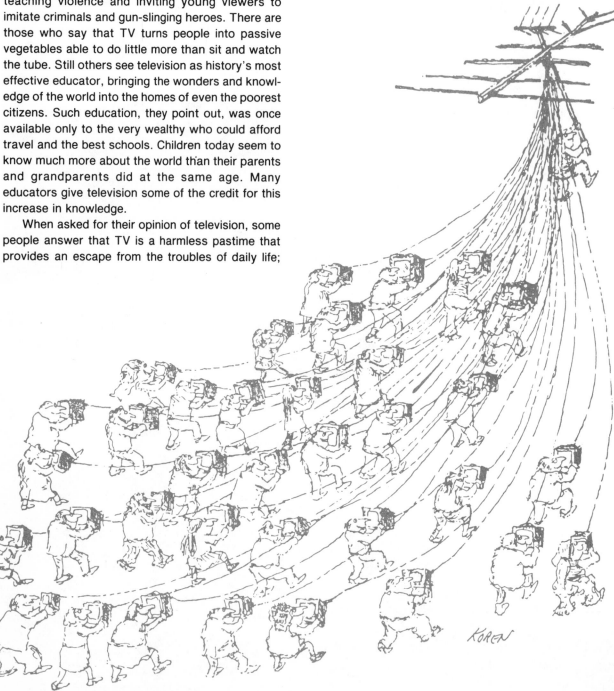

KOREN

argument about its benefits. Television is a controversial subject—but one on which everyone must take a stand. That glass-windowed box sitting in almost every household in the land demands a daily decision. To watch or not to watch, that is the decision. And each time that decision is made, a person reveals what values are important.

It is clear that as a nation we have long since decided that watching television *is* an important activity. Ninety-eight percent of American homes have at least one TV set (a percentage higher than for homes with indoor plumbing). The average set is on for seven hours a day, and most children begin regular watching by the time they are two or three years old. Studies show that the typical 16-year-old has spent as much or more time in front of the TV set as in school. The average American watches television 52 hours a week. Women watch more than men (weekly average is 33 hours for women ages 35-54 and 28 for men), and the less educated watch more TV than the more highly educated. In a lifetime, the average American will have spent almost nine years in front of the television set.

KOREN

There is no doubt that we consider television important. There is hardly an American who does not have a strong opinion about television. You probably have an opinion about television, though perhaps you haven't stopped to think about it. Take some time now and write your opinion in about 50 words. Begin with "I think television is. . . ." Do not give your opinion of any particular program on television; rather evaluate television as a mass medium. When you have finished, sign your paper and hand it in. You will need to use it later in this chapter.

After the opinions are written and collected, discuss the advantages and disadvantages of watching television. You might do this by listing on the board "good points" and "bad points" about television.

After the discussion of existing opinions, continue with this chapter. It deals with five important questions:

1. How does the television system work?

2. What kinds of programs succeed?

3. How would life change without television?

4. What does television teach?

5. Who should have access to television time?

I think
Television is...

TV QUIZ

Here is a test you can take to see how much you already know about the workings of commercial television in the United States. The correct answers are given on the following pages. Take the test before reading beyond this page, note your answers on a separate piece of paper, and check them as you read on.

1. TRUE FALSE Some large cities have as many as ten VHF stations from which to choose.

2. TRUE FALSE The three networks (CBS, NBC, ABC) own most, but not all of the TV stations in the country.

3. TRUE FALSE Television stations are subject to more government control than newspapers.

4. TRUE FALSE Newspapers are public servants; however, television stations are established mainly to provide entertainment.

5. TRUE FALSE One television network is supported, in part, by taxpayers' money.

6. TRUE FALSE TV stations are owned by the Federal Communications Commission but operated as private businesses for a profit.

7. TRUE FALSE There are more newspapers than television stations in the United States.

How Does the Television System Work?

There are currently about 1,194 television stations in the country. This is a small number in comparison to the 8,000 radio stations and about equal to the number of daily newspapers. Television stations operate on channels 2–13 (VHF) and channels 14–83 (UHF). Adjacent VHF channels (2 and 3, or 7 and 8, for example) in the same city could interfere with each other and so are usually separated by an unused channel. This means that even large metropolitan areas have only about five VHF (*Very High Frequency*) stations. UHF (the *Ultrahigh Frequency*) has many more channels available but is still in the early stages of development. UHF stations have a smaller coverage area than VHF stations because of the higher frequencies on which they operate. Since they reach fewer people, such stations are not as attractive to advertisers. Currently they tend to be smaller stations with smaller audiences than VHF.

VHF stations operate on frequencies similar to those of FM radio stations (in fact, TV sound is FM) and can therefore reach only an area in a 50–100 mile radius from the transmitting tower. If you had a TV set that could tune between channels 6 and 7, you could listen to local FM radio stations on the TV set; FM radio could be considered channel 6½.

Cable television is not really a mass medium. Only homes or apartments wired to the station can receive the programs. Cable television operates like a telephone except that instead of just sound, pictures and sound are transmitted over the wires.

Broadcast television sends pictures over the airwaves; anyone with a set can tune in. Of course, this limited reception could change if the whole country becomes "wired" for cable. For now, when we speak of television, we mean broadcast television. We will treat cable TV in greater detail in Chapter Twelve.

Television stations are privately owned businesses just like newspapers, radio stations, or publishing companies. Unlike these other communications industries, however, television stations are licensed by the Federal Communications Commission (FCC) to serve the "public interest." Every three years a station's license must be renewed, and to keep its license, the station must prove that it has served the public.

According to court-supported decisions, the channels belong to the people. TV stations are licensed to use those channels only to serve the public in their viewing area. If any person or group can prove that a station has not served the viewing public, then that station could lose its license. For instance, stations are required by the FCC to provide fair coverage of important local issues. In theory, a TV station that broadcasts only network shows and old movies could lose its license for failure to treat local issues. In practice, the FCC has refused license renewals only a few times since the beginning of television.

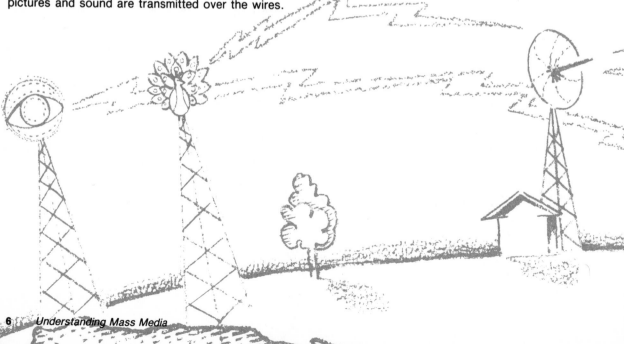

Eighty-five percent of all television stations are affiliated with (but not owned by) one of the three major networks—Columbia Broadcasting System (CBS), American Broadcasting Company (ABC), and National Broadcasting Company (NBC). The most profitable stations are generally those affiliated with these three commercial networks. A TV station that does not belong to a major network is either an independent or a member of the Public Broadcasting Service (PBS). Independent stations as a rule mainly show old movies, local sports, and reruns of TV shows from a few years ago. PBS stations, sometimes called "educational TV," carry cultural and educational programming. PBS is supported by a Congressional grant of money, by foundation donations, and by contributions from viewers. PBS is the only network that does not carry advertising.

Networks are not television stations; they do not broadcast programs. They supply programs to the local television affiliate by using specially rented television lines. Each local TV station is ultimately responsible for its own programming. A station can refuse to broadcast a network-supplied program but rarely does so. Networks supply local stations with programs for the morning (morning news, game shows), the afternoon "soap operas" (so called because they were originally sponsored by the soap companies), evening news, and night-time programs. Local stations must fill in with their own programming (usually movies, local news, or reruns) when the networks do not supply programming.

The networks provide programs to the affiliates free and are paid for the advertising time they can sell during the program. A 30-second "spot" commercial in network "prime time" (the desirable evening hours) sent to all the network affiliates in the country can cost an advertiser thousands of dollars per second. A 30-second spot on the first TV showing of a major movie can cost well over $300,000. The exact cost depends on how popular the program is that the ad interrupts; the more viewers, the higher the cost.

A small amount of time during each program is left for the local station to sell to local advertisers. This advertising constitutes the main source of income for local stations. Local stations also receive some of the money their network receives for national commercials.

Networks obtain their programs either by making them on their own (news and documentaries), by covering live events (special news events, sports), or by purchasing the programs from producers. Most prime-time programs and weekly programs are supplied to the networks by producers. The producers (or sponsors of an event such as the National Basketball Association or the National Football League) receive money from the networks, the networks receive money from national advertisers, local stations receive money from local advertisers.

The three major networks compete with each other to attract the most viewers. The number of people who watch each program is measured by rating systems, particularly the one developed by A. C. Nielsen Company. Nielsen ratings are used to determine advertising rates and can spell life or death for programs or series.

What Kinds of Programs Succeed?

Television programs serve to gather an audience for the commercials. For this reason there has been surprisingly little change in programming since the beginning of television. Networks tend to stick with what has worked in the past.

When a certain type of program proves successful on one network, the other two often rush to produce a similar one. This "success copying" accounts for the waves of popularity in certain types of shows from season to season. One season medical shows may be popular; the next, ethnic humor or dramas about rural families; the next, police stories or westerns.

Most commercial TV programming can be placed in one of the following categories:

News and documentaries
Sports
Movies
Music/Variety shows
Westerns
Crime shows
Talk shows
Quiz and game shows
Soap operas
Situation comedies
General and family dramas

MEDIALAB

Televiewing

1. How does the amount of television watched by people in your class compare with the national average? Determine some method to measure accurately the TV viewing of class members. (Assume that people cannot accurately answer the question "How much television do you watch?")

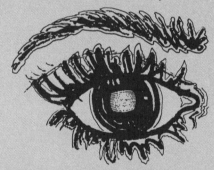

2. Why do you think women tend to watch more TV than men? Why do those with more schooling watch less TV than those with less schooling?

3. With which networks are your local channels affiliated? Are there any "independents?" Who owns them?

4. Why do you think newspapers are not licensed by the government but radio and television stations are?

5. Form teams to inspect the "public file for license renewal" at each local TV station and report on what that file contains.

6. Why do you think such a large percentage (85%) of stations are affiliated with one of the three major commercial networks?

7. Report on the history of television broadcasting in the United States.

8. Arrange a tour of a local television station.

9. Look in your local TV listings or in a magazine such as *TV Guide* and determine whether a program is provided by a network or by the local station.

10. Find out how much advertising time costs on local television stations. Your library may be able to supply a copy of the *Standard Rate and Data Service* book giving spot TV information.

11. Either by yourself or in a group prepare a report on the rating systems used to determine which programs are watched the most. Write to A. C. Nielsen Company and ask for their literature on the rating system.

12. Which category of programming listed on page 8 is currently the most popular?

13. Find some current examples of "success copying."

14. Sports programs are among the most successful and profitable television presentations. Discuss how television has influenced sports in the United States. Consider how television has helped sports; whether television encourages or discourages adults from participating in sports; whether watching sports on TV might replace watching them in person (football games in the future played in empty stadiums and videotaped for later broadcast just like any other TV show); and which sports are most and least successful on television.

MAINLINING SOAPS

No one knows before a show is broadcast how many viewers it will attract. Very few series last more than three years; many are cancelled after a year or less. One of television's most profitable, long-lived, and dependable type of broadcasting is the soap opera. The functioning of soap operas reveals quite a bit about television in general. Soap operas are morality plays in miniature; they are quite important to those who watch regularly.

The following article reveals much about television in its behind-the-scene examination of the world of soap operas. A student of television must study what is typical of television rather than what is exceptional. Some teachers will encourage or even assign students to watch educational specials, believing that this is television at its best. But in this study of TV programming, it is more revealing to look at typical programming, and nothing is more typical than the soap opera.

The Allure of Daytime Television Drama

by Stephen West

Soap operas have large, devoted audiences. It is profitable, dependable broadcasting. Why do so many people watch? Here are some answers.

Every weekday morning at 10:30, the first of 16 soap operas broadcast daily by the three major networks appears on between four and five million television screens across the country. By one o'clock in the afternoon, when the networks are simultaneously offering ... soap operas, recent Nielsen ratings show that over 13 million American homes (or about 21%) are being filled with the sights and sounds of this particular form of entertainment.

Why is this so? Why do the networks broadcast programs which almost everyone, including the viewers, seems to think are so terrible? And, more to the point, why do so many people go ahead and watch these shows anyway? The most obvious answer is that there's not much else on the air during the daytime, except for the game shows. But this can hardly be the com-

plete answer; for in spite of the fact that it's hard to find someone who will admit to watching soap operas regularly, much less *enjoying* them, there is a good deal of evidence that we have millions of covert soap opera freaks living in our midst.

These people may say they would rather watch something else, something "better." It is, after all, a common assumption that soap operas are trivial, silly, a waste of time. But I'm not convinced. I do not believe that anything which can command such religious devotion from so many people is a trivial phenomenon. That quality of addiction, of some need which must be satisfied, deserves a serious examination.

The networks' reason for offering these programs is quite simple: they make a lot of money at it. Along with the game shows, the other main program format

for daytime broadcasting, the soap operas are the most profitable part of the television business. Although audience size—and thus, advertising income—is perhaps one-third the size of a nighttime show, the production costs of games and soaps may run only *one-tenth* as much as the expensive prime time offerings. According to one industry source, "On the average soap opera today, we make back the production expenses for the whole week on the first day, Monday. So Tuesday through Friday's advertising is pure profit for the network. Or to put it more dramatically: for every dollar of profit which CBS makes at night, they make seven dollars of profit in the daytime. If there were no daytime, there would be no network."

... But this need to keep production costs low has important limiting effects on daytime television. The number of hours to be filled with *something* is more than twice as great as during the evening. For the 9:00 a.m. to 6:00 p.m. period, each network must come up with 45 hours of material every week, not counting Saturday and Sunday. Every year, the number of daytime half-hour slots to be filled approaches 4,700. No wonder the networks resort to formula programming.

Soap operas are cheap because you can produce one every day with the same basic personnel and facilities. On "As the World Turns," for example, everything is shot in one studio, on four sets erected from a total pool of 29. Every day, the cast comes in early in the morning for several hours of rehearsals and technical preparations. Blocking, camera angles, cutting, sound, pacing—everything is finalized, so that when 12:30 rolls around, this four act playlet is ready to be broadcast live to an audience of almost ten million people. Unlike "As the World Turns," however, most soap operas are not, in fact, broadcast live, but are produced by a method known [as] "live on tape." In this case, the episode which is recorded on videotape today will be broadcast a few days from now. The pressure of a live performance still remains, though, because "you don't stop that tape and waste money by starting over unless an actor literally drops dead on the set," according to one technician.

After the day's performance, the crew begins work on erecting a new group of sets, while the actors and director spend the afternoon reading through the next day's script. That evening, the cast must memorize their lines for a new half-hour epi-

sode, since the whole cycle starts again the next morning. With this kind of production schedule—compared to the week required to make an evening program, or several months for a two-hour movie—the mere fact that a coherent, reasonably polished performance can be pulled off every day is an awesome feat.

Because of these technical constraints, soap operas resemble the legitimate theater more than nighttime television or films: they are rougher, more spontaneous, more uncertain. Most are produced in New York, because Broadway has an unending supply of actors trained to memorize large sections of dialogue and to cover mistakes by improvisation in an ongoing performance, while Hollywood does not. Without background music and with relatively little cutting from scene to scene within an "act," soap operas project an intimate, almost documentary feeling, as if you're observing a few minutes of real time in some real people's lives. Somehow the clanking of forks against plates comes through much more clearly in an eating scene; the pauses, the coughs, the uncertain glances aside, all the seams in an interaction remain unclosed in these programs. They have a flatness, a looseness which resemble the tone of everyday life and which is very different from the more frenetic, tight, "flawless" productions on prime time.

Around the studio for a soap opera, everyone is concerned with only two things: maintaining a reasonable level of technical polish and keeping the Nielsen ratings high. They simply have no time to consider the

broader implications of what they're doing, beyond delivering a certain number of viewers to the sponsor and thus earning a living for themselves. A question about how they think their program may be influencing its viewers will be met by a blank, puzzled stare. Hopefully, they think, the viewer will be influenced to buy the sponsors' products and to tune in the program again tomorrow; but beyond that, who cares what the viewer thinks?

The actors, director, and technical crew for a soap opera are the implementors of the script, and the pace of their job is so relentless they can hope for little more than avoiding disaster. Their chances of improving the script, of creatively enlarging its meaning through their craft, seems to be rather limited, except insofar as an actor is able to clarify the personality of his character, bit by bit, over a period of months or years. And even here the opportunities are limited. There just isn't enough time to do much more than learn your lines.

The scriptwriter himself, the creator of what seems to be the substantive core of the series, is also plagued by many of these same problems of time pressure. The language of the script is no more smooth or coherent than the acting, but the scriptwriter is responsible (along with the producer) for making choices about the plot as well as the dialogue. And it is the plot—the concrete actions which the characters make, the incredible problems which they must confront—which keeps the viewer hooked to the program.

According to Robert Shaw, a soap opera scriptwriter for over

Soap operas project an intimate feeling, have large devoted audiences, and are filmed daily on sets such as this scene in progress from ''The Young and the Restless.''

20 years and a man who probably knows as much about the genre as anyone in the business, there are basically two parts to writing a successful series: creating major characters—especially including the heroine—for whom the viewer can feel empathy, and working out a complex, disaster-laden, but finally optimistic plot. Soap opera viewers . . . are overwhelmingly female; the men who watch daytime television, on the other hand, greatly prefer the game shows. (Eight of the top ten programs watched by women are soaps, while nine of the top ten watched by men are games.)

Thus, Mr. Shaw explains, "The key to daytime serials is empathy. If we can't build empathy in a character, we haven't got a show. Empathy means, in a way, identifiability, likeability

. . . and this hasn't changed since the first ones on the radio 45 years ago. There is a theory—which I believe, to a considerable extent—that women tune in soap operas to watch someone who has more misery than she does. It makes you feel good to discover that somebody else has it worse. We have found, by trial and error over the years, that one of the things that's almost impossible to do is to make a sympathetic character out of a rich woman. . . ."

The leading women, for this purpose of building empathy, are generally young, attractive, and stylish, but they still retain a good bit of that small town Protestant modesty which is so much a part of almost every soap opera series. (Consider the names of the mythical, generally Midwestern towns where the

action normally takes place: Shadyside, Sunnyview, Oakville, etc.) "The ideal soap opera heroine," Shaw says, "is a woman's image of herself, which is not necessarily the truth. It's how she *thinks* of herself. A woman can be flopping around the house in a flannel bathrobe, with her hair in curlers, doing the ironing. She sees my heroine doing the ironing in a $400 tailored suit, and somehow she transfers, she thinks that's the way she looks."

In Shadyside, moreover, it is the women who are running the show, according to their own domestic set of values. It is a world of weak men and strong women, a world in which the housewife heroines know that the important things in life are *interpersonal*, not material, and certainly not political. . . .

The implicit message of all soaps, both during the show and during the commercials as well, is that any problem can be solved. Things may be pretty messed up these days, but the system is basically sound. . . . I hardly need to add that the sponsors of these programs have enormous vested interests in the *status quo,* in the maintenance of American housewives' optimism.

The problems which beset a soap opera heroine, and they are many and varied, basically fall into two overlapping categories: the disruption of health and the disruption of social/sexual relations. According to Robert Shaw, cancer . . . is probably the single best problem a writer has at his disposal for beefing up his ratings. "Of course, murder is always good, provided you murder someone the viewer cares about," Shaw says. "It has to be one of the main character's favorite brother or sister or uncle, somebody who can hold the viewer's attention for quite a while. And, of course, this is a good way to write out an actor who's leaving the show . . . Then there's infidelity, which is almost basic to *all* serials."

Disease is a common problem in the soaps because it's something everyone can identify with, an irrational threat beyond one's control. In Shadyside, if not in the rest of the world, disease is democratic: it can strike anyone, regardless of position. The doctor is held in great esteem here because, unlike most other professions, he is intimately connected to the domestic world of bedrooms, children, house calls. (Where else, except on television, do doctors still make house calls?)

Various kinds of psychological problems have recently become standard themes for these programs. Child psychology and the problems of the "disturbed child" are especially big these days, along with runaway children, amnesia, . . . drug addiction, you name it. In the social/sexual disruption category, there are still more possible disasters. . . . And finally, says Shaw, "If you're really stuck, you can always bring in the Bad Sister, the one nobody's heard from for years. That's tried and true, along with the in-laws as heavies, and what to do with your invalid parents. There's really no end to the possibilities."

Through all of these problems, of course, the heroine maintains her basic optimism. She lives in a totally uncertain world, but her faith in the idea that her problems will eventually be solved is never in doubt. For the viewer, this one certain feature of the program changes its entire character; it becomes like a mystery story, . . . in the sense that the final outcome is never in doubt. The interest in the story exists in means, not in ends, and this is why the viewer's appetite for more and more can never be satiated. A soap opera is an open-ended narrative form, like folk legends or our experience of our own lives. Were it to end, it would cease existing entirely.

By definition, there is no end to a soap opera, unless it gets taken off the air. "As the World Turns" has been churning along now for over [25] years, and it's just as superficially uncertain and basically predictable as it ever was. "I am absolutely convinced," Robert Shaw says,

"that there is some relief in watching these serials . . . I think the viewer feels better after having watched, for the very reason that she's seen someone more miserable than she is. Also, our women *do* solve their problems: cancer *is* curable, husbands *do* come back . . . We're selling hope, really, and it's not much more specific than that. We stay away from the problems of the country, we'd never mention a depression or the stock market." Then he adds, wistfully, "They live apart from it, really."

Finally, in spite of all the personal problems which living in Shadyside inevitably entails, most viewers would probably be glad to exchange their own lives for those of the soap opera's characters. There may be a lot of problems, yes; but boredom and loneliness are not among them, and these are clearly what the viewers suffer from most. At least the characters in a soap opera have engaging, crucial problems in their lives, not an endless stream of minor frustrations and indignities, like broken washing machines, dirty dishes, and screaming kids.

The soaps open up the viewer to another world where things seem to matter. At least they provide the viewers with gossip material for times when they run short on other subjects. I have a feeling there are millions of little networks of friendships in this country based on arguing the merits of a soap opera heroine's latest move, on filling each other in on the details of a missed episode, on trying to second-guess what the scriptwriter will do next week. And given the viewer's entrapment, this is probably better than nothing. ■

MEDIALAB

The Soaps

1. If your class meets while a soap opera is scheduled on any of the networks, be sure to watch and discuss at least one episode.

2. In 1971 and 1972 M. L. Ramsdell and other researchers at Rollins College watched 600 hours of soap operas and concluded that one of the messages the soaps teach is that "the good life can be achieved by anybody who is a white male professional or a white female who marries the professional and subsequently becomes a mommy." Is this message still being taught by the soaps today?

3. Why do you think soap operas are so popular?

4. Explain in your own words how the acting, camera work, and sets of soap operas are different from those in nighttime dramatic shows.

5. What would happen if the soaps were shown at nighttime instead of during the day? In answering this question consider how the daytime and nighttime audiences differ.

6. Talk with someone who watches soap operas regularly. Try to find out why that person watches them and why certain ones are favorites.

7. Why do soap operas rely so much on tragedy and disaster in their plots?

8. Do you think soap opera characters are believable and real?

9. How is programming influenced by the need for the networks to make a profit?

10. Stephen West, author of the article on soap operas, says that "A soap opera is an open-ended narrative form, like folk legends or our experience of our own lives." Explain this in your own words.

11. Soap operas can easily be criticized by those looking for high dramatic art, but they are a unique form of drama. What does a soap opera offer in terms of plot and character that no other plays, movies, or books supply?

12. Stephen West quotes scriptwriter Robert Shaw as saying, "The key to daytime serials is empathy." Explain empathy and why it is so important to the success of soap operas.

13. What prime-time shows might be considered "nighttime soaps"? In what ways do they borrow from the soap opera formula and in what ways are they different?

Life Without Television

One way to measure how television influences the way we live would be to find a community (perhaps a town of at least 1,000) where people are *not* exposed to television. We could watch these people very closely to see how their lives are different because of their lack of television. But finding such a community is nearly impossible, for there is hardly a place in the United States that is without television. Even in the most remote and mountainous areas at least 90 percent of the households have television. Since there is no city that would suit our experiment in tubelessness, perhaps we could look for 1,000 average people who don't watch television. But since these people are such a minority, they can hardly be considered average. To measure the effect of television is indeed difficult precisely because television has become so much a part of ordinary life in America.

One experiment in the absence of television was conducted in Germany, where 184 volunteer television viewers were paid to give up TV for one year. At first the volunteers reported that they spent more time with their children, went to movies more frequently, read and played more games, and visited friends and relatives more than they did before they gave up television.

But within a few weeks things began to change. Even though the people were paid not to watch, one man dropped out after only three weeks. No one lasted more than five months. Why? Tension, fighting, and quarreling increased among families without television. When the experiment was over and the television sets were back on, these effects disappeared.

Television is like a drug. Habitual viewers are addicted to television and need their daily fix in order to get along. When television is not available, the addicted become nervous, restless, and irritable.

MEDIALAB

How TV Influences the Way We Live

1. The experiment described on the preceding page took place in Germany. Do you think the results would be any different if it were conducted in the United States?

2. How do you think your family would react to such an experiment?

3. What positive aspects of television did this experiment reveal?

4. Why did tension, fighting, and quarreling increase within the TV-less families? The psychologists who conducted the experiment made an educated guess at the answer. Stop and think of your own reasons before reading any further.

One of the psychologists who conducted the experiment believes that watching TV tends to cover up conflicts and disagreements between habitual viewers. That is, instead of working out problems, people avoid them by watching TV. TV works as sort of a buffer between people, helping them to be together without having to work out their conflicts. Take away the TV set and the rough edges begin to show.

5. Write a very short fictional story describing what happens "The Day Television Disappeared." Base your story on the unlikely happening of huge sunspots or some other unknown phenomenon that wipes out all television reception in the world. Your story should tell what might happen when people discover what has happened and then how things might change without television. You might want to include in your account some of the effects of TV on the following: family life, movie attendance, libraries, newspaper and book reading, sports, advertising, radio programming.

6. Recall the last time the family TV set broke down. How long was the set out of order? Take a survey in the class and find the average number of days or hours the set remained out of order. (If a family has more than one TV, the answer should be about the main set, the one used most often.) What does the class average say about the importance of television?

7. Find someone in the class who either does not have a TV or who lives in a family where someone almost never watches TV. Find out from that person why he or she does not watch TV. What is the extra time spent on instead?

8. One of the undeniable effects of television is that it takes up a lot of time. The "average" person watches TV for six to eight years during a lifetime. If TV were to vanish, a lot of extra time would be available to do other things. How might people be different if they had this extra time to fill? How would you spend your time if you had no TV?

9. Talk to one or two people who remember the days before television. Ask them how they think television has changed family life and the way people spend their time.

10. Television is a rather recent invention. Imagine an invention that could capture the public's interest and time as much as television has. Would it be like television or something very different? How would it change people's lives?

What Does Television Teach?

If you were to interview people selected at random and ask them, "What did you learn from television this past week?" the answers would probably fall into two categories. One common answer would be "nothing." People would say they didn't watch any TV the past week or they would think that you were asking about educational television which they didn't watch. The other common answer would be from people who would tell you something they learned from a newscast, a documentary, a special, or some program on the educational channel.

But there is another kind of *teaching* that television provides. Even the advertising and the entertainment programs on television teach—they teach what products are acceptable to use and what products promise to bring happiness. They present images of what the police are like and what kind of people are criminals. They teach how rich people live and what a happy family looks like. Television shows nice things—cars, furniture, houses, clothes—and presents them so that they appear desirable, even

necessary. Thus, people want the "good life" they see on television and allow TV to shape their desires. Television teaches how people supposedly live, talk, dress, and behave. Television programming helps make the products advertised in the commercials appear necessary or desirable.

This kind of "learning" is difficult to detect. If all television is educational, we must ask what kind of education this "School of the Tube" provides. Does television present a realistic picture of the world or does it show only fantasies and fiction?

George Gerbner is a television researcher who constructed a test to measure the kind of education provided by television. Before explaining what he found, take the test yourself. The test on the next page is a simplified version of Gerbner's test. Write the answers on a separate sheet of paper. At the top of the paper, before you begin the test, write the estimated number of hours you watch TV in an average week.

TELEVISION & YOUR WORLDVIEW

1. What percent of the world's population lives in the U.S.? (a) 1% (b) 5% (c) 10% (d) 15% (e) 20%

2. What percent of American workers are in law enforcement jobs? (a) ¼% (b) ½% (c) 1% (d) 2% (e) 5%

3. What are your chances of being the victim of a serious crime this year? (a) 1 in 100 (b) 2 in 100 (c) 3 in 100 (d) 5 in 100 (e) 10 in 100

4. What percent of the victims of crime are under 30 years old? (a) 70% (b) 55% (c) 40% (d) 25% (e) 10%

5. What percent of the victims of crime are black? (a) 70% (b) 55% (c) 40% (d) 25% (e) 10%

6. What percent of married women work at jobs outside the home? (a) 60% (b) 50% (c) 30% (d) 20% (e) 10%

7. What percent of U.S. workers are employed in managerial or professional jobs (white collar)? (a) 5% (b) 10% (c) 15% (d) 20% (e) 25%

8. What percent of workers have jobs in professional athletics or entertainment? (a) ¼% (b) ½% (c) 1% (d) 2% (e) 3%

(Answers and scoring system on page 35.)

Your teacher or test scorer will take the papers and arrange them into piles according to the amount of TV viewing reported. The papers should be grouped in four piles according to number of hours watched: 0–3 hours per week; 4–7 hours; 8–11 hours; and more than 11 hours a week. Then find the average test score for each group. The higher the test score, the more inaccurate a view the person has of the world and U.S. situation. The lower the test score, the more accurate and realistic the view. As a class, draw some conclusions from the results.

In giving this test to adults, Gerbner found that people who watch a lot of television tend to overestimate the percentage of world population made up of Americans much more than do light TV viewers. He found that heavy viewers also overestimate the number of people employed as professionals or managers. In general he found that the more hours people watched television, the more inaccurate were their answers to the questions (the higher their test scores). Those who watch a lot of TV are much more likely to fear they will be the victims of a crime than those who watch little TV. What explanations can you offer for these findings?

1. The original TV test found that people who watch the most television have the least accurate idea of what the real world is like. Other polls have shown that the answer most people give to the question "Where do you get most of your information about the world?" is "Television." How can you explain both these findings?

WHO me WATCH TV?

2. The same experimenter who composed the test found that people who read newspapers frequently (even if they also watched a lot of TV) were much more likely to choose correct answers. What does this finding say about both newspapers and television?

3. Can you conclude from this test that "watching television makes people stupid"?

4. What types of programs give viewers a *more* accurate picture of the world?

5. Examine the chart on page 21, "Percent of Household TV Usage per Day." What does the graph show as the national pattern of television viewing? Why do you think that is the case every year?

6. According to the "Percent of Household TV Usage per Day" graph, at what two hours of the day does television have the largest audience?

7. Examine the graph on page 21, "Hours of TV Usage per Week by Household Characteristics." How is the amount of time spent viewing TV influenced by:
    (a) household size?
    (b) household income?
    (c) availability of cable?
    (d) the presence of children?

8. Graphs give only numbers, not reasons. Discuss why and how household size, income, and the number of children influence television viewing.

9. The graph shows that more people were watching television in July than in February. Why do you think that is the case every year?

TV VIEWING STATISTICS

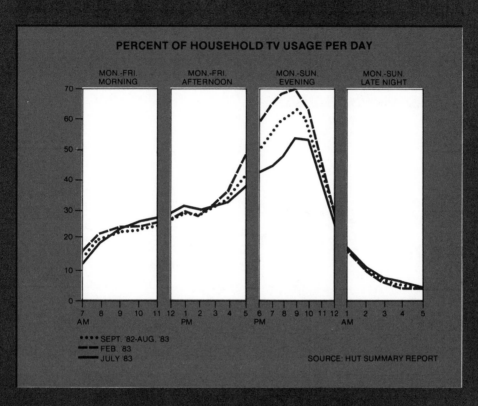

PERCENT OF HOUSEHOLD TV USAGE PER DAY

MON.-FRI. MORNING MON.-FRI. AFTERNOON MON.-SUN. EVENING MON.-SUN. LATE NIGHT

•••• SEPT. '82-AUG. '83
——— FEB. '83
——— JULY '83

SOURCE: HUT SUMMARY REPORT

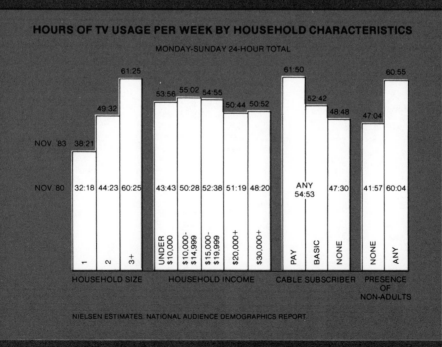

HOURS OF TV USAGE PER WEEK BY HOUSEHOLD CHARACTERISTICS

MONDAY-SUNDAY 24-HOUR TOTAL

NOV. '83

	61:25						61:50				60:55
49:32		53:56	55:02	54:55				52:42			
38:21					50:44	50:52			48:48	47:04	

NOV. '80

| 32:18 | 44:23 | 60:25 | 43:43 | 50:28 | 52:38 | 51:19 | 48:20 | ANY 54:53 | | 47:30 | 41:57 | 60:04 |

| 1 | 2 | 3+ | UNDER $10,000 | $10,000-$14,999 | $15,000-$19,999 | $20,000+ | $30,000+ | PAY | BASIC | NONE | NONE | ANY |

| HOUSEHOLD SIZE | HOUSEHOLD INCOME | CABLE SUBSCRIBER | PRESENCE OF NON-ADULTS |

NIELSEN ESTIMATES: NATIONAL AUDIENCE DEMOGRAPHICS REPORT

TV in the News

The test results of researcher George Gerbner suggest that television viewing and a highly accurate picture of the world do not go together. Sometimes the teaching television does is very obvious and can be seen in small news stories. Here is a sort of scrapbook of news stories related to the teaching done by television. Read the stories and attempt to draw some further conclusions about the educational effect of television.

TV film on air pollution starts panic in Germany

Agence France-Presse

BONN — A particularly realistic television film on atmospheric pollution started a wide-scale panic among West German viewers when it was screened Sunday night.

The film, directed by Wolfgang Menges and titled "Smog," showed the catastrophic situation which could be brought about by a saturation of carbon dioxide in Dortmund, a city in Germany's heavily industrialized Ruhr district. It showed children asphyxiated, people struck down on the streets and traffic brought to a complete halt.

After the film was shown, telephone switchboards at the television station were practically blocked. One man asked how to save his children, while another asked how to get gas masks.

In Dortmund, the biggest blast furnace in Europe had to slow down production two weeks ago because of the pollution hazards when it was going full blast.

RANCHO CORDOVA, May 31 [UPI]—Two teenage gunmen surrendered to

police today after a tense, seven-hour drama in which they held more than 20 persons hostage in a suburban bank, received a $1 million ransom, and appeared on television to tell their story.

The hostages—most of them women and children —all were released unharmed.

Michael D. Madigan, 18, and Brian James Young, 19, walked out of a suburban shopping center bank surrounded by more than 50 deputies, agents of the Federal Bureau of Investigation, and police after they were promised they could watch themselves on television.

Coroner's Jury Blames Alice Cooper Stunt For Boy's Self-Hang Death

Calgary, Alta, June 25.

A Calgary boy's death by hanging in March resulted from his attempt to imitate a mock-hanging performed by a rock music star during a television program, a corner's jury has ruled.

The jury, investigating the death of 14-year-old David Andrew Coombs, ruled it accidental and called for banning of television programs which depict simulated hanging or similar violent acts. This was a reference to a program seen by the youth on the Canadian Broadcasting Corp. network in which rock star Alice Cooper performed his hanging stunt.

Dr. John Butt, a pathologist, told the jury that youthful experiments with hanging have been "widely reported" among adolescent boys recently, and he suggested public attention should be called to what he termed "this dangerous practice."

Coroner Dr. W.M. Wilson said he had called the inquest to bring the practice to public attention to "let youngsters know how lethal this can be."

The boy's father told the inquest his son and daughter saw the television hanging routine and afterward the boy was heard to tell his sister it was just a trick he could do himself.

After seeing the show, the jury was told, the boy attended a party where several youngsters emulated the mock hanging act.

Gorillas going ape over television

By William Hines
Sun-Times Bureau

WASHINGTON—In some quarters it might be considered cruelty to animals, but the keepers of the nation's largest collection of great apes have started letting their anthropoid charges watch television during the day.

Public-spirited citizens and business firms in Atlanta contributed 19 TV sets to the Yerkes Primate Research Center at nearby Emory University after an appeal by Yerkes' director, Dr. Geoffrey H. Bourne.

The 136 gorillas, chimps and orangutans were getting bored, Bourne explained, and TV seemed to be the answer. By all indications,

Bourne said in a telephone interview, the experiment is a huge success.

One of the apes, a chimp named Dobbs, was a ready-made TV fan by virtue of two six-month stays in the home of a woman in Santa Barbara, Calif. He got hooked on Westerns—the more violent the better, Bourne said.

"Dobbs can even tell the bad guy," Bourne related. "He associates the bad guy with violence, and sometimes he starts jumping up and down even before the bad guy starts anything rough."

Lest anyone doubt the effects of TV on impressionable minds, Bourne told of one occasion when an animal show depicted two chimpan-

zees making a shambles of the inside of a house.

"Next day Dobbs tore up his room," Bourne said.

Except for the veteran tube-boob, Dobbs, the primate colony hasn't been exposed to TV long enough yet to develop tastes in entertainment. Nor are the animals allowed to sit up till all hours watching the box, as a questioner learned when he asked Bourne if they had watched President Nixon and the three commentators on Wednesday night.

"I don't think so," he said, "We usually just let them watch from 9 to 5."

TV serves a useful, humane purpose when it is necessary to isolate the animals for long periods to conduct metabolic tests, Bourne

explained. "They're locked away by themselves sometimes for months at a time and get terribly lonely," he explained. "We feel that TV is a real contribution here."

Bourne was asked whether the center uses closed-circuit TV or videotape machines to document activities or to entertain the animals by allowing them to see themselves as others see them. He said funds weren't available for such equipment but that he would be more than delighted to accept it as a gift if offered.

"We'd like to be able to run tapes and films of our own choosing," Bourne said without elaborating on the type of TV fare he would offer his charges if he were in charge of programming.

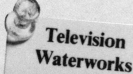

Television Waterworks

When the Super Bowl is on, the workers at Chicago's largest water pumping station can tell how massive the viewing audience is simply by charting pumping pressures at the plant. During the game, the water pressure will be down. At half time, it suddenly builds up tremendously. "That's about the time that the beer drinkers flush their toilets," explains chief engineer Bob Powers.

Employees at all the city water plants have to watch the game to anticipate the sudden demand. Extra power is necessary to lift tons of water from Lake Michigan to replenish the supply.

"You can tell when there's a blockbuster movie on television," says Powers. "There's always a big demand for water during commercials on the Sunday play-offs, for the Miss America Pageant, for the World Series, and other TV highlights."

Lost boy survives on berries, cacti

FLAGSTAFF, Ariz., Oct. 16 [UPI]—A California teenager survived for five nights in wild country by eating berries and cactus pulp as he had seen television cowboys do, and licking the morning frost from leaves and logs. John Shubin, 16, of Whittier, was found beside a highway Monday by a tourist. "He is in surprisingly good condition for the ordeal that he's gone thru," said Coconino County Sheriff Joe Richards. Shubin lost 17 pounds.

Murders set in fit of passion

REDDING, Cal., May 21 [Reuters]—Gerald Bishop was so angry because the San Francisco Giants lost a baseball game he pumped 17 rifle bullets into his television set.

The bullets went thru the walls of his mobile home and penetrated a house 300 yards away.

Lula Jorgenson, in her 70s, was sitting quietly at home knitting, but fled in panic when bullets began whizzing round her room.

After his arrest, Bishop asked Policeman John Grimes: "Haven't you ever wanted to shoot your TV set?"

Opinions by Cartoon

Another view of the effects of television is sometimes seen in satirical cartoons. Take a look at the cartoons on these pages and discuss what statement about television they make. Do you agree or disagree with each viewpoint? Make a cartoon of your own that shows your opinion of television.

"KID'S ESPECIALLY LIKE THIS MODEL... IT DOESN'T HAVE AN 'OFF' SWITCH!"

MEDIALAB

What TV Teaches

1. Many of the news stories describe how TV inspires people to imitate what they see. Do you think these cases are rare or rather common?

2. Can you recall imitating TV characters or shows when you were younger? Do you see your smaller brothers and sisters doing that today?

3. If you believe that TV does encourage certain kinds of behavior, do you think it encourages good or bad behavior? What kinds of actions does it encourage most?

4. Do you think that television is specifically to blame for the fact that some people may imitate what they see and hurt themselves or others? Might something else influence them just as strongly? Or is TV's impact unique?

5. One news story is about a film on air pollution that started a near panic in Germany. Could something like that happen in the U.S.? Did it ever happen in the days before television?

6. Consider television as a kind of educational system, a sort of informal school of the airwaves. What lessons in living does regular commercial TV teach?

7. What opinion about television is expressed in each of the cartoons?

8. Why do you think there are more cartoons drawn and published that are critical of TV than cartoons that point out the advantages of television?

9. Draw your own cartoon about television. If you don't want to draw, use cut-outs or photographs.

BLOOD ON THE TUBE:

The Violence Question

The critics of television often point an accusing finger at television's role in teaching about violence. Perhaps you already have an opinion on the question of whether or not television encourages violent behavior.

How much violence is presented on television programs? Perhaps you believe that the make-believe violence does not affect viewers. The slambang fights and wild chases that take place in cartoons may seem harmless, but researchers have found various effects on children. On the following pages one person presents a strong argument that *TV violence is harmful.*

" IT'S BLOOD!! "

TV VIOLENCE *IS* HARMFUL

by Jesse L. Steinfeld, M.D.

Dr. Jesse L. Steinfeld has been a professor of medicine at the University of Southern California and an official of the National Institute of Health. He has also served as Surgeon General of the United States.

Every day some 40 million American children ages two through eleven tune into their family television sets for an average of 3½ hours of watching. By age 12, they total an estimated average viewing time of 13,500 hours apiece—far more than double the time they spend in the schoolroom. In the process, they will have watched 101,000 violent episodes, including an estimated 13,400 deaths.

What is the effect of all this television mayhem on our young people? Consider these recent findings:

• At the University of North Carolina Child Development Center, researchers recently paired ten preschoolers who had similar television and play habits. Then, over an 11-day period, one child was shown a violent Saturday-morning television offering, while his partner watched a nonaggressive show. The five exposed to violent programming became remarkably more aggressive, some even tripling their violent acts (kicking, choking, hitting, pushing), while their mates' scores remained largely unchanged.

• Two Penn State researchers carefully recorded the level of physical and verbal attacks among 92 kindergartners, then divided them into three groups to watch different half-hour television films over a four-week period. One group saw "Superman" and "Batman" shows, each containing several physical and verbal assaults. A second group saw "Mister Rogers' Neighborhood," whose puppet vignettes teach youngsters how to cope with anger, jealousy, fear and frustration. As a control, the third group saw neutral shows. Among children who had measured initially low in aggression there wasn't a significant response one way or another. Children from the lower socioeconomic backgrounds who saw "Mister Rogers" improved strikingly in cooperation, obedience to rules and daily relations with others. However, among those who were above average in aggressiveness—fully half the total—exposure to the violent films caused a sharp increase in their attacks on playmates.

• In 1959, New York Department of Mental Hygiene researchers evaluated both television-violence viewing and aggressive behavior of 184 third-grade boys. In a follow-up study of the same group ten years later, they discovered an astonishing long-term effect. "Regardless of whether the individual's behavior at age eight was combative or nonaggressive, if he watched high levels of television violence he was likely to rank high in aggression ten years later," concludes Dr. Monroe Lefkowitz, the senior researcher.

• Survey teams studied 2900 junior- and senior-high-schoolers and 1500 graduates from almost 100 schools throughout the nation. In each group the researchers found a correlation between television-violence viewing and a wide range of troublemaking behavior.

Research Proves the Point. These studies—and scores of similar ones—make it clear to me that the relationship between televised violence and antisocial behavior is sufficiently proved to warrant immediate remedial action. Indeed, the time has come to be blunt: We can no longer tolerate the present high level of televised violence that is put before children in American homes.

Many citizens and parents have long fretted over the impact of television on our youth. Therefore, in March 1969, Sen. John O. Pastore (D., R.I.), chairman of the Senate communications subcommittee, asked that the Surgeon General create a Scientific Advisory Committee on Television and Social Behavior to determine "what harmful effects, if any, these programs have on children." Three years later, the work of hundreds of scientific investigators, spelled out in 2500 pages of studies, left no doubt that televised violence adversely affects our younger generation. Dr. Robert M. Liebert, State University of New York expert in imitative learning and child development, best summarizes the researchers' findings: "We have impressive evidence that watching television violence causes a significant increase in aggressive behavior. It is not the only or even the most significant cause of antisocial behavior, but it certainly is one of the major contributors. It also happens to be one cause we *can* change."

The high level of violence is truly appalling. For six years, Dean George Gerbner, of the University of Pennsylvania's Annenberg School of Communications, studied violence levels on all three networks. The combined output contained incidents of physical force intended to hurt or kill at a rate of about eight per hour. And cartoons—the mainstay of children's programming—averaged 22 such incidents hourly.

Indifference to Harm. Gerbner's study is supported by Boston University Prof. F. Earle Barcus. In 1971, Barcus monitored all the Saturday children's programs of his city's three network stations and one UHF independent. He found 71 percent of the stories had at least one instance of human injury or killing, and about a third of the dramatic segments were "saturated" with violence.

Why? To find out, Prof. Muriel G. Cantor of American University, interviewed 24 Los Angeles producers and scriptwriters—a group responsible for nearly all the cartoons and live-action programs aimed at the Saturday-morning children's market. None had any specific academic background for preparing children's programs. Over half had been in entertainment, advertising, promotion or publicity. Most displayed an appalling indifference to possible harmful effects of their output on children. "As long as we are on the air," said one producer, "I don't care." Always, the ruling consideration seems to be audience size.

Yet the violence-equals-ratings-equals-profits formula is not infallible. A survey in England showed that children overwhelmingly prefer humor to "action" or "adventure." Could this be true also in the United States? We don't know. Our commercial broadcasters have never bothered to conduct extensive research, and thus American audiences simply have had little choice. ■

MEDIALAB

TV Violence

1. Conduct a class study to measure the amount of violence currently shown on television. Divide the class so that a group of students is assigned to each local TV channel. Each group should divide viewing time among its members so that the entire prime-time schedule of its station can be monitored during one week. In addition to evening hours, also assign someone to monitor the Saturday morning children's shows. Each person should keep a written record of all the televised violence that would include the following information: date, time, channel, name of program or programs viewed. Note each act of violence committed during viewing and write down a description of each act in a few words. Also note why the violent act was committed (for example, self-defense, to escape the police, etc.). List each weapon seen and keep track of the number of people wounded and killed.

After one week of watching for TV violence, each group should gather its data and compile a record of that channel's "violence report" for the entire week.

Once these are compiled, compare the local stations and programs to determine which is the most and which the least violent.

2. Judging from your statistics in the study above, how many killings appear on television in an average year?

The article by Jesse Steinfeld quoted a study that found an average of eight incidents per hour on TV of "physical force intended to hurt or kill." How does this compare with your more recent findings?

Which programs seem to depend the most on stories in which killing is involved?

3. What kind of violence is most common on Saturday mornings? Is there more or less than on prime time?

4. What are among the most common reasons for the violent acts shown on television?

5. Reach some conclusion from your violence study.

6. Think of at least one good argument in favor of the opinion that "TV violence is *not* harmful." Discuss these arguments in class. If you cannot think of one reason, do some library research using the *Readers' Guide to Periodical Literature* under the heading, "Television."

7. The article tells of experiments by "two Penn State researchers." Read this section (fourth paragraph of the article) carefully and discuss their findings.

8. What studies mentioned in the article conclude simply, "Watching television makes children more violent"?

9. Is there any kind of control on your television watching or on that of your younger brothers or sisters in regard to violent programs?

10. Write a short essay in which you state your own opinions about violence on television.

Who Should Have Access to Television Time?
A Debate

Television stations are all licensed to serve the public. The station management must decide who deserves valuable air time. The following pages give information for a debate based on a situation that really happened.

The next page shows a print version of a television commercial that Mobil Oil wished to telecast on three networks. Two of the major networks refused to accept the ad; only NBC agreed to broadcast it.

The question under debate is this: Who deserves time on national television to express a viewpoint? That is, who should have access to television? Should access be controlled completely by the three networks? Should only advertisers who can afford the necessary tens or hundreds of thousands of dollars be allowed on the air? Should anyone with a cause be given time? Should access to television be government controlled?

One idea causing much controversy within the broadcast industry comes from a new interpretation of the right to free speech. According to this idea, the Constitutional right to free speech means little in a mass media society unless citizens have access to the mass media to express their opinions. Television (and, to a lesser extent, newspapers, magazines, and radio) is limited in the number of opinions it can present. Therefore, the question becomes: Who has

access to the limited time on TV to express their opinions? So far, the answer has been "anyone with the money to buy the time; namely, corporations selling products." But what if a corporation wants to buy time to influence public opinion? Enter Mobil Oil versus the networks.

For this debate, three students should represent Mobil Oil; three, ABC; three, NBC; and three, CBS. Three more students should represent a citizens' clean-air group that has been refused air time to present a message urging people to walk and ride bikes whenever possible, instead of driving. The remainder of the class will be members of a fact-finding commission who will vote on the question according to their beliefs and the arguments presented in the debate. Decide on your own structure, time limit, and rules for the debate. Devise some kind of voting procedure to end the debate. Allow a day or two for the debaters to prepare their positions.

The following written statements of position are presented here as they appeared in writing when the ad was originally presented to the networks. These positions should be viewed only as starting points by the debate teams. The CBS and ABC teams must argue against allowing the ad on TV, the NBC team in favor of allowing it, and the Mobil team must argue in favor of the ad.

 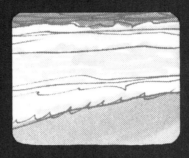 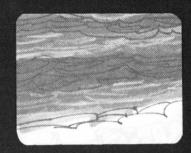

OPEN ON WIDE SHOT OF BEACH AND
OCEAN.

TURN TO WATER: CAMERA MOVES
OVER WATER AT RAPID PACE.

FRAME FREEZES

ANNCR. VO: "According to the U.S.
Geological Survey, there may be
60 billion barrels of oil or more
beneath our continental shelves."

"Some people say we should be drilling
for that oil and gas. Others say we
shouldn't because of the possible
environmental risks. We'd like to
know what you think."

"Write Mobil Poll, Room 647, 150
East 42nd Street, New York 10017."

SUPER CONTINUES ON SCREEN

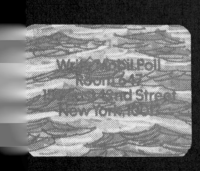

CUT TO LOGO

ANNCR. VO: "We'd like to hear from
you."

Why do two networks refuse to run this commercial?

CBS: ABC: NBC:

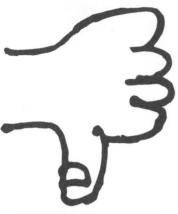 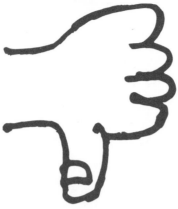 

SUMMARY OF THE CBS POSITION:

"We regret that the subject matter of this commercial . . . deals with a controversial issue of public importance and does not fall within our 'goods and services' limitation for commercial acceptance."

SUMMARY OF THE ABC POSITION:

"This will advise that we have reviewed the above-captioned commercial and are unable to grant an approval for use over our facilities. It is against our policy to sell time for the discussion of controversial issues of public importance. Such matters are most responsibly handled in our news and public affairs programs where both sides of an issue can be presented. We have reported on the energy crisis and have run 14 Mobil commercials which were within our accepted guidelines."

SUMMARY OF THE NBC POSITION:

"Approved as submitted."

SUMMARY OF THE MOBIL OIL POSITION:

As you can see from the storyboard we want to ask the public how it feels about offshore drilling.

But the policies of two national television networks prevent us from asking this question.

This is dangerous, it seems to us. Any restraint on free discussion is dangerous. Any policy that restricts the flow of information or ideas is potentially harmful.

The networks say that the public's need for information is best served in news programs prepared by broadcast journalists.

Behind the networks' rejection of idea advertising may be the fear that demands for equal time will be made. We have a reasonable answer to that. We offer to pay for equal time, when the request is legitimate.

We think *more* discussion, not less, is needed of vital issues such as the issue of America's energy needs. We're willing to buy the time to say what we should be saying. We're willing to buy time so you can hear opposing views.

But two big networks aren't willing to make time available, in this case.

You know the principle at stake here. You've seen it in writing, more than once: *"Congress shall make no law . . . abridging the freedom of speech."*

You've seen it in the First Amendment to the Constitution of the United States. So have we.

Scheduling TV Time

1. Design a TV schedule for one day of programming of your own experimental television station. The schedule should reflect the prime purpose of every station to "serve the public interest of those in the viewing area." Your schedule should run for one 24-hour day, should contain *only programming that cannot be found on other TV stations* in the area (no movies, reruns, or network shows allowed), and should reflect an active imagination. Here is part of one such "Experimental TV Schedule":

Evening
5:30-6:00
30 Minute Meal. Turn the TV on in the kitchen, follow the directions of the TV chef, and 30 minutes later you have dinner. Necessary ingredients are listed in the newspaper each day.

6:00-7:00
Newsmakers in the City. While other stations are having news reported by announcers, this station has a one-hour news program in which there is no announcer. If a robbery is in the news, the entire report will consist of the person robbed telling the story of what happened. All-film presentation.

7:00-10:00
Citizen Access. Groups and individuals with something important to say will be given free time to speak. Videotape equipment will be provided along with instructions on how to make the presentation interesting. Detailed contents of the program will be listed each day in the newspaper.

10:00-10:30
Consumer Guide. Guide to where to get the best prices in the city on various products. This show will name names and give prices. Also it will give warnings about shoddy merchandise or unethical salespeople working in the city.

10:30-11:30
Crime Beat. Portable camera will ride along with squad car or follow detectives while they work. Other weeks this show will follow people in other occupations to give an idea of what it is like to be a computer programmer, radio disk jockey, construction worker, etc.

11:30-1:30
Night Life. Portable cameras visit city night life (night clubs, popular hangouts, etc.) to show what happens at night.

1:30-3:00
Insomniac's Special. Soothing music and hypnotic visuals especially designed to induce sleep.

2. Take a survey of the class to find out which program is watched by the most class members. Discuss why that program is the most popular and what it teaches.

3. Write a critical review of a television program that you have watched. Point out both the weak and strong points of the program.

4. Arrange to have in class as many TV sets as there are local stations (or as many as possible). Turn all the TV sets on at once (each tuned to a different station), with the sound off. Watch the sets during class. Be able to tell the difference between a live or videotaped program and a film program. What part of the programs has the fastest visual pace, the most

MEDIALAB

changes of picture per minute? How is the effect of TV without sound different from that with sound? How is televiewing different when multiple sets are used?

5. If the school has videotape equipment, arrange for as many people in the class as possible to produce their own TV program. Three people can work as a team to make one program. So that all the programs can be seen, limit each to one, three, or five minutes in length.

6. The project teams formed at the beginning of the course should now present their reports on the image of various groups as television portrays them. Allow plenty of time for each report and for questions from the class. Teams include those on the images of law enforcement personnel, doctors, elderly people, teenagers, women (or men), criminals, or any topic chosen by a project team.

7. Explain the cartoon illustration used on page 2. What comment about television is the artist making?

8. Attempt to group television programs by types: situation comedies, soap operas, quiz shows, talk shows, etc. First draw up a list of as many types of programs as you think exist. Next test your list of types by attempting to classify all TV programs according to the list. Use the daily newspapers or a TV schedule magazine such as *TV Guide* to provide program names.

9. Select one TV show to watch during prime time (evenings). On a sheet of paper make two columns: "How the Program is Realistic" and "How the Program is Unrealistic." Fill in both columns as you watch and then report or discuss your findings with the class. This project can also be done by having the entire class watch the same program (or programs) and compare and discuss their lists.

10. Those who have no television at home should write about the advantages of having no TV.

11. Watch some TV programming intended for young children and make a written or oral report. Select either entertainment-type programs such as those seen on Saturday mornings or educational programs such as "Sesame Street" or "Electric Company," or, watch both kinds and compare them.

12. Prepare a report on how televised sports programs affect family life.

13. Prepare a report on television censorship. Use *Readers' Guide to Periodical Literature* if you wish to find material on recent censorship cases. General books on the history of television would be better sources of information on past cases.

14. Find out how much time in each television hour is given to commercials. Note how many different commercials are given in one time period. The percentage of time devoted to ads will vary accord-

ing to the time of day—daytime, prime time, and late night. Keep track of these differences.

15. Studies have found that well over 50 percent of people who watch TV in the evening do not bother to change channels. They start on one channel and remain with it for hours at a time. Do you believe this? Can you explain why it might happen?

16. Watch one hour of programming on your local Public Broadcasting Service station (educational TV). Note similarities and differences to commercial television.

17. Read a chapter in any of the following books or any other book about television. Report on its contents:

> *Television: The Business Behind the Box*, by Les Brown.
> *The Age of Television*, by Leo Bogart (third edition).
> *The Crowd-Catchers: Introducing Television*, by Robert Lewis Shayon.
> *Remote Control*, by Mankiewicz and Swerdlow.
> *Tube of Plenty*, by Erik Barnouw.

18. Prepare an information sheet on all your local TV stations. List (a) the channel and call letters of all TV stations in your area; (b) the network each belongs to, if any; (c) the location of the station's studio and transmitting tower; and (d) the owner of the station.

19. The *Standard Rate and Data Service* book (found in the reference section of many libraries) gives information about spot advertising on television. Check in the book to find out how much each local TV station charges for advertising. Report the findings to the class.

20. If you enjoy and understand electronics, report on how television works. What makes color in a TV picture, and how does a picture travel from a TV studio to the home TV set?

21. Have a class discussion/poll and select the three worst programs on TV. Explain and defend your choices.

22. Examine the opinion about television you wrote at the beginning of this chapter, and rewrite it based on what you have learned in this chapter. You do not have to change your opinion.

ANSWERS TO TV TEST:
The most correct answer to each of the eight questions is *b.* For every answer in which you chose *a* or *c*, score 2 points. For every *d* you selected, score 5 points; for every *e*, score 10 points. Add up your total score.

On another piece of paper write:

1. Number of hours a week you watch TV

2. Score on TV test

Do not put your name on the paper.

Student Presentations

The following is a list of forty possible research topics or sources. The topics should be distributed among class members who will each prepare a 1–3 minute report for the class. Find and read one relevant magazine article or book chapter on your topic. (Research for topics should not be done in an encyclopedia.) Research sources are magazine articles that should be available in libraries. Most of the research for these presentations will have to be done in a public library.

Be sure to take into account when the article was written. Some titles are of interest mainly because they were written ten or more years ago.

1. Violence on television

2. Television ratings

3. Televised sports

4. Educational television

5. Advertising on television

6. Children's television

7. Advertising on children's programs

8. Moral aspects of television

9. Television news

10. Censorship of television

11. CBS

12. ABC

13. RCA

14. How television works

15. Television as presented in Ray Bradbury's novel *Fahrenheit 451.*

16. Television as presented in George Orwell's novel *1984.*

17. Television as presented in Aldous Huxley's *Brave New World.*

18. Television as presented in Jerzy Kosinski's novel *Being There.*

19. "To Grab Viewers' Attention, TV Ads Aim for the Eardrum," by John Koten, *Wall Street Journal,* January 26, 1984.

20. "How to Make TV Commercials That Sell," by David Ogilvy, in Chapter Eight of *Ogilvy on Advertising.*

21. *The New York Times* of March 19, 1939. Report on television at the World's Fair. It contains the following judgment: "The problem with television is that the people must sit and keep their eyes glued on a screen; the average American family hasn't time for it."

22. "Study Shows Most Viewers Misunderstand TV Programs," in *Editor & Publisher* magazine of May 24, 1980.

23. "Television vs. Progress," by Les Brown in *Saturday Review* of September 16, 1978.

24. "The Videophobes," in *Time,* November 8, 1968.

25. "Here's What TV Is Doing to Us," by Edwin Kiester, Jr., in *TV Guide* of December 17, 1977.

26. "Are TV Commercials Insulting to Women?" in *Good Housekeeping,* May 1971.

27. "The Structure of Televised Football," by Brien R. Williams in *Journal of Communications,* Volume 27, No. 3, Summer 1977.

28. One chapter from *The Plug-In Drug* by Marie Winn.

29. One chapter from *The Show and Tell Machine* by Rose K. Goldsen.

30. One chapter from *Television: The Business Behind the Box* by Les Brown.

31. One chapter from *The Crowd-Catchers* by Robert Lewis Shayon.

32. "It Was Just a Joke, Folks: How a Casual Remark from Johnny Carson Emptied Supermarket Shelves All Over the Country," in *TV Guide,* May 18, 1974.

33. "Your Money *and* Your Life," by David Cook in *Columbia Journalism Review* of July/August 1979.

34. Two articles on cable television from the May 1984 issue of *Consumer Research* magazine.

35. "TV's Impact on Adults: It's Not All Bad News," by David Loye in *Psychology Today* of May 1978.

36. "The Visibility and Image of Old People on Television," by Marilyn Petersen, in *Journalism Quarterly,* Autumn 1973.

37. "How TV Producers Sneak in a Few Extra Commercials," in *The New York Times* (Arts and Leisure Section) of August 11, 1974.

38. "The Technology of TV Violence," by Roger Field, in *Saturday Review,* June 10, 1972.

39. "Media Mentors," by John L. Caughey in *Psychology Today* of September 1978.

40. "Plugola: What the Talk Shows Don't Talk About," by Terry Ann Knopf in *Columbia Journalism Review* of January/February 1977.

Television:

TV
or
Not
TV

Let's look at some of the arguments for television and at some of the criticisms commonly aimed at it. One of the following articles stresses the value of the common collective experiences we have shared by watching live televised events such as the moon landings, the manned space shuttle flights, and the Olympic Games. These shared experiences are seen as important in an era when a sense of community seems to be slipping away.

The other article reminds us that television programs are often not well written, well acted, or competently produced. Addiction to television is not uncommon and a belief that life's problems can be solved by changing channels is pervasive and disturbing.

Television is probably somewhere between the most wonderful gift ever bestowed upon humanity and the source of all evil. Let's look at the two views of television that follow.

In Defense of Television

by Peggy Charren and Martin W. Sandler

Shared experiences are one of the most important aspects of television viewing. Here are some ideas about the benefits and opportunities of television.

In March 1939 a New York *Times* reporter, assigned to the World's Fair, at which television was introduced, offered a prediction about the new invention. "The problem with television," he wrote, "is that the people must sit and keep their eyes glued to a screen: the average American family hasn't time for it. Therefore ... for this reason, if no other, television will never be a serious competitor of broadcasting."

The reporter was one of the first of a long line of people who predicted that, as the novelty of television wore off, TV-watching would decline. They could not have been more wrong. Since 1948, when television first became widely available to the American public, TV-viewing has risen so steadily that today Americans spend more time watching television than doing anything else except sleeping. Television has become such an important part of our lives that by the age of 65 the average American will have

spent 9 full years watching TV.

Television is this nation's common denominator, its shared experience. Millions watch the same programs every night, laughing at the same jokes, absorbing the same information, being subjected to the same points of view. And chances are that the next day at school or the office or the factory much of the talk will center around the characters and stories of television dramas and situation comedies, the antics of Howard Cosell or Johnny Carson, or one of the many "specials" that appear throughout the year. Wherever we go in the nation we take this experience with us. If we begin watching a week-long mini-series in Chicago one night and we need to make a business trip, we turn on our set in Boston or Los Angeles or New Orleans the next night and tune in Part Two. For millions of people, not to watch television is to be out of the flow of American life. More than one set of parents in this country, after years of forbidding certain TV programs in their

home, have relaxed their rules, concluding that they could not continue to keep their children out of touch with what their classmates talked about.

Television's unique strengths lie in the way it is able to present people with interesting topics of conversation and in its ability to transmit pictures of events to all parts of the world at the moment they are happening. Someone once said that the best thing on television is golf—because no one can write a script for the ball. Television thus far has been most effective when it has gone outside the studio. The highest ratings throughout television history have not gone to situation comedies, soap operas, mini-series, or even lavishly promoted network spectaculars. They have gone to what Israeli sociologist Elihu Katz calls the "live broadcasting of history" or "the high holidays of mass communication." Time and again in the last two decades the activities of the entire nation have come practically to a halt as we have shared a common collective experience by watching a live televised event.

Some of these events have been awe-inspiring—the moon landings, the manned space shuttle flights, the victory of the underdog United States hockey team at the 1980 Olympics. Televised events of this type take on the quality of holidays. In an era when a sense of community seems to be slipping steadily, these occasions have given us the opportunity to share together, rejoice together, and exult in our accomplishments as a nation and as human beings.

This shared experience is one of the most important aspects of the televised event. Just as television has allowed us to share our joy and pride, witnessing triumphs and discoveries, so have we found collective solace in viewing together the tragedies of the nation. Somehow—by sharing the experience of the Kennedy and Sadat funerals, the plight of the Iranian hostages, the assassination attempts on our Presidents—we have been able to comfort ourselves, renew our commitment to democracy, and carry on.

If television binds us in joy and sorrow, it also unites us as creatures dependent on an electronic box for many human needs. In less than four decades, television has become educator, comforter, entertainer, baby-sitter, titillator, salesperson, patriot, investigator, *paterfamilias* to the nation, and psychiatrist to the individual. We watch television when we are bored and when we are anxious, alone and together, to laugh and to cry, to learn and to avoid learning. Even so, watching television is like sex in Victorian England. Almost everybody does it, but

few brag about it. As one critic has said, "Disparagement of television is second only to watching television as a national pastime."

Television, like comic books and the movies before it, has been blamed for all the ills of society—from the quality of our candidates to crime in the streets. This is not a particularly happy time in history. Populations are growing so quickly, resources are being used up so rapidly, and poverty is such a significant problem that the very survival of the human race is in question. Yet, terrorism and crime are probably no more commonplace and pervasive than in certain other times in history. The difference is that with TV, the world now has a messenger that brings the actual sights and sounds of these disruptions into living rooms night after night. Our tendency is to place the blame for these disruptions not on their complex causes but instead on the messenger.

If television is not entirely to blame, neither is it the innocent messenger. The truth is that television both reflects and affects behavior, and it does neither perfectly. TV does not cause poverty, but it does affect our attitudes toward the poor and their condition. It does not cause crime, but it affects our attitudes toward the role of violence in our society. To say that television didn't invent the most serious problems and isn't responsible for most of them is not to say, however, that this infant medium has not presented us with a myriad of significant problems of its own.

... In an age when, as a nation, we have come to regard TV

as one of the essentials of life, it is vital for us to learn how to make the most of it. Television is here to stay. And today more than at any other time in its history, it is growing and expanding. . . .

"Once I thought the most important political statement we could make about television was to turn it off. But television can instruct, inform, and inspire, as well as distract, distort, and demean. And turning it off rejects the good with the bad. My family wants its voice added to the summons for quality, and I urge you to speak up, too, in every way possible. This marvelous medium, with all its potential for laughter and light, is worth fighting for." Bill Moyers

"There are times, and today was one of those times, when television approaches the truly magical, when it becomes the sort of instrument that, 50 or 60 years ago, would have been regarded as supernatural. . . . This has been, without question, one of the more memorable days in our nation's history; and television, much maligned television, which frequently does numb the brain and dull the senses, today produced a technological miracle. Never has any generation of Americans had greater reason to claim they were eyewitness to history." Ted Koppel, "Nightline," January 20, 1980

"Television is a medium of expression which permits millions of people to listen to the same joke at the same time, and yet remain lonesome." T. S. Eliot ∎

MEDIALAB

In Defense of Television

1. Notice that "In Defense of Television" does not deal with specific programs on television, it treats television as a mass medium. What is the main benefit of the medium of television as explained in the article?

2. What does it mean to say that television is this nation's "common denominator, its shared experience"?

3. What kind of programming does the article claim is the strength of television?

4. Every few years there is some event that seems to unite the country, an event shared by television. The event could be an Olympic celebration, a funeral or tragedy, or even a televised mini-series. What event in your memory has been a nationwide emotional experience shared through the medium of television?

5. When asked, "Why do you watch television?" you would probably respond with a simple, "Because I like some of the shows." But there are deeper reasons for watching. The article points to some uses for television as follows:

educator
comforter
entertainer
baby-sitter
titillator
salesperson
patriot
investigator
paterfamilias (Latin for "head of the
    household")
psychiatrist.

Discuss each of these roles and give examples of how television is used for each.

An Attack on TV

by Jeffrey Schrank

Most arguments against television concern possible harmful effects of certain types of programming. But these criticisms could also be made of similar presentations in movies, books, or comics. Here are some ideas about the negative effects of television as a medium.

By the time a typical person reaches the deathbed (very likely placed beneath a TV set in a hospital room), he or she will have spent almost nine years watching television. Without television, nine years would be added to the average person's "activity life." It is difficult to believe we have freely chosen to spend so much of a lifetime watching dancing phosphers on a glass screen.

For millions of regular viewers, television is no longer one choice among many to occupy a weekday night. The option has become which programs to watch, not if the set should be on. On any given weekday night, year after year, no matter what programs are presented, there is a fairly constant TV audience of one hundred million people.

People do not watch television because of certain shows they find exciting. If the show they claim to enjoy is not on, they watch some other show. Paul Klein, former vice-president for audience measurement at NBC, claims that viewer choice is based on the L.O.P. theory—the least objectionable program.

The L.O.P. theory states that people don't watch particular programs—they watch television. The set is turned on for the same reason people climb mountains—it's there. The program viewed at the time is the one that is considered least objectionable. To garner high ratings, all a show has to do is be less objectionable than its competition. A show does not have to be well written, well acted, or lavishly produced. Network programmers know that some well-received programs are stupid, but they also know that a program doesn't have to be good, it only has to be less objectionable.

Our language further supports Klein's L.O.P. theory in that we read THE newspaper, listen to THE radio, read A book or A magazine, but simply watch television. There is truth buried in this linguistic habit, for we do watch the medium of television, and that is significant no matter if the program is about culture or crooks.

Many people watch television simply because they are addicted to the tube. Addiction, normally thought of in terms of drugs, has two necessary components—tolerance and a withdrawal illness or abstinence syndrome. Tolerance means the body gradually adapts to the drug so that constantly larger doses are required to produce the same effect. A withdrawal illness is a negative physical reaction to a lack of the drug. In other words, without the drug, a person becomes very ill. Abstinence syndrome refers to usually minor ailments (running nose, sweating, tremors, irritability, etc.) when the normal dosage is delayed or missed.

Both these elements of addiction can be seen in viewing habits. The component of tolerance can be seen in the gradual increase of the "average daily dose" self-prescribed by viewers over the past eleven years. In 1963, the average household had the set on for five hours and twelve minutes daily; by 1974 that figure had increased to six hours and fourteen minutes; and by 1985 the daily dose had increased to over seven hours.

Television's power to addict might spring from its ability to involve us emotionally.

We have all experienced deep

emotions in front of TV screens; we have all learned about the world we will never visit in person or experience "live." We watch television in order to be manipulated into feeling. We want those images on the screen to be frightening, to make us cry or howl with laughter, to help us feel vicarious thrills and excitement, to stimulate awe at the ability of others. Our nervous systems do not distinguish between the fear of a mugger lurking ahead on the deserted street at three in the morning or the fear aroused by the midnight creature feature. In both cases our heart throbs, the pulse quickens, and the body sensations are real. The feelings are real, only the televised stimulus is lacking a third dimension.

People have always sought out games and theater to experience feelings normally missing from daily life. But when the seeking takes six to eight hours a day, it is a sign of an absence of a rich emotional life based on reality. The shadows become substitutes for reality. A Los Angeles soap opera addict explains: "Without these programs going on, I wonder if I would go on. People seem to forget me. . . . These people are my company. My real friends. I have it [TV] on because I feel people are talking to me."

This woman is an extreme case of TV-as-reality-substitute, but her symptoms are common to millions. By watching television, the feelings and sense of companionship can be enjoyed without responsibility, without the need to share these feelings with others or express them in public or even to "own" them as ours. These TV-generated feelings come from skilled writers

"George, one of these days you're going to turn into a vegetable from all that TV."

and producers and not from within ourselves—they are safe and nonthreatening. Television encourages habitual viewers to avoid responsibility for their own recreation and feelings of aliveness. Responsibility slips into the willing hands of corporations who control TV content as well as the supply of goods presented as means to "come alive."

A professional polling organization conducted a survey of the attitude of readers of the *National Enquirer*. Of the responders, 76 percent agreed that "TV makes me feel tired," 75 percent agreed that it "makes me eat more," and 56 percent claimed that TV causes them to "sleep more." Less than half rated entertainment programs as "satisfactory." Yet this box that shows mainly unsatisfactory programs and makes viewers hungry and sleepy is one of the few experiences we as a nation have in common.

The medium itself teaches values, regardless of the pro-

grams. Children who grow up on "Sesame Street" learn early to be regular consumers of TV programming. They also learn to accept as normal the fast cutting of "Sesame Street" and fail to learn the value of watching any one scene or visual for more than a few seconds. Television in general teaches the value of frequent change. Images change constantly, programs change, and there is always that knob to change the channel.

Some psychologists believe TV may be partly to blame for the belief that life's problems can be solved by changing the channel. Los Angeles psychiatrist Dr. Lawrence Friedman explains one tendency of the channel-changing personality, "I'm convinced that at least fifty percent of all divorces in this country are unnecessary. And it's all because TV teaches us simple solutions to complex problems. People tell me, 'If only I could get rid of this marriage, everything would be all right.' Nonsense!" ■

MEDIALAB

An Attack on Television

1. Summarize each of the following "attacks" against television as given in the article:

TV as a time-stealer
TV as an addiction
TV as an emotional substitute for reality
TV as a passive medium
TV as a teacher of simple solutions.

2. The article points out that saying "TV is addictive" is more than a figure of speech. In what way is the "addiction" to television like the addiction to drugs? Be sure to discuss tolerance, withdrawal illness, and abstinence syndrome.

3. One of the reasons we watch television is to experience emotions. This is often called "vicarious experience." In what main way is vicarious experience from television different from that experienced from theater or books?

What danger does the article point out in regard to television as a supplier of emotions?

4. How are the emotions you experience while watching television (or movies) different from emotions in "real" life? How are they the same?

5. Explain the L.O.P. theory in your own words.

6. How do you explain surveys that show we find TV unsatisfying coupled with constant increases in the time spent watching television?

7. The TV program "Sesame Street" is often given as an example of helpful educational programming. What "hidden teaching" of the show is pointed out in the article? Do you think television shows in general have such "hidden lessons"?

Some Questions to Ask Yourself About Your Own TV Watching

Peggy Charren and Martin W. Sandler

TV programs, like an addictive drug, have a built-in failure to satisfy. They provide only enough pleasure to bring viewers back for more. What does television teach? Television teaches you to watch more TV.

• Are you upset with the amount of time you spend in front of the TV set? How much time *do* you spend with TV? How does this compare with national viewing statistics? (The average American watches 6 hours and 44 minutes per day.)

• What kinds of things have you stopped doing because of your TV watching?

• Do you find yourself watching selected programs that you look forward to, or do you simply watch whatever is on?

• Has television affected your life positively? Negatively?

• Do you find that your buying decisions in the supermarket or the department store are helped by TV commercials? Hindered?

• Do you *automatically* turn on the television set when you walk into your home? Is the TV set on in your bedroom right up until the time you fall asleep? When else do you *automatically* turn on TV? For example, as soon as you enter a hotel room? Whenever you're home alone with a couple of hours to kill?

• For the most part, do you watch TV alone or with other people? When you watch with others do you ever discuss what you have seen with them? When you have finished watching a program alone do you ever ask yourself what you liked or did not like about it?

• Do you feel yourself adjusting your own personal schedule in order to watch TV? Do you avoid going out on Friday evenings so you won't miss "Dal-

las"? Do you show up late for engagements because you had to see the end of "60 Minutes" or "Family Feud"?

• Has television affected the quality of time you spend with your family? Do you do less together because of televised weekend sports? What about mealtimes? How many meals do you eat in front of the tube?

• Is television a major irritant in your home? Do you fight about what to watch, about turning it off?

• Do you have cable or a video recorder? If you do, do you find that you're watching even more television than you did before? Have the increased options made your TV viewing more enjoyable? ∎

Chapter 2
ADVERTISING

Advertising is the fuel that powers mass media. Television is free for the viewing audience—while advertisers gladly pay thousands of dollars a second to reach those who are watching. Newspapers, magazines, and radio stations would cease to exist if advertisers deserted them for other media.

(The blank spaces in this paragraph are intentional. As you read, supply your best guess at the answers; later research will provide more accurate ones.) When you watch television _____ percent of the time is devoted to "messages." Your favorite radio station gives about _____ minutes in every hour to ads, and in the morning paper _____ percent of the space is advertising. A mass circulation magazine will be about _____ percent advertising.

It would be unrealistic to study mass media without taking a very careful look at the world of advertising.

THE HISTORY OF ADVERTISING

No one knows who was the first advertiser. Perhaps thousands of years ago one of our ancestors carved a sign in a rock announcing a fire restarting service for the reasonable fee of one carved ax handle. But mass advertising didn't exist back in prehistoric days for the simple reason that there was no need for advertising.

Advertising exists to solve a problem: the presence of more goods than are needed. In a society of scarcity, where there is not enough to go around, there is no need for ads. Everything that is grown or made is put to immediate use. Advertising requires a surplus of goods or services. It exists to create a demand. There is no need for advertising if the demand already exists far beyond the supply.

As long as goods were supplied locally, hand-made as needed, there was little need for advertising beyond an occasional announcement or sign. A shoemaker would hang a sign outside his house (which was also his workshop), but had no need to advertise. All he could do was make a few pairs of shoes a week. Each shoe was custom-made for a specific person—there was no back room filled with inventory; there was no surplus of shoes to be moved before the "new fashions" could be introduced.

Even if our humble shoemaker could hire workers to turn out a surplus of shoes, how would he advertise? The technology of printing was not a mass medium until around the year 1500. Only with printing could he make handbills to pass around the village. Before printing he would have to rely on a town crier or perhaps a strolling minstrel to sing a jingle about his shoes.

Modern advertising had to wait for a surplus of goods. And a surplus of goods came about only with machines that could turn out more than one at a time—not until the Industrial Revolution. Only after the Industrial Revolution were there enough products and money to support mass advertising.

So mass advertising required the technology of printing and the Industrial Revolution. But there was a third requirement—literate customers. During the 1800s laws were passed both in England and the United States requiring children to attend school. These laws were important to advertising since they raised the literacy level of the general population to the point at which printed advertisements could be understood.

Printers were quick to see that handbills were a profitable source of business. By combining handbills with news, printers produced what would eventually become the modern newspaper and magazine. Printers realized they could make money both by selling their paper to readers and by charging merchants to print advertisements.

But printers found they spent too much time soliciting ads from merchants, so they hired agents to sell advertising space. These agents were not paid a salary; they were paid a commission on each ad they sold. The size of the commission became standardized at 15 percent of the cost of the ad and often remains that today.

As more newspapers, newsletters, and magazines were printed, merchants were besieged by advertising agents. "Which publication is best for my goods?" each wondered. The agent knew the most about advertising and so became a kind of selling consultant. In 1870, two competing agents, J. Walter Thompson and N. W. Ayer realized that they could best serve their clients by writing effective selling copy and planning which publications would be best. These agents created the age of modern advertising. Large advertising agencies still bear their names.

Advertising changed as new media became available—color posters, radio, and television. But the purpose of advertising changed as well as its media. Advertising went through a series of refinements, each representing a new approach to selling. At first, advertising was only information. Next, advertisers saw the value of capturing reader attention before presenting the information. In general, advertising progressed through eight stages:

1. information
2. attention
3. repetition
4. association
5. product benefit
6. motivation
7. entertainment
8. behavioral

These eight stages did not follow in orderly steps, and a new step did not completely replace the previous step. Tracing these eight steps helps give a clear picture of the role of advertising today.

INFORMATION APPROACH

Before the nineteenth century most advertising was merely informative. It consisted of price lists, signs on walls, printed announcements, and even the calls of the town crier. Supply and demand were in balance and there was no need to produce new products. People bought what they needed and needed what they bought. There was limited competition among merchants.

ATTENTION APPROACH

By the start of the nineteenth century, factories were turning out goods that needed some attention in order to sell. The goods had to be sold in markets away from the factory. Manufacturers found it necessary to use various devices to attract attention.

To call attention to the "advertisement," devices such as borders, headline type, and increased white space were used. Today, we take these devices for granted. But remember, the earliest ads were considered more like news. "A shipment of tea arrived by ship yesterday and is available for sale at dockside" is both news and an ad. In fact, the word *advertise* first meant "to announce." Many early newspapers (and some today) were named the "Advertiser," not because they carried ads, but because to advertise meant to announce.

Consider page one of the *Boston Evening Transcript* of April 9, 1840. On its front page were three-line notices for Italian cravats, money to loan, potatoes, two teens who wanted work in a "Publik House," and shares of bank stock. The page was a solid mass of small type, broken only by a large capital letter here and there. Ads and news were not separated, nor were ads "classified" according to type of merchandise.

Only in the mid-nineteenth century were large sizes of type and simple designs used to gain readers' attention.

REPETITION APPROACH

Many influential large city newspapers objected to large size type for some announcements. They felt it would be unfair to others. The "agate rule" stated that all announcements had to be set in agate type, which was this size.

> S MALL BAGGS to hang about Children's necks, which are excellent both for the *prevention and cure* of the *Rickets*, and to ease Children in breeding of Teeth, are prepared by Mr. Edmund Buckworth, and constantly to be had at Mr. Philip Clark's, Keeper of the Library in the Fleet, and nowhere else, at 5 shillings a bagge.

If the type could not be made larger, it could be repeated to attract attention. Repetition as an advertising device was created to get around the "agate rule." It is still used today as perhaps the most common of all persuasive devices.

Robert Bonner, an early publisher, took a whole page of the *New York Herald* in 1856 and repeated his message 600 times. P. T. Barnum was a master of the art of repetition. In 1841 he ran the ad on this page for his museum of Americana:

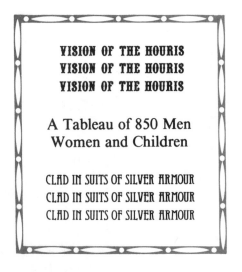

VISION OF THE HOURIS
VISION OF THE HOURIS
VISION OF THE HOURIS

A Tableau of 850 Men
Women and Children

CLAD IN SUITS OF SILVER ARMOUR
CLAD IN SUITS OF SILVER ARMOUR
CLAD IN SUITS OF SILVER ARMOUR

Barnum believed in the power of repeating an ad and wrote:

"The reader of a newspaper does not see the first insertion of an ordinary advertisement; the second insertion he sees, but does not read; the third insertion he reads; the fourth insertion, he looks at the price; the fifth insertion, he speaks of it to his wife; the sixth insertion, he is ready to purchase; and the seventh insertion, he purchases."

While Bonner and Barnum were practicing repetition, technology made it possible to sell food in glass containers or tin cans. Prior to this time, merchants scooped food from huge bins or barrels. There was little room for the development of a name brand. But cans and bottles made possible the sale of small quantities of food under a brand name. The method of repetition was ideally suited to making the public aware of brand names.

Repetition as a means of persuasion still thrives today. It received a boost from the scientific work of Ivan Pavlov and J. B. Watson in the 1920s. Pavlov and Watson introduced the idea of the "conditioned reflex." The theory held that learning involved the association of a response with a stimulus. A response to a specific stimulus was learned if the stimulus was repeated often enough. Pavlov demonstrated that a dog learned to lift its paw at the sound of a bell if the dog had been repeatedly rewarded for doing so.

J. B. Watson was hired by the J. Walter Thompson Advertising Agency to apply these theories to advertising. So advertising quickly learned to repeat often and to treat the purchase as a reward for the consumer's correct response.

By the 1930s repetition meant using a catchy claim or jingle that was repeated almost to the point of irritation. A classic example was the phrase and jingle "LS/MFT." The entire country knew these initials stood for "Lucky Strike Means Fine Tobacco."

The repetition approach thrives today, not only for products. Celebrities also know that keeping a name before the public breeds familiarity and acceptance.

ASSOCIATION APPROACH

By the end of the nineteenth century, advertisers began to suspect that pure repetition was not enough. Advances in color printing and techniques developed by French poster artists led to the next phase in advertising—association.

Artists such as Aubrey Beardsley, Toulouse-Lautrec, and Edward Penfield showed that paintings of attractive people in poster ads created pleasant associations for the product. Even today, pleasing graphics and appealing pictures lead to favorable product associations.

PRODUCT-BENEFIT APPROACH

As products became more complex, advertisers found it necessary to explain what the products were and why the consumer would benefit from their use. In the 1950s, Rosser Reeves developed the phrase "unique selling proposition" to show that every ad must present the product as unique. The "USP" had to be a product benefit that no other brand could offer.

Reeves' agency took Colgate toothpaste and coined the word *Gardol* for its decay fighting ingredient. It didn't matter if the ingredient was unique to Colgate, it was sufficient that the name *Gardol* be unique. Colgate was unique because it alone had Gardol; and it alone had Gardol because its ad agency made up the word.

MOTIVATION APPROACH

By the end of the 1930s, the fledgling science of motivational research was discovered by ad agencies. Products were seen to have psychological meanings. Advertisers realized that people bought goods not only because they needed them but also because of various and often hidden psychological needs.

During this time the work of Sigmund Freud was recognized in the United States. Although few advertisers completely understood his theories, they realized that people often bought products for unconscious motives. In other words, before this time advertisers assumed that people bought a certain brand of soap because it cleaned best or cost less. From Freud's work they realized that a brand may be bought because the buyers feel the brand makes them more powerful, more loved, or more socially acceptable.

Motivational research learned, for example, that women would not pay more than a dollar for a bar of soap to make them clean. But they would pay many dollars for a "cream" that promised to make them beautiful. In other words, don't sell soap—sell dreams. Don't sell oranges—sell health and vitality. Don't sell automobiles—sell prestige and power.

Ernest Dichter became the leading proponent of motivational research, and his ideas still exert a strong influence on advertising. One of the most popular books on advertising, *The Hidden Persuaders* by Vance Packard, became a best-seller in the late 1950s. The book "exposed" motivational techniques and promised to explain:

> "Why your wife buys 35 percent more in the supermarket than she intends to."
>
> "Why your children like cereals that crackle and crunch."
>
> "Why men wouldn't give up shaving even if they could."

But even with the techniques "exposed" in a best-seller, they are still used today to create new products and repackage old products to look new.

ENTERTAINMENT APPROACH

In the middle of the 1950s, the Doyle Dane Bernbach agency realized that advertising could also be entertaining. The history of advertising so far assumed ads were to be informative. But the Doyle Dane Bernbach television commercials entertained. TV commercials today take entertainment value for granted, but keep in mind that the only good commercial is one that sells.

BEHAVIORAL APPROACH

By the 1970s consumers were more critical and better educated. They were becoming increasingly skeptical about commercials.

Behavioral research studied consumer needs and buying patterns to present a product image that would be seen as satisfying a real consumer need. An example of the behavioral approach can be seen in the long running Virginia Slims cigarette campaign. The campaign seemed to illustrate an understanding of the changing role of women in society and presented a product that fit this changing self-image. Another example of this approach is the ads for reduced calorie soft drinks as a product produced for active, weight-conscious people.

MEDIALAB

The History of Advertising

1. What type of society is needed before mass advertising can become commonplace?

2. What three conditions does the article explain are needed for mass advertising?

3. Explain how the first advertising agencies were formed.

4. Discuss each of the eight stages of advertising. Explain them in your own words.

5. Find advertisements that illustrate each of the eight stages of advertising. You do not have to find eight separate ads; many ads contain illustrations of more than one stage.

P. T. (Phineas Taylor) Barnum, America's greatest showman, publicized his American Museum in New York City (1842) with extravagant advertising and exhibits such as a bearded lady. By 1871 his circus had become an American institution. In the course of his career Barnum managed many attractions such as the ever popular Gen. Tom Thumb. He also managed the successful American tour of the world-famous singer Jenny Lind.

Claims Analysis:
The Fine Art of Deception Detection

By the time you are 60 years old, you will have seen and heard about 50 million advertising messages. Most will be ignored, some will prove helpful, and others will mislead.

Advertising can help you discover new products or show you where to buy goods at the lowest price. But it can also mislead you into buying what you don't want or into thinking a particular brand is better than it really is. To be able to tell the difference, you need to become a skilled reader of ads.

You must learn to determine exactly what facts are presented in an ad. Also, you must recognize how the ad tries to make the product look appealing. These may seem to be two simple skills, but advertising experts spend millions to make the job difficult.

Looking for facts in ads and commercials requires the mind of a Sherlock Holmes and the logic of a computer. Almost every advertisement makes what is called a product *claim*. The claim is simply what the ad says about the product. For example, "Jumbo pens write longer than any other ballpoint pen" *claims* very clearly that the Jumbo pen writes longer than any other pen. That sounds simple, yet claims are rarely as clear as that made for the Jumbo ballpoint pen.

Advertising Claims

There are two basic kinds of claims—one that provides information useful in making a purchase decision, and one that tells little or nothing factual. Here are some advertising claims similar to ones that have been used repeatedly on radio and television and in print advertising.

Look at each ad claim and then write (on a separate piece of paper) what you think the commercial "claims" about the product. Rate each claim as either (a) one that provides useful information or (b) one that gives little or no useful information. After you have done this with each of the four ads, go on and read the comments made by a skilled ad reader.

CLAIM 1

"Everbright toothpaste helps get your teeth whiter and cleaner. Its special ingredient XT-40 fights tooth decay."

CLAIM 2

"Brushing with Goodteeth toothpaste helps fight tooth decay. Nine out of ten dentists interviewed agreed that brushing with Goodteeth is effective in combating decay."

CLAIM 3

"New improved Blubbers bubble gum now has twice as many sticks of gum. New Green Blubbers is chewed by more professional football players than any other bubble gum. Look for Blubbers in the bright green package wherever good gum is sold."

CLAIM 4

"Strictly controlled scientific tests by an independent testing laboratory show that Imperial gasoline with PowerTane® outperforms any gasoline made without PowerTane. Get Imperial gasoline with Power-Tane to help your car run quieter, smoother, and get more miles per gallon."

Comments of a Skilled Ad Reader

(Do not read this until you have made your own comments about the four fictional ads on the previous page.)

CLAIM 1

This ad contains no useful information. Many ads make use of comparative adjectives such as *whiter, cleaner, quieter,* etc., without saying whiter or cleaner than what. Cleaner than if you used mustard as toothpaste? Whiter than if you used licorice paste? The ad doesn't say. Perhaps the ad means only that brushing teeth is better than not brushing. The claim invites the reader to supply the missing comparison by saying "cleaner and whiter than any other toothpaste." But the ad does not say this, and to believe it does is to misunderstand it. The ad is not misleading only if it is read very carefully.

Another claim made in the ad is that Everbright contains a special ingredient—XT-40—to fight tooth decay. What is XT-40? It could be something that has always been in the toothpaste; it could be something that all toothpastes contain.

The claim "fights tooth decay" is very carefully worded. It doesn't say "stops" tooth decay. If Everbright could stop tooth decay, the ad would say that. Brushing with water also "fights tooth decay"; so does using toothpicks.

CLAIM 2

The word *helps* is used thousands of times in advertising. Remember that "helps" does not mean "does"—it means "helps." It would be perfectly accurate to say that "a bucket of water helps fight forest fires." But that is not the same as saying that a bucket of water can put out a forest fire.

"Nine out of ten dentists" (or doctors, athletes, or whomever) means simply that the company was able to find nine who agreed. Note that dentists would agree that brushing with anything would help fight decay; brushing is more important than what is put on the brush. Dentists know that the proper brushing technique is more important than the brand of toothpaste. The statement doesn't say that Goodteeth itself stops or fights decay—it says that *brushing* with Goodteeth "helps" (remember that word) fight decay.

CLAIM 3

The word *new* (or *revolutionary*, or *improved*, or *all new*) is another of the advertiser's favorites. "New" does not necessarily mean better—it simply means different.

The fact that Blubbers has twice as many sticks is not the same as saying twice as much gum. They may have simply cut the same amount of gum up into smaller pieces. If the amount of gum had doubled, the ad would probably state that very clearly.

The claim that pro football players chew Blubbers means little. Perhaps each player was mailed a case at the beginning of the season. It would be a very hard claim to either prove or disprove. Also, there is no real connection between chewing gum and playing football well.

CLAIM 4

Be careful with this claim. Begin with the knowledge that gasolines are all pretty much the same. The claim here sounds good, but if you read carefully you can see that you never find out exactly what "PowerTane" is (remember "XT-40"). If "PowerTane" is simply a trademarked name for some common ingredient, then it would certainly be honest to say that "Imperial gasoline outperforms any gasoline made *without* PowerTane." In fact, all gas does have the same ingredient that Imperial calls PowerTane. But Imperial has registered the name "PowerTane" so that no other company can use it—this is called a registered trademark. The claim amounts only to saying that "our car with wheels rides smoother than any car made without wheels."

The ad encourages the unskilled reader to think that Imperial outperforms any other gasoline. But the ad does not actually say that. If Imperial did indeed outperform any other, you can be sure the ad would say so very clearly. Notice that the ad never uses untruth. Also notice that the final sentence again contains comparisons without an ending. Quieter, smoother, and more miles per gallon than what?

A Short Course in Advertising Claims

If your analysis of the four fictional claims was not as perceptive as that of the "advertising expert," you need at least a short course in advertising analysis.

One basic rule to remember in analyzing ads is that if any product is truly superior, the ad will say so very clearly and will offer some kind of convincing evidence of its superiority. If an ad hedges at all about a product's superiority, you can suspect that it is not really superior. You will never hear Standard Oil (or any other brand) say "Standard gasoline in your car gives you four miles per gallon more than any other brand." Standard would love to make such a claim, but it simply isn't true. Comparable types of gasoline are all pretty much the same. Although there were some clever and deceptive gasoline ads a few years ago, no one has yet made an outright claim that one brand of gasoline is better than any other brand.

To create the necessary illusion of superiority, advertisers usually resort to one or more of the following eleven basic techniques. Each is common and easy to identify.

I. The Unfinished Claim

The unfinished claim is one in which the ad claims that the product is "better" or has "more" of something but it does not finish the comparison.

Samples:

"Magnavox gives you more." (More what?)

"Supergloss does it with more color, more shine, more sizzle, more!"

"Twice as much of the pain reliever doctors recommend most." (Twice as much as what?)

"You can be sure if it's Westinghouse."

"Scott makes it better for you."

"Ford LTD—700% quieter."

2. The Weasel Word Claim

A *weasel word* is a modifier that makes what follows nearly meaningless. The term *weasel word* comes from the habits of weasels who suck out the inside of a raw egg through a tiny hole. An unsuspecting person picks up what looks like a whole egg only to find it is empty. Weasel word claims sound convincing at first, but upon closer examination turn out to be empty claims.

The most common weasel words include *helps* (perhaps the most used), *virtual* or *virtually*, *like* (used in a comparative sense), *acts* or *works, can be, up to, as much as, refreshes, comforts, fights, the feel of* (also *the look of*), *tastes, fortified, enriched, strengthened.*

Samples:

"Helps control dandruff symptoms with regular use" (This claim is an accurate statement about the product. A consumer would be wrong to think that the claim is the same as "cures dandruff.")

"Leaves dishes virtually spotless" (An unskilled ad reader will remember the claim as being "spotless" and not *almost* ("virtually") spotless. We hear so many weasel words that we tend to tune them out—which is exactly what advertisers want.)

"Only half the price of many color sets" ("Many" is the weasel here. The ad does not claim that this set is inexpensive, only that there are some that cost twice as much.)

"Fights bad breath" (This is much like "helps control dandruff"; it does not say "stops bad breath.")

"Lots of things have changed, but Hershey's goodness hasn't." (This claim does not say that Hershey's chocolate has not changed.)

"Bac*os, the crispy garnish that tastes just like its name." (This does not say that Bac*os tastes the same as bacon.)

A Special Weasel—"better" and "best"

The reason so many ads need to use weasel words and the other techniques described here is that they are applied to *parity products*. A parity product is one in which all or most of the available brands are nearly identical. Since no one superior product exists, advertising is used to create the illusion of superiority. The largest advertising budgets are devoted to such parity products as beer and soft drinks, cigarettes, soaps, and various drugstore pain remedies.

In parity claims, the words *better* and *best* take on unique meanings. In such claims, *better* means "best" and *best* means "as good as." Here's how this word game works: Let's say that in a given product category there are a number of brands that are alike. Legally this means that each can claim to be best—they are all "superior." Since they are all equal, they must all be best. So "best" means that the product is as good as all the other superior products in its category. If one orange juice says "the best there is," this means only that it is as good as (not better than) any other orange juice on the market.

On the other hand, the word *better* has been legally interpreted as being comparative and therefore becomes a clear claim of superiority. That orange juice ad could not legally have claimed "better than any other brand." The only times "better" can be used are (a) if the product is indeed better than anything else; (b) if "better" is actually used to compare the product with something else ("our orange juice is better than powdered drinks"); or (c) if "better" is part of an unfinished claim ("the better breakfast drink").

Samples of "better" and "best" weasels:
"Better Shopper brand cocoa is the very best."

"Tests confirm one mouthwash better against mouth odor."

3. The "We're Different and Unique" Claim

This kind of claim states simply that there is nothing else quite like the product advertised. For example, if a lemonade manufacturer added blue food coloring, it could advertise, "There's nothing like new blue Tarttaste." The uniqueness claim is supposed to be interpreted by readers as an indication of superiority.

Samples:
"There's no other mascara like it."

"Only Inca has this unique filter system."

"Panther is like nobody else's car."

"Either way, liquid or spray, there's nothing else like it."

"If it doesn't say Goodyear, it can't be Polyglas." ("Polyglas" is a trade name copyrighted by Goodyear. Goodrich or Firestone could make a tire identical to the Goodyear one and yet they couldn't call it "Polyglas"—a name for fiberglass belts.)

4. The "Water Is Wet" Claim

"Water is wet" claims say something about the product that is true for any brand in that product category (e.g., "Schrank's water is really wet"). The

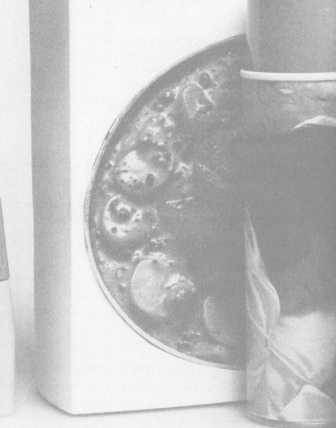

claim is usually a statement of fact, but not a real advantage over the competition—though it is made to sound like one.

Samples:
"The Detergent Gasoline" (true of any gas)

"Brasilia: The 100% Brazilian Coffee" (Most American brands import coffee from Brazil.)

"Great Lash greatly increases the diameter of every lash." (Any mascara does.)

"Skin smells differently on everyone." (as does all perfume)

5. The "So What" Claim

This is the kind of claim to which the careful reader will react by saying "So what?" A claim is made that is true but that gives no real advantage to the product. This technique is similar to the "water is wet" claim, except that it does claim an advantage that is not shared by most of the other brands in the product category.

Samples:
"Campbell's gives you tasty pieces of chicken and not one but two chicken stocks." (What good are two stocks?)

"More than twice the iron of ordinary supplements" (But is twice as much any better?)

Strong enough for a man but made for a woman" (This deodorant claim says only that the product is aimed at the female market.)

6. The Vague Claim

The vague claim is simply not clear; this category often overlaps others. The key to the vague claim is the use of words that are colorful but meaningless, as well as the use of subjective and emotional opinions that defy verification. Most of these claims contain weasels.

Samples:
"Lips have never looked so luscious." (Can you imagine trying to either prove or disprove such a claim?)

"Lipsavers are fun—they taste good, smell good and feel good."

"Its deep rich lather makes hair feel new again."

"For skin like peaches and cream."

"The end of meatloaf boredom"

"Take a bite and you'll think you're eating on the Champs Elysées."

7. The Endorsement or Testimonial

This technique uses a celebrity or authority in an ad to lend his or her stellar qualities to the product, whether what the person is known for is related to the ad or not. Sometimes the people actually claim to use the product, but very often they don't. Some agencies survive by providing "names" for testimonials.

Samples:

"Don't leave home without it." (Karl Malden for American Express Travelers' checks)

"They make money the old fashioned way; they earn it." (John Housman for Smith-Barney, Inc.)

"Play to win with Ram." (Tom Watson for Golden Ram Golf Equipment)

"So easy even I can do it." (John Newcombe for Canon Cameras)

8. The Scientific or Statistical Claim

This kind of ad refers to some sort of scientific proof or experiments, to very specific numbers, or to an impressive-sounding mystery ingredient.

Samples:

"Wonder Bread helps build strong bodies 12 ways."
(Even the weasel "helps" did not prevent the FTC from demanding this ad be withdrawn. But note that the use of the number *12* makes the claim far more believable than if it were left out or replaced by, say, "many ways.")

"Mrs. Molly's Oven Cleaner has 33% more cleaning power than another popular brand."
("Another popular brand" translates simply as some other kind of oven cleaner sold somewhere. What the claim probably means is that Mrs. Molly's Oven Cleaner comes in a can ⅓ larger than the can used by another brand.)

"Special Morning—33% more nutrition" (also an unfinished claim)

"Certs contains a sparkling drop of Retsyn."

"Sinarest. Created by a research scientist who actually gets sinus headaches"

9. The "Compliment the Consumer" Claim

This kind of claim butters up the consumer by some form of flattery.

Samples:

"We think cigar smokers are someone special."

"You've come a long way, baby."

"You pride yourself on your good home cooking. . ."

"The lady has taste."

"If what you do is right for you, no matter what the others do, then RC Cola is right for you."

10. The Rhetorical Question

This technique demands a response from the audience. A question is asked that is worded so that the viewer or listener is supposed to answer in a way that affirms the product's goodness.

Samples:

"Plymouth—isn't that the kind of car America wants?"

"Shouldn't your family be drinking Hawaiian Punch?"

"What do you want most from coffee? That's what you get most from Hills."

"Touch of Sweden: Could your hands use a small miracle?"

"Wouldn't you really rather have a Buick?"

11. Incomplete Information

The ad can make some claim which is accurate but incomplete. Some important bit of information is withheld from the consumer, thus increasing the chances for misunderstanding.

Samples:

"Made with wool" (This claim does not mean "made entirely out of wool" or "100% wool." It means only there is some wool in the garment.)

"Now with Nutrasweet" (When the sweetener Nutrasweet was first introduced in soft drinks, many people understood this claim to mean that Nutrasweet had taken the place of saccharin in the soft drink. In reality, Nutrasweet had replaced only some of the saccharin.)

"BINGO cereal is part of a nutritious breakfast." (This claim does not mean BINGO is nutritious. If you serve pure junk food with milk and fruit, you could claim it is "part of" a nutritious meal.)

Advertising Claims

1. As a class, go through the list of claims below and note for each (a) what a casual or non-expert reader might believe each ad says, and (b) what an expert ad analyst would say about the claim:

"Built better, not cheaper."

"You're not getting older. You're getting better."

"The taste of extra freshness."

"Five of these six top shipping pros are more than satisfied with the new Pony Express Shipping System."

"New lemony Woodwright gives you the look of hand-rubbed wood beauty instantly."

"Hair Beauty shampoo is enriched with protein and conditioners to make hair look healthy."

"Custom Blend Coffee lets me be different."

"If you care enough to serve the very best, you serve Crystal Springs natural water."

"Super-Clean works to eliminate unwanted odors. It works faster and smells fresh."

"Give an acne pimple something to worry about. Use Wipeout medicated soap. Fortified with AR-2."

2. Take about one week to find examples of each of the 11 advertising techniques pointed out in this chapter. Tear the ads out of magazines or newspapers or quote directly from TV or radio.

3. Select one or more products and devise a way to compare the advertising claims made for that product with the product itself. Construct a test (or a series of tests) to verify or disprove the advertised claims.

4. Rewrite some ads so that they change from ads presenting little or no information to ads that are genuinely helpful to consumers.

5. What kinds of products do you believe have the most useful and honest advertising? Which have the least useful? Is it possible to generalize?

6. Write letters to the manufacturers of some products whose advertising you believe is deceptive. Explain your case in writing. As a class, decide on the best letters and mail them.

7. Write some advertising copy that accurately describes a product you really believe to be of high quality. Make your ad useful to consumers and completely honest—but at the same time make it one that will sell the product.

Understanding Emotional Appeal

Once you are able to evaluate ad claims so that they don't mislead you, you are ready for the second important skill necessary to deal with advertising. You need to be able to see how the ad appeals to you, how it involves your feelings, wishes, and dreams. Ads attempt to make products look luxurious, sexy, grown-up, modern, happy, patriotic, or any one of dozens of other desirable qualities.

Nearly every ad (except purely factual advertising such as that of a grocery store listing its prices) attempts to give the impression that the product advertised will make the user one or more of the following:

Of course, toothpaste or shampoo or soap or deodorant will *not* make their users any of these things. But the advertiser tries to say that the user will *feel* loved or popular or whatever if he or she uses the product.

A product claim is an attempt to convince potential buyers that a certain product is better than any other and that it works. The appeal in the ad is to feelings and emotions. Many studies have shown that a person's choice of a specific product and brand is more often based on feelings than on specific product claims. Most ads have both a reasonable-sounding claim and an appeal to feelings. The careful viewer or listener should be able to see in any ad not only what claim is being made, but also what emotional appeal is being used.

Here are some descriptions of ads or portions of ads. Read each and determine what feelings the ad implies the product will give its users. After you have done this, read the comments of a skilled ad reader that follow.

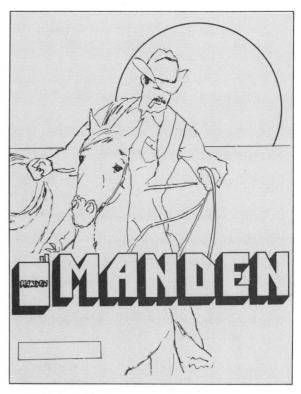

APPEAL #1:

Cigarette ad: picture of a cowboy riding a horse across the prairie with a sunset in the background. Cowboy is smoking a Manden cigarette.

APPEAL #2:

Automobile ad: the auto is parked in front of a huge mansion. A uniformed chauffeur stands nearby as a man in a tuxedo and a woman in a formal gown get into the car.

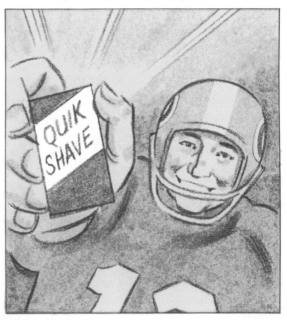

APPEAL #4:

Razor ad: a football player in uniform is holding up a package of Quik-Shave razor blades, saying ''If Quik-Shave can shave me close, it can shave anybody.''

APPEAL #3:

Ad for any one of many possible products: picture of a handsome man and a beautiful girl hugging each other while looking over a lush green valley.

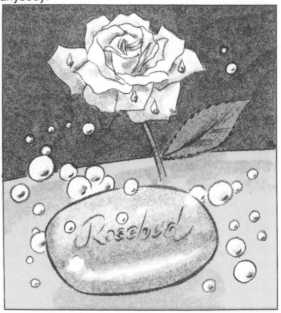

APPEAL #5:

Soap ad: picture of a beautiful rose with fresh morning dewdrops on its petals. The rose is growing out of a sink filled with soapsuds. Somewhere on the ad are the words: ''For hands soft as roses use Rosebud.''

CU--Man with dandruff on his coat.

MS--man looking at his dandruff.

    man: Billy, Why don't you use. . .

CU--Man and woman.

    Man: Jeanie, I don't know what I would
do without you.

LS--Family in living room. Father
taking pictures.

CU--Camera with chromakeyed sunset.

CU--Film and logo. Chromakey of sunset.
Music over.

APPEAL #6:

TV commercial: a man is unable to get a date with a girl he likes. A friend tells him that he has bad breath (or dandruff or body odor or acne or messy hair, or wears the wrong kind of clothes, or any one of dozens of such evils). He takes the advice of his friend, switches to the product being advertised, and in the end he and the girl are together.

APPEAL #7:

TV commercial for a certain kind of film: a happy family is together in front of a fireplace. The father is taking a picture of the rest of the happy family.

The Ad Reader's Comments

APPEAL #1:

The picture in this cigarette ad suggests the romantic ideal of the old West where every man was his own boss—a rugged individualist. It further suggests wide-open spaces and freedom. The ad appeals to people who wish to be considered rugged and strong, to people who feel a longing for freedom such as that suggested by the wide-open spaces of the wilderness. The ad suggests that smoking a Manden is somehow associated with these feelings. It also suggests that, since this rugged individual smokes Manden, if you consider yourself that kind of person, you too should smoke this brand. The ad does not say that people will think you are a rugged masculine man if you smoke Manden, but the picture implies it.

APPEAL #2:

In looking for the emotional or feeling hook in an ad, always notice the setting in which the product is placed. Placing the automobile by the huge mansion with a chauffeur and people in expensive clothing says that this is a car for wealthy people: if you want to feel wealthy or be considered wealthy by others, then buy this car. The ad would never come out and say "Buy this car and people will think you're rich," but that is what the picture implies. Always look for the setting in which the product is placed for a clue to the feeling hook in each ad.

APPEAL #3:

This picture could be used for perhaps hundreds of different products. Probably the ad would show a bit of ad copy (written claims) at the bottom and a picture of the product somewhere. The picture suggests love, beautiful people, freedom, the beauty of nature, and even a certain "naturalness" and youth. The picture might be used in an ad for shampoo, deodorant, clothes, hair spray, or even cigarettes or jewelry. The emotional appeal of the ad is that by using the product advertised you will somehow be associated with the feelings the picture suggests. At the very least, the picture creates a good mood, so that the reader will experience a pleasant feeling when seeing the product's name.

APPEAL #4:

Famous people are paid large sums of money to appear in advertisements holding, or sitting in, or wearing, eating, or drinking certain products. If you view such ads carefully, you will see that the celebrity rarely says he or she uses the product all the time. Advertisers can pay for famous people to appear to endorse their products. They will pick the person according to the feeling this person communicates— it should be a feeling the advertiser wants to be associated with the product. In the Quik-Shave ad, the maker assumes that men like to think of themselves as rough and tough, and the football player is an excellent choice to suggest such a person.

The idea behind endorsements is that some of the heroics and fame of the star become associated with the product and, therefore, with all the users of that product. The ad suggests that you, too, can be like this famous person just by using Quik-Shave.

APPEAL #5:

The rose suggests softness, beauty, and delicacy. By placing the rose in the soapsuds, the ad suggests that your hands will feel as soft as rose petals if you use Rosebud. The picture says this far more appealingly than words could.

APPEAL #6:

This is a very common kind of commercial. The suggestion is that simply by using a certain product, the user will become popular, be accepted where he or she was rejected before and will instantly solve a personal problem. The ad appeals to people who feel "left out" or unpopular. People who are popular know that their popularity has nothing to do with which brands they use.

APPEAL #7:

This ad creates good feelings by showing the happy family around the fireplace. The suggestion is that by using the kind of film being advertised, you too can achieve such family joy.

MEDIALAB

Advertising Analysis

1. Make a portfolio of ads from magazines illustrating the various types of emotional appeals. Write an explanation of each ad's appeal.

2. Pick either an ad in print (magazines, newspapers) or a TV or radio commercial that best fits each of the following categories:

The World's Most Honest Ad.

The Forked Tongue Award—for skill in sneaky, misleading, and deceptive use of language in ads.

The At-Least-It's-Fun Award—to the most entertaining ad.

The Foot-in-the-Door Award—to the most persuasive ad found.

The World's Worst Advertisement.

My Favorite Ad.

3. Write and/or draw an ad you consider to be honest, helpful, and important. The ad can be for some service or quality—peace, the elimination of poverty, love, better education, ecology, justice, etc. You may pick your own topic for the ad or use one of the following:

A horse is better than a car.

Garbage is valuable—save your garbage.

A toothpick

A button is better than a zipper.

No one over 21 should hold public office.

The legal age to vote should be 14 years.

Water

A machine that dispenses a whiff of fresh air for 25¢

An automatic watermelon deseeder

A new invention—black and white television

Old, warped phonograph records

4. Find some old advertisements either in magazines (at least ten years old) or in books that reprint old ads. Bring some to class and examine how advertising has both changed and remained the same over the years. You might also want to consider whether the changes in ads mirror the changes in people.

5. In some European countries that have commercial television, the ads are lumped together at the beginning of a program segment. If a one-hour program is shown, the first 8 or so minutes contain

FOOT IN DOOR AWARD

FORKED TONGUE AWARD

all the ads, and the program then runs uninterrupted for the next 52 minutes. What do you think of this system? How might it affect the ads themselves?

6. In many countries the television and radio stations are run by the government. They contain no advertising at all. Do you think such a system (one in which the government provides all the money) has any advantages over a system in which advertisers provide the money? Are there disadvantages?

7. What kinds of ads are most commonly found in comic books? Why do you think advertisers choose these books?

8. One of the most important selling techniques in advertising is repetition. Repetition is used within an ad, and ads themselves are repeated frequently. A common means of repetition is to repeat the selling message several times within each ad. Ads on TV and in magazines are used dozens or even hundreds of times. Do you think this repetition irritates people or increases the likelihood of the ad's being successful? How is repetition used in a similar way in school?

9. Which of these do you think benefits most from good advertising: a product truly superior to its competition? A product no better and no worse than its competition? A product obviously worse than its competitors?

10. What would happen if all advertising were abolished?

11. Read and report on one chapter from any one of the following books:

The Promise and the Product by Victor Magolin and Ira and Vivian Brichta.

Thirty Seconds by Michael Arlen.

The Hidden Persuaders by Vance Packard.

Down the Tube by Terry Galanoy.

I Can Sell You Anything by Paul Stevens.

Reality in Advertising by Rosser Reeves.

Ogilvy on Advertising by David Ogilvy.

Motivating Human Behavior by Ernest Dichter.

12. The project team's report on "The Image of Women/Men in Advertising" could be presented now.

The Appeal of Television Commercials

The images in television commercials often are so bright, so wonderful, and so exciting that we fail to find out just how they are created. We want to believe that people and products are as clean and shining as the images we see. The following article shows the ways in which highly skilled directors give us gorgeous scenes full of action and excitement to whet our dreams and appetites. The images in commercials often appear almost magical. A cucumber slice appears as a UFO and a bar of soap seems as majestic as the Grand Canyon. How does a television commercial make the genuinely artificial food substitute look deliciously real? Here's how.

OF DIRECTORS, MAGIC AND WATERFALLS OF SALAD DRESSING

by Jonathan Price

The art of making consumer products appeal to the casual television viewer is part of the skill of TV commercial directors.

In primitive times Celtic kings hired sorcerers to cast a "glamour" over a hill to make the enemy imagine a fortress where there was only a hut. Nowadays the strategists of commercials seek such magical interference with our vision from a director. For approximately $2,000 a day a director is expected to add a glow to the idea. The director sets up bright-bright lights and brings wrap-around lenses in for giant close-ups of superactive scenes, featuring realer than real consumers. The best directors hypo the hype.

Unlike a real movie director, the director of a commercial does not work with the writer during the process of writing; he is not consulted about a script before it is submitted to him for a bid; and often he does not meet the cast until the day of the shoot. He may not change the basic story, or the characters, during the shoot. And although he may have the right to try his own editing, he almost never controls the final version, since the ad agency steps in, choosing the shots they like and ordering those shots the way they like.

Because his control is cramped in so many important ways, a director of commercials has a limited range of decisions to make (lights, camera, acting, sets), but even in this restricted field a good director can make the difference between humdrum and startling appearance. Directors add gloss. Directors work in film, which still provides slightly sharper images, clearer depth of field, stronger colors than videotape, because it is fast, cheap, and relatively easy to edit, these commercials *look* better than the shows. . . .

The personality of a director tends to show up in his choice of specialization. You might not think it, but each major product category has its conventions (wine ads are misty; shampoos require brilliantly back-lit showers), and some directors polish those conventions to a slick gleam. One director excels at food, another at cars; a third can handle animals and kids well; still another actually works with grown-up human actors to get a strong performance. (This is known as "people-directing.")

Tony Ficalora, for instance, shows us food the way it might appear to a baby rolling in it or to a starving man hallucinating in the desert. Ficalora can make a salad dressing seem like a waterfall and a salad like a jungle. In one spot we move through the lettuce leaves slowly—as moisture from above drips into the camera—nosing our way to the heart of the greenery. Only when red dressing slops down onto these giant bushes do we realize that our sense of scale has been fooled and we are actually in the bowl. In another spot for Kraft, giant eggs roll toward us, lumbering left and right, until one gets picked up and cracked at the end. That frame freezes motion in glistening white while the mayonnaise label appears. . . .

Ficalora likes vast banquets. His home economist (a director who works with food has to have one) knows how to cook for looks—and how to keep the food looking luscious despite hours under the hot lights. She will bake ten chocolate cakes, a dozen chickens, in succession, bringing each out of the oven at intervals so that there will always be a fresh one in front of the camera. And in his best films, Mateus rosé comes surrounded with slippery hot lobsters and misty grapes; Celeste pizza drips oil and cheese as we lift a slice; another hand-size food becomes a basketball for Tropicana.

Such directorial exaggeration enlarges our appetite, encouraging us to dream of jumping into our food as if it were a pile of hay. When a Ficalora orange flies open, so many giant drops of juice fly out in a medium-size TV that, if they were real, we could use up a whole sheet of Bounty cleaning the screen. Surreal? He seems medieval to me, like an archetype of the Glutton, whose eye is bigger than his belly.

Andy Jenkins, by contrast, likes to work outdoors, shooting supposed "locals" and "real people," making fake scenes seem more real than any hand-held documentary ever could.

Following the maxim that seeing is believing, Jenkins persuades us by his attentive work with actors, generating whole lives for people who appear for only three seconds, and building a complete town or home for them, even if we see only one corner. Often these grizzled inhabitants are actors, but with Jenkins, they woof and scratch and go around looking like "jes folks." He set fire to an abandoned farm for Metropolitan Life. We see chickens run from an old-fashioned fire truck; we see geezers staring; we hear the grateful farmer hold out his thanks to the firemen—"You boys want a couple of chickens?" Except for the fact that every shot is gorgeous and full of active detail, we might think this brief film had been shot during a real fire. Jenkins' most spectacular shot shows the misty dunes of Kitty Hawk or Cape Hatteras; we see the tan plane clearly, it comes toward us, it takes off, then we soar with it, over the first hill of sand. The mood is gentle, lovely, gray. Jenkins likes intricate construction: he built the Wright Brothers' plane for that spot; and for Owens-Corning, he built an igloo in the Mojave desert and insulated it with their Fiberglas. It did not melt.

Bob Giraldi, a popular director, costs five to ten thousand dollars more than a nonstar director, but he can give you a dreamy "look" that will glamorize your product. He once did an antique spot for Barney's, showing how the men's store started; he used forty suits from the period and shot the whole in sepia; only when we come up to the present do we enter a world of color. Giraldi shot a karate dojo in yellowish light, showing

slow-motion turns and kicks, then went to a bar for the after-workout drink of Miller's; the bar is darker, crowded with reds and browns, and the beer seems to light it up. Lots of smiles, daps, and handshakes here; so we get two spaces, two moods. For Arrow shirts he re-created an upper crust British garden party in such detail that a regular movie director would wince with envy; for Pioneer he made beautiful pictures of the interior of Carnegie Hall.

. . . One of the few directors who does keep the kind of total control a Hollywood pro does is Dan Nichols, and he started out as a writer. . . . Nichols' involvement with the writing allows him to plan the high volume of scenes in his spots; in one sixty-second McDonald's spot he showed sixty-five scenes, and in most spots he crams in fast cuts, zooms, and reverses. For one commercial about McDonald's take-out food, called *Ice Nine,* he figured out sixty-four potential snow scenes and listed them in categories; under "Down-hill Skiing," for instance, he listed these shots:

1) Aerials of skis, flip, spread eagles, layouts, crossing
2) Ski race start at timing gate
3) High-speed powder skiing
4) High-speed slalom
5) Mogul head bops
6) Kite
7) Ski jump (high speed)
8) 36-degree pole swings
9) Cross-country skiing
10) Hot dogging . . . ballet

After that ten seconds, we go on to look at ice skating, snow chores, sledding, snow romps, snow school, snow sports, picnickers in the snow eating McDonald's take-out food, and girls indoors, "nice and warm."

One McDonald's spot is titled *Quick Cuts,* and that is Nichols' style. To be seen and recognized in half a second, each scene must be clear, well-lit, and carefully planned. If we pan left in one scene, we often pan right in the next; if we are moving forward for one second, we may pull back in the next. His editing established a rhythm of movement: two stills, a move forward, a move back, a still, then the camera holds still while someone moves past it to the right, then back to the left. He uses frozen frames like dotted notes, or syncopation, holding one image for a while so that the next one is more sharply emphasized. They mark the end of one sequence of ski sports, the beginning of ice hockey scenes; they give us a rest. In another one, each frozen frame shows us a person, the target of the song "You, you're the one." Nichols comments, "My formula is energy. You have to keep it going."

Such complex, baroque visions make McDonald's seem dense with life—lots of physical movement, lots of memorable snapshots. But ultimately such spots are as artificial as a McDonald's shake. Perhaps that very artificiality—the "madeness" of the spots—appeals to Americans at least as much as the whetted-up vitality. There are two men who disagree: David and Albert Maysles believe people want to look at reality, and they have made grimy documentary films like *Salesman,* in which they trail Bible salesmen around the country. Their films seem unrehearsed. As David Maysles says, "The viewer never really

knows what's coming up next because that's the way it was shot. The photographer doesn't know what's coming up next." When they make a film, they pay for it themselves, so they keep complete control. But they pay for these feature films by making spots.

They do not charge the advertiser much because they just take their cameras out on location and talk to real people who use the product or make it. "The transition from documentaries to commercials wasn't as difficult as you'd think," says David Maysles. "The copywriters and art directors did most of the research in picking the people we were going to work with, and then we shot as we normally do." Bob Judd and Jerry Weldor of J. Walter Thompson located a Champion Spark Plug dealer who would let them film him; we see him chat with customers, go out to service a broken-down car, wave at the camera. He seems friendly, at ease. Evidently it took a few hours for him to relax, but after a while he just went ahead with his work without "acting" and the results seem casual and comfortable. Nothing hard-hitting, but something fairly intimate. Then there's the spot they did for IBM in which we see one employee after another wishing us Happy New Year—it's moving because there are so many and they seem to be having such a good time with the cameraman. Advertising coffee, the Maysles shot an impromptu basketball game in a gym; as guys came off the court to relax, they were asked if they had drunk coffee for breakfast. Yes, indeed. It looks like luck, but a lot of the casual, friendly mood comes

from the down-home directness of the men behind the camera.

Reality, then, is a certain "look." "You've got to give the Maysles their head, or you shouldn't hire them," says Howard Rieger of Young & Rubicam. That could apply to any of these top directors. But the Maysles lived with one family for three days just to get a picture of them eating Jell-O. "For Jell-O we wanted spontaneous, natural, believable dialogue," says Rieger. "If you're looking for reality, they're the guys."

Perhaps. But once "reality" is sliced into a commercial selling a dream of coffee as a high-energy food, we reenter the fantasy realm. Perhaps, as Aristotle suggested, we want to believe in dramas and get angry only when forced to face their open falsity. So a high premium gets put on making the lie believable, shiny, hypnotic, luscious, active, and arresting. In a commercial, it seems, the director is the person who makes the genuinely artificial food substitute look more deliciously real than steak. And Americans love it—we eat dreams. ■

MEDIALAB

The Magic of Images

1. In what way are some directors of television commercials like magicians?

2. Describe some current television commercials in which ordinary objects (autos, ice cream, salad dressing, etc.) seem to glow or appear larger than life and very inviting.

3. Debate the following proposal: "There ought to be a law forbidding advertisers to show their products in an unreal way. Advertisers are not allowed to tell lies in print or spoken words; they shouldn't be allowed to deceive in pictures either."

4. The article concerns television commercials. Much of what is said about TV ads, however, is also true of magazine advertising. Find examples of visual persuasion in magazine advertising.

5. Discuss how people are chosen for commercials so as to be the most convincing. Be sure to discuss the value of people with no professional acting experience.

6. The article talks about one sixty-second McDonald's spot containing sixty-five scenes. What current commercials use such fast-paced editing? Why?

7. Are there some products that are better presented in longer, slower moving shots?

8. Examine some television commercials and explain the various ways in which the director makes the product attractive.

9. Describe how a commercial for milk would look if directed by Tony Ficalora. How would it be different if directed by Andy Jenkins or the Maysles brothers?

10. Directors of TV ads do not receive on-screen credits. Discuss some currently popular ads that have similar "looks" to those discussed in the article.

SO YOU THINK YOU UNDERSTAND FILM!

A Test

If you can correctly answer six out of the following nine questions before reading this chapter, you already know so much about film that you should be making films instead of reading about them. If you cannot answer at least six correctly, you need to read the rest of this chapter.

The questions are not the most important ones that can be asked about film, but they do require a firm understanding of film.

1. A recent feature film produced by a major Hollywood studio left the audience sitting in front of a blank screen for 45 of its 90 minutes. The blank screen was part of *every* showing and was not caused by equipment failure. The film was a box office success and played in your area. What was the film and why did the audience put up with the blank screen?

2. The film version of *Fiddler on the Roof* was shot almost entirely with the camera lens covered by an ordinary nylon stocking purchased in a local department store. Why was this done?

3. If you watch a feature film for one hour, how many separate still pictures do you see? (Assumption: You don't fall asleep or leave for popcorn.)

4. You have a reel of film about two minutes long containing pictures of a rather expressionless face. How could you show this film in such a way that an audience would believe the face shows a variety of emotions? You may add additional film but cannot change the two-minute film you have.

5. Define (a) a scene, (b) a cut-away, (c) an establishing shot.

6. Which arts do not have "editing" as part of the creative process?

7. During which years did people go to movies and watch films without sound? (Pick any one year for your answer. If that year is one in which people watched films in silence, the answer is correct.)

8. When were movies invented? (Answer must be accurate within five years of the exact date.)

9. How many pictures does a professional movie camera take in one minute of shooting?

ANSWER KEY:
Answers to the test questions can be found on the following pages of this chapter.

1 on page 86
2 on page 110
3 on page 87
4 on page 97
5 on page 93
6 on page 96
7 on page 112
8 on page 86
9 on page 86

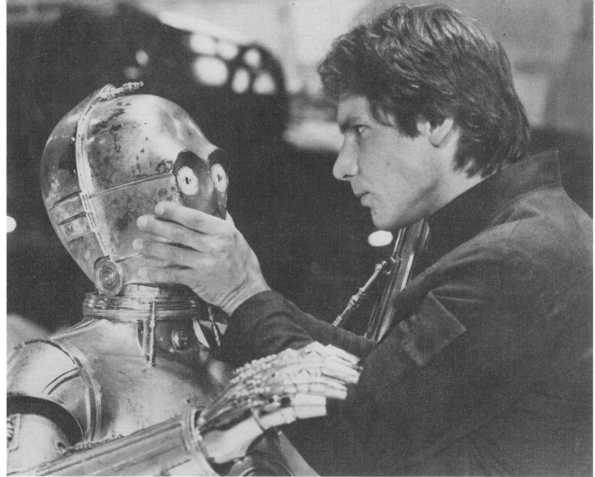

Han Solo (Harrison Ford) uses primitive means to deactivate C-3PO's (Anthony Daniels) voice mechanism in a scene from *The Empire Strikes Back*, the successful sequel to *Star Wars*. (© Lucasfilm Ltd. (LFL) 1980, all rights reserved.)

"IT" THE FILM MEETS "I" THE VIEWER

Critics writing about *Star Wars*, the first installment of George Lucas' intergalactic trilogy:

. . . warmed-over 'Wizard of Oz,' Flash Gordon, Jack Armstrong, and World War II dogfights all rolled into one.

—P. RULE (*America* magazine)

Lucas has rather left his audience out in the cold, with only regularly administered shots of special effects to keep them warm.

—R. BOMBS (*Monthly Film Bulletin*, a British magazine)

. . . . so strong and so refreshing that it takes a crusty person indeed to resist its charms.

—K. TURAN (*The Progressive*)

This is the trippiest, most convincingly technological science-fiction film ever made.

—D. ROBBELOTH (*Audience* magazine)

. . . . fundamentally dull and misconceived . . . an empty thing . . . the biggest exploitation movie of them all.

—M. MOORCOCK (*The New Statesman*)

This is the kind of film in which an audience, first entertained, can later walk out feeling good all over.

—*Variety*

You might think that six professional critics should be able to decide whether a major film is a crashing bore or an exciting masterpiece. But as the excerpts from film reviews show, opinions on *Star Wars* were quite divided. Six jewelers would not disagree on whether a necklace was made of diamonds or glass. But six film critics can look at the same film and judge it anywhere between "dull" and "extraordinary."

Critical opinion of almost any film, whether by professional critics or the weekend filmgoer, will vary from those who consider it the best film they have ever seen to those who find it puts them to sleep. Often a film widely praised by critics will play only to the projectionist and empty seats, while another film generally conceded to be junk will break box office records.

One explanation for this wide range of opinions about film is that no two people "see" the same film. Each viewer enters into the world of the film and becomes part of that world. Comments made about films are often not comments about the film at all, they are comments that people make about themselves.

To help explain the special problem of talking about film, take a look at the drawing on this page and quickly (in five seconds or less) describe what you see.

Some will say the picture is an old woman, while others see a fashionable young woman. The problem is not one of disagreement about age. If you look at the picture long enough, you will see it change from young woman to old woman and back again. To see the gnarled old woman, focus on the neck band of the young woman—this is the old woman's mouth. The young woman's chin is the nose of the old woman.

The picture is no more an optical illusion than any other picture—or any movie. In looking at any object, we see selectively and are often surprised to find that others looking at the same picture or situation see something completely different.

You cannot accurately say the picture is of an old woman any more than you can say it is of a young woman. You *can* say, "I see an old woman" or "I see a young woman." Or "First I saw the young woman, then I saw the older one." In other words, you can make a statement about yourself that is accurate. The same is true in film.

After watching a film, listen to an audience as it leaves the theater. You will overhear some say the film was terrific, good, artistic, perhaps a master-piece. Others will call it a bore, dumb, meaningless, or simply bad. Some will leave the theater and have a long discussion, perhaps an argument, about whether the film was good or bad. But such a discussion is similar to an argument about whether the picture is of an old or a young woman.

Most likely the participants in such a discussion are not talking about the film at all; they are making statements about themselves but disguising the remarks as film criticism. In other words, most people do not distinguish between revealing person-al reactions to film and criticizing the film itself. Let's say you watch a film and later tell someone, "It was a bore." What you really mean is, "I was bored." There is a big difference between the two. Your comment is about *yourself* and not the film. Probably there were some people in the audience who were not the least bit bored. There is no commonly agreed-upon standard by which to judge whether a film is boring or not. But it is easy for you to recognize your own feeling of boredom.

In talking about films, you should be able to distinguish between comments about the film and comments about your reactions to the film. When

Opinions about films vary widely. *The Old Man and the Sea* is one of the films regarded anywhere from "flawed" to "extraordinary." Copyright © Warner Bros. Inc.

talking to friends, you will probably stay on the level of speaking in terms of yourself—unless you want to impress someone with your knowledge of film. When attempting film criticism, especially in communicating with an audience who does not know you, making statements about yourself is of limited value. If someone tells you that a certain film is "sickening," that does not mean you will find it "sickening"; you might enjoy the same film. If you know the person well, you might be able to say, "If that person found it sickening, I wouldn't like it either." A most common error in film discussion is to confuse statements about the film with statements about oneself.

The following statements were taken from overheard remarks or from written film criticism. Each statement is presented in terms of talking about the film. Imagine you are the person who made each statement and change each comment into a statement about yourself. Do *not* do this by adding "I think" to the beginning of the statement. For example, the statement "It was good but too long" could be changed to "I enjoyed the film but was bored toward the end."

"It was a sick film."

"It was a confused movie with a stupid and complicated plot."

"A moving work of art that will drive you to tears."

"This flick is really fantastic; you just *have* to see it."

"A collection of clichés long overused in science fiction films."

"The film drives home an important message that will make you think deeply about the problem of honesty."

"A dumb, idiotic film that didn't make any sense."

"A brilliant comedy marked by a sparkling sense of humor."

presenting in
SUPER PANAVISION!!
QUINTAPHONIC SOUND!!
3D!!

1. Explain the different feelings you have when you talk about a film in terms of yourself and when you comment in terms of the film alone. Which is most difficult? What special skills or attitudes are needed for each kind of statement?

2. Reread the critical comments about the film *Star Wars* on page 76. Which are statements about the film and which about the critic? Do you think any of them are statements about the critic "disguised" to look like statements about the film?

3. Some film critics write more about their personal reactions to films, while others attempt to be more objective and judge the film on its merits as a work of art or entertainment. Examine several film reviews by any critics (such as those in a local newspaper or a magazine you read) and decide which approach they use most. Which do you prefer? Which would you use if you were a professional movie critic?

4. We could call those who write mainly in terms of their own reactions "subjective critics" and those who write about the film as "objective critics." Why is it not possible to be completely objective about a film? Is it possible to be completely subjective?

5. During this chapter, the project team that selected a number of short films for classroom use should look at these films and talk about them with the class and in smaller groups. Talk about them in terms of yourself at first. As you gain more of the knowledge and vocabulary needed, talk about the films more objectively. Never have a discussion in which all you do is talk about "it"—the film.

6. Write two film reviews of some feature film you have seen recently or a short film shown in class. Review 1 should present you, the subjective critic, providing personal reactions to the film. Review 2 should present you, the objective critic, talking mainly about "it"—the film.

APPROACHES TO CRITICISM

Gene Siskel (left) and Roger Ebert (right) are co-hosts of ''At The Movies,'' the nationally syndicated weekly movie review program. Their witty reviews are as individually opposite as the two critiques reprinted here.

Read the two samples of film criticism/commentary that follow. The first is by Richard Corliss and appeared in *Time* magazine shortly after the release of *Indiana Jones and the Temple of Doom*. The second article is by *Denver Post* film critic Michael Healy and appeared a short time later. These critics view the Indiana Jones film from different perspectives, and each raises questions that show the value of film criticism. Both articles illustrate that film criticism goes far beyond a mere pronouncement of ''I like it'' or ''I don't like it.''

Keeping the Customer Satisfied

by Richard Corliss

Indiana Jones and the Temple of Doom provides sophisticated, familiar pleasures to millions of moviegoers. George Lucas and Steven Spielberg have found a way to update old Hollywood formulas. But do their movies touch the heart?

May 25, 1990. George Lucas and Steven Spielberg today announced plans to build a giant theme park called Star World, with attractions based on scenes from their films. Between them, Spielberg and Lucas have directed or produced the dozen top-grossing movies of all time: Jaws (1975), Star Wars (1977), The Empire Strikes Back (1980), Raiders of the Lost Ark (1981), E.T. The Extra-Terrestrial (1982), Return of the Jedi (1983), Indiana Jones and the Temple of Doom (1984), Gremlins (1984), Close Encounters: The Final Edition (1985), Indiana Jones Phones Home (1987), 1942 (1988) and The Gremlins Eat Princess Leia (1989).

A spokesman for the film makers' corporation, Luke Spielberger Ltd., said that the attractions will include a Poltergeist funhouse, a scuba dive through shark-infested waters, an American Graffiti drag strip, a Millennium Falcon journey through the Twilight Zone, an E.T. flying-bike ride and an Indiana Jones snake pit. The restaurants, or cantinas, will feature gremlins serving popcorn and candy bars. Each afternoon the Ewoks Marching Band will parade through the park playing the works of John Williams.

The spokesman would not confirm reports that Lucas and Spielberg intended to buy all six major Hollywood studios, and then raze the back lots, as sites for Star World. But he struck fear into moguls' hearts when he asked, "Why settle for the Force when you can have the Empire too?"

For now they are content to make movies—movies that careen from thrill to giggle and back to thrill again at 24 frames per second. Nobody does it better; no one has ever done it with quite so much relentless ingenuity. They broke out by going back. Lucas proved with the *Star Wars* trilogy that the Old Hollywood formula of moviemaking, cagily updated, could work wonders at the box office and in the toy store. His movies are Hardy Boys tales for the space age: they shine like Plexiglas, are as durable as Teflon and have the aftertaste of Tang. Spielberg has tapped into the moviegoer's childlike imagination with *Close Encounters of the Third Kind, Poltergeist, E.T.* and his upcoming production of *Gremlins*—fables of the sort that touch every eight-year-old just before he falls asleep. Or just after.

Put it this way: the boys have credentials. So of course *Indiana Jones and the Temple of Doom* (glorious, goofy title) will be a summer smash. Of course this new adventure, second in the series that Executive Producer Lucas and Director Spielberg began with *Raiders of the Lost Ark,* will provide sophisticated, if largely familiar pleasures to a few hundred million moviegoers. Of course *Temple of Doom,* a crackerjack swash of voodoo and derring-do, will create demand for another sequel. Some things are just written. . . .

The main plot, about the search for a sacred stone stolen by a coven of Indian thugs and used to augment sadistic black-magic rituals in the bowels of the temple of doom, need not concern us here. Suffice it to say that

George Lucas and Steven Spielberg have combined talents to update the Old Hollywood formula of the adventure story. Typical of their final product are these scenes from *Indiana Jones and the Temple of Doom*. Left, a fast-paced, action-packed chase scene, and right, the adventure-prone hero, Indiana Jones (Harrison Ford) (© Lucasfilm Ltd., all rights reserved. Photos by Keith Hamshere).

the new film is more an embellishment than an improvement on the snazzy *Raiders*. If you enjoyed seeing skeletons rise on spikes, or Indy snap his trusty bullwhip around a steel-willed woman, or the two of them trapped in a cave with ugly crawling things, you should be amused to see them again. Again you will savor the Indiana Jones schizophrenia: by day a bow-tied, bespectacled archaeologist; by night a resourceful swaggerer, whom Ford brings to life as a modern blend of Bogie and the Duke, with just a glint of misfit psychopathy in his eyes. Again you will slip easily into the care of some expert masseurs, now stroking, now pummeling, as *Temple of Doom* heads for a climax that is a literal cliff-hanger.

Snaking through the movie is a familiar Spielberg theme: the disappearance, and then the welcome return, of children. It illuminates his three most personal movies *(Close Encounters, Poltergeist* and *E.T.)* and affirms his belief in movies as a Mechanized Fountain of Youth. Toward the end of *Temple of Doom,* Indiana leads hundreds of enslaved Indian children out of an underground quarry and into the light. Spielberg means to be another kind of Pied Piper: leading grownups into the darkness of a moviehouse to restore, for a couple of hours at least, the innocence of childhood in all its wonder and terror. The wonder may reach as deep as *E.T.;* the terror may be as slick and exhilarating as *Temple of Doom's* climactic underground tram ride. If Lucas and Spielberg ever

do open a Star World, this combo of Disney World's Space Mountain and Big Thunder Mountain Railway rides should be the hottest attraction.

This is brilliance that rides on narrow-gauge tracks. One is tempted to demand of these two spectacularly talented film makers that they raise their sights beyond the Saturday-matinee refreshment stand. Lucas seems happy to produce pictures that affect the heart rate but not the heart; and Spielberg, when working with Lucas, concentrates his nonpareil directorial gifts on energizing each frame, keeping his boss and the customer satisfied. But perhaps the young moguls can brush aside such criticism. They know what sort of edifice they want to build. You don't fault a theme park for not being a cathedral. ∎

SUMMER MOVIES

by Michael Healy

Do big, blockbuster movies like *Indiana Jones and the Temple of Doom* herald the dehumanization of fun? Are the people in the movies less interesting than the special effects? Here is the opinion of one film critic.

Just about all the big summer movies are out now, and almost all of them doing very nicely. "Natl B.O. Sizzles; New Records Set" as it says in *Variety,* the show business periodical that keeps track of such things.

Producers are happy. Directors are happy. Stars are happy.

I am not happy, and for two reasons.

First, most of the summer blockbusters have not been very good.

Second, because the summer movies have been so successful, we're going to see many more films just like them. The Hollywood movie companies are a very conservative lot, and past performance is the main criterion for what new projects are given money to proceed. More of the same is better—that's the movie industry's motto. . . .

But the multiplication of sequels isn't the main worry I have about this year's crop of big money-makers. I'm more concerned about what's been omitted from most of these movies, with no discernible affect on their ability to draw audiences.

What's been left out, by and large, is humanity. I think of the process as the dehumanization of fun, since art is hardly a concern at all in most of these pictures.

To start with the biggest of the big, look what happened to Harrison Ford's character of Indiana Jones in the "Temple of Doom." In "Raiders of the Lost Ark," Jones was a kind of Clark Kent college teacher, an unlikely adventurer who seemed as surprised as everyone else that he could turn into a superman when need be. When asked how he plans to rescue the ark from a column of Nazi soldiers, Jones answers, "I don't know. I'm making this up as I go along." His vulnerability is what made him likeable.

There's none of that self-deprecating humour in "Temple of Doom." Jones has become a stereotypical tough guy, with a sneer on his lips and weapon in his hand at all times.

Much has been made of the lousy way Jones and his snotty little kid sidekick treat the film's dumb blond reluctant heroine, Willie Scott, in the film (she's an even flatter character than he is). But I don't think this is just a case of the usual sexism cropping up in a traditional male adventure story. Jones has become such a robot that he treats *everyone* as mere annoyances and obstacles in fulfilling the dictates of his programming.

Even when he's off duty, Jones can't soften up and act less goal-obsessed. . . . Maybe chivalry was a self-serving male lie, but it wasn't as callous and dehumanized an attitude toward women as the one the Indiana Jones character displays in "Temple of Doom."

Much has also been made of the film's excessive violence, but I think that all the ketchup, upsetting as it may be, is merely a symptom of the movie's essential, deeper hard-heartedness. All the human beings are just props in the story, and not nearly as interesting to the filmmakers as their whoop-dee-do special effects.

That's why the malnourished Indian children in "Temple of Doom" were so disturbing to me. I mean, think about how nastily they are used—as cheap atmosphere. Doesn't anyone look at these skinny little kids being beaten and think how horrific an image it really is? There *are* starving children in India and elsewhere at this moment, and if you actually see them, actually think about their individual lives, it makes their use as Steven Spielberg scenery all the more obscene.

Ralph Macchio (left) and Pat Morita (right) portrayed a sensitive student-teacher relationship in the 1984 film *The Karate Kid.*
(Movie Still Archives, New York.)

Of course, we're not supposed to think about that when watching "Temple of Doom." This is supposed to be escapist fun. But the price of escape in this movie is a good part of one's humanity, and it's simply not worth it. Spielberg treats his story as if it were a big machine, and if human beings happen to get ground up in the machine's workings, well, that just makes it an even more interesting mechanism.

"Gremlins," which Spielberg produced and Joe Dante directed, shows an equal disregard for the simple movie wisdom that human life is somehow important, and that human pain is not usually funny. The gremlins are not simply mischievous, but are cruel and murderous little malignities. They put people in real danger for their lives, as we know after they've killed off a couple of people in clever ways.

Dante seems to be after the kind of comic effect cartoon violence elicits, for he peppers the film with unreality, constantly referring to other movies and quoting whole scenes from "E.T." and other of his boss's works. Dante keeps peeking through the fabric of the story, whispering, "I'm only kidding."

But the problem is that he still shows images of human death and suffering realistically, so that we end up laughing at slaughter simply because it's set in an unreal world. That's brutalizing, as far as I'm concerned. . . .

The summer season started so promisingly, with "Romancing the Stone," a terrific action-adventure movie that actually had likeable human characters, a clever script, plenty of derring-do and, overall, a nice spirit about it. Since it was released in the early spring, the only big movies that have been nearly as

much fun have been "The Karate Kid," "Star Trek: The Search for Spock" and "Beat Street," the break dance film produced by Harry Belafonte. Though they are vastly different kinds of pictures, what those films have in common was an interest in characters as human beings, and a little respect for their individuality and a sympathy with their pain.

Those movies have a certain humanity, in other words, that most of the summer's cinematic roller-coaster rides have not. They focus on the riders, not the wonderous machine that's whipping them around.

And such films, concentrating more on character than on movie technology, more concerned with the anecdote than the wisecrack, seem to be getting scarcer. ∎

MEDIALAB

Approaches to Criticism

1. How do Healy and Corliss differ in their opinions of *Indiana Jones and the Temple of Doom?* What does Healy object to in the film? What quality does Corliss point to in the film that "keeps the customer satisfied"?

2. Healy's article is less a film review than a criticism of a trend in film that he saw in the summer of 1984. What is the trend he saw? Do you think the observations are valid? Does the trend still exist today?

3. Corliss begins his review with a fictional account of an announcement that filmmakers Lucas and Spielberg plan to build a giant theme park called Star World. The account is fiction, but what truth does it capture?

4. Both critics agree that technology overwhelms emotion in a film such as *Indiana Jones and the Temple of Doom.* Find the sentence(s) where each critic makes this observation. Do you sense that one critic is more upset by this than the other?

5. Corliss and Healy make very different observations about the enslaved children in Indiana Jones. How do their views differ on this subject?

6. Write your own film criticism on one of the following topics:

- current trends in popular movies
- recurring themes in the films of Steven Spielberg
- recurring themes in the films of George Lucas

How Still Pictures Become Movies

I would say that there is no art form that has so much in common with film as music. Both affect our emotions directly, not via the intellect. And film is mainly rhythm; it is inhalation and exhalation in continuous sequence.

—INGMAR BERGMAN, Swedish filmmaker

Motion pictures are an art form, but they are also a mechanical process. The beginnings of all the other arts are lost in early history. No one knows who discovered sculpture, who made the first painting, or who wrote the first music. Film (and its cousin— photography) are the only art forms whose beginnings are known to us. The reason for film's unique position in the arts is that in order to have an art of film someone first had to invent photography and then find a way of showing photographs to create the illusion of movement. The invention of movies is often credited to Thomas Edison around 1895.

Let's take a look at the machinery of film—at what makes movies move.

Would you go to see a movie that sounded entertaining and exciting but featured a sign at the theater entrance that read:

"For One Hour Of This Two Hour Film The Audience Will Look At A Blank Screen!!"

Maybe you wouldn't, but you already have. In fact, every time you go to a film you spend half the time watching a blank screen. Perhaps an explanation is in order.

If you look at a piece of motion picture film, you see that it consists of a series of tiny pictures, one on top of another, each divided by a thin black line. Home movie film is 8 millimeters wide, film used in school and on television usually is 16 millimeters wide, and film in movie houses is 35 millimeters wide, but they all work basically the same way. Looking at the piece of film, you will notice that each frame is a picture of the same thing in a slightly different location each time. The illustration on this page is 24 frames long and therefore shows movement over a one-second period of time.

One side of the film has holes, the other carries the sound track. The holes fit the sprockets and claws of a projector that moves the frames between the projection bulb and the magnifying lens 24 times each second.

The illusion of movement in movies comes more from the projector in the theater than from the camera used to make the film. A movie camera takes only still pictures, just like a snapshot camera. The main difference is that the movie camera takes 24 ''snapshots'' every second while a still camera, operated by hand, takes pictures only as fast as the photographer moves. A movie camera is a rapid-fire still camera; it doesn't actually take ''moving pictures,'' it takes still photographs.

Films become moving pictures only because our process of seeing is sluggish. The retina of the eyeball (which sends images to the brain) retains images for about 1/30 to 1/10 of a second after an object is out of sight. A most extreme example of this after-image (often called "persistence of vision" because the image "persists" for a time) is the white or blue spot you see after someone has taken a picture of you with a flashbulb. This after-image persists much longer than most images because of its intensity and brightness.

When you watch a film, you are "seeing" what was on the screen a fraction of a second ago. The movie projector has gears and claws that jerk the film in front of the lens in a stop-and-go-motion. Each frame stops in front of the projector light for about 1/24 of a second. Then the projector shutter (a whirring disk with holes that alternately block light and let it through) blocks the light while the next frame is pulled into place. In the course of a film, the projector shutter blocks out the picture for about 50 percent of the time, so that the audience is really sitting in front of a blank screen. During a two-hour film, the audience will see 172,800 individual pictures (24 frames per second, 60 seconds per minute, for 120 minutes), but the projector shutter will have blocked off the light for about one hour of that time. During that time, the audience is watching the after-images.

Every film you see is, in a way, an optical illusion. The movement in movies comes from the combination of the slowness of your seeing process and the rapid movement of the film through the projector. Anyone who can push a camera button and thread a projector can make a movie.

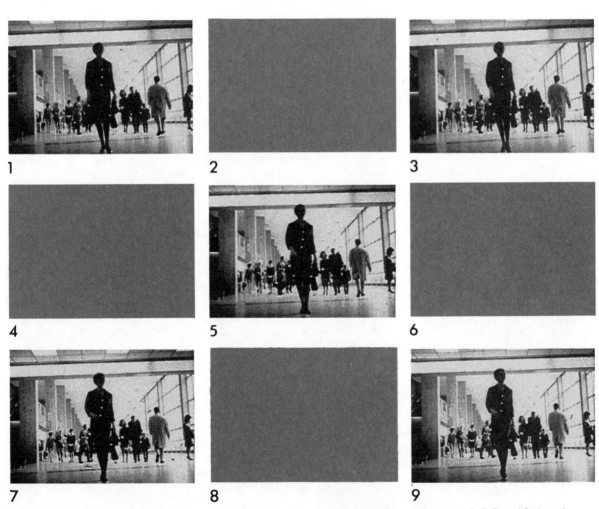

Frames 2, 4, 6, and 8 illustrate the positioning of blank frames in a series of nine frames. Frames 1, 3, 5, 7, and 9 show the individual pictures that will make up a film sequence. The entire sequence will last less than one half a second.

MEDIALAB

How Movies Move

1. Look at the inside of a movie projector and find the place where the light passes through the film; also find the lens that magnifies the tiny picture and the claw that stops and pulls the film in jerks past the lens. Find the device that turns the sound track into sound.

2. Devise an experiment that demonstrates persistence of vision. Library research might be helpful in designing the demonstration.

3. *A Problem:*

(a) What would happen if the camera used to make the film took 48 pictures each second instead of the normal 24? Note: the question is about the movie camera, not the projector. Assume the film will be projected at its normal 24 frame-per-second speed.

(b) What would happen if the camera were run at 12 frames per second instead of 24?

How Pictures Are Connected to Give Meaning

To make a film that people will enjoy, the filmmaker has to know how to put together the thousands of pictures that make up the illusion of movement. Anyone who reads knows that a book is made up of words formed into sentences and then grouped into paragraphs. We could say this is the basic structure for a book. A person may have a huge vocabulary, but if he or she doesn't know how to put the words together into sentences and paragraphs, that person will never write a book. The basic structure of a film is less obvious but just as real and necessary.

SHOTS AND SCENES

The basic building block of a film is the "shot." A "shot" is simply what happens in front of the camera from the time the camera starts until it stops. The "shot" is to a film something like the word is to a book. Just as words are put together to make sentences, shots in a film are put together to make "scenes." A "scene" is a single shot or a group of shots usually unified by time and place. Both a sentence and a scene are difficult to define but easier to demonstrate. Let's take a look at the making of just a few seconds of film that will eventually become part of a feature film. Here is the script for two scenes (numbers 114 and 115) from a film:

114 LONG SHOT—Bank building on busy street Entrance to bank is clearly visible. Pedestrians pass by, uniformed guard standing on left side of door. Charley is standing to the right of the revolving door.

Cut to

115 MEDIUM SHOT—Charley
Charley is chewing his ever-present toothpick and glancing around nervously. He checks his watch.

Cut to

CLOSE-UP—Charley
His hands move to his belt in a nervous gesture. We see a glimpse of the gun in his shoulder holster.

Scene 114 calls for only one shot—a long shot. A long shot is one in which the camera is set up a long way from the subject. This particular shot establishes the fact that Charley is standing in front of a bank and not just any downtown building. A long shot that "establishes" a location is called an "establishing shot." Establishing shots set the stage for the action to follow. The camera for scene 114 will probably be set up across the street from the

bank or perhaps in a third-story window of another building across the street.

In the final film, scene 114 will last no longer than three seconds. To shoot the scene, however, the camera will be set up and as much as two to ten minutes of film will be shot. From this the director or editor will select the best footage and decide if the pace of the film requires the long shot of the bank to be shown for two seconds or five seconds or maybe not at all.

Although this scene is very short and simple, it can be used to illustrate the work, cooperation, and patience needed to make a full-length feature film.

For instance, if the ordinary people walking by the bank can be identified when the film is projected, they must give their written permission in the form of a "release" that allows their pictures to be used in the film. This is done to protect those who might find it embarrassing or somehow damaging to be recognized in a particular place by the public or those who simply wish privacy.

Most often the pedestrians and crowds you see in movies are paid to be there. They are called "extras" and are hired for films on a per-day basis. They are hired only to walk by a bank front, to stand on a corner, to carry a bunch of bananas through a fruit market, or to jump rope on a sidewalk. If the script called for a flock of pigeons to be on the sidewalk and to scatter when the hero approached, they, too, would be hired from an animal rental specialist (for perhaps $100 or more a day).

If a film were being shot in your city, you might find an ad in the local newspaper asking for extras for crowd scenes. If you applied and were accepted, you might find yourself in a scene such as 114.

Long before actual shooting, the film's producers would have obtained the permission of the bank to film in front of it. The work would probably be done on a day the bank was closed. If the film is about a bank robbery, the bank might not like its name associated with the film. In this case the property department ("prop" for short) would have a fictional nameplate made so the bank would not be identified in the film.

As the actual shooting of scene 114 begins, the director yells, "Quiet on the set," and an assistant holds a slate in front of the camera reading "Scene 114, Take 1." The camera will run for several seconds or several minutes and then stop at the director's order. The slate board appears on the film as identification so that when the film is edited, a particular shot can be found easily. The actual film of the slate board is then discarded.

If the budget for this film is limited, the director might decide to save money by using a "stock shot" for scene 114. Film studios and special film libraries have large collections of footage of almost every conceivable situation, which they sell for use in films. If a director needs a picture of a house exploding, a ship sinking, a forest fire raging through thousands of acres, the skyline of Rome, a jet taking off or landing, these stock libraries will provide the needed footage.

One of the most commonly used stock shots, especially in television films, is the jet plane landing and taking off. These shots are used to indicate the movement or action of characters from one city to another. Some of these stock shots are supplied by the airlines, who realize that their name on the plane is free advertising.

So scene 114, one which will appear on the screen for a few fleeting seconds, requires much time and effort to shoot. Selecting just the right bank (which means first of all deciding whether the scene will be shot on a studio lot or "on location" on a public street); setting up the camera position; obtaining all the needed permissions; transporting the crew and actors to the right place at the right time; enlisting police permission to block off the sidewalk and perhaps the street (if the film takes place in the 1930s, the director can't have 1980s cars driving past the bank); taking the light readings and supplying any artificial light needed; planning costumes and makeup; and finally directing the scene itself—all these take hundreds of hours of labor.

For scene 115, the camera will move closer to Charley, and again the filming will begin with the slate board. The director may decide to shoot this scene from two different angles and pick the best one later while editing the film. If so, the second angle will be slated as "Scene 115, Take 2." If, during the second take, Charley sneezes or a jet roars overhead or a member of the stage crew drops a hammer with a loud clang, that take will have been ruined. It will then be started over, with the slate reading, "Scene 115, Take 3." The director's quest for perfection can result in scenes being shot and reshot four, six, or even twenty times.

After the entire film has been shot, the editing begins. The editor, or the director, or both working together, select the best footage and make the crucial decisions of how long each shot should remain on the screen, which footage should be used and which thrown in the scrap pile, and in what order the shots should be arranged to tell the story best. The three shots in scenes 114-115 will pass across the screen in a matter of a few seconds. Few people in the audience will appreciate the time, work, and effort that went into those few seconds of very ordinary filmmaking.

SEQUENCE

In our description of the structure of a film, we have compared a shot to a word and a scene to a sentence. The next larger division is a "sequence," which is a grouping of scenes joined by a common purpose or setting. When people speak of the "chase scene," they really mean the chase *sequence.* The two scenes used to illustrate "shot" and "scene" were part of a sequence informally called "Charley's Arrest." The arrest sequence will run in the film for about three minutes and will have about twenty scenes.

We can use the example of a football game to make these terms clearer. Let's say that a real football game is being filmed (or televised) as it happens—the director cannot control the action, so instead the cameras must be directed to cover what happens on the field. One of the sequences of the football game is the "Goal Line Stand."

SCENE 225—FIRST DOWN AND GOAL TO GO

Teams take positions with the ball on the six yard line.

LONG SHOT of players lining up.

Cut to

MEDIUM SHOT of quarterback barking signals and receiving the ball from the center. The quarterback steps back to pass and throws the ball.

Cut to

MEDIUM SHOT of intended receiver over goal line. The ball misses his fingertips by inches.

SCENE 226—SECOND DOWN AND GOAL TO GO

LONG SHOT—team huddle

Cut-away to

Cheerleaders

LONG SHOT—team breaks huddle and enters formation.

Cut-in to

EXTREME CLOSE-UP of football in center's hands.

Cut to

LONG SHOT—Ball is snapped to quarterback who is immediately tackled. Players untangle and the quarterback walks dejectedly back to huddle.

Scenes 227 and 228, we can guess, would show unsuccessful attempts at the third and fourth downs. Scene 229 would begin a new sequence, perhaps to be called "94-Yard Touchdown Drive."

Notice that scene 226 uses a shot called a "cut-away" and one called a "cut-in." A *cut-away* is a shift of attention from the main action to some related action. Shots of the crowd or the cheerleaders during a sports event on TV are cut-aways.

They cut away from the main action. A *cut-in* directs the viewers' eyes to some very specific action or object within the main focus of attention. A close-up of a football sitting on the goal line or a close-up of a basketball hoop during a free-throw attempt are cut-ins.

Cut-ins and cut-aways are used in television sports to provide visual variety. But they are also used in film because that is the way we look at things. If you attend a football game, your own eyes will spend most of the time watching the action on the field, but occasionally they will cut away to catch some of the action in the stands. In a classroom you might cut in to watch the teacher's hand as he or she picks up a piece of chalk. You might cut away to look out the window at the passing clouds.

The cut-away is also useful to the director in manipulating time in a film. Film time and real time are different. If a film were made in real time, you would almost certainly find it boring. If the character were to fly from Chicago to Washington in a real-time film, you would have to watch the plane in the air for an hour—a scene that would quickly empty any theater. In a film-time film, you see the plane take off and a second or two later the traveler is standing beside the White House. Because you have learned to accept film time, this causes you no problems. Time in films is both compressed and expanded.

The cut-away is used to compress time. Take as an example a script that calls for a scene of a boat steaming up a river and docking at a wharf. In real time this action takes about 20 minutes, far too long

for a film. The director solves the time problem by filming a long shot of the boat out in the river, cutting away to someone walking along the wharf to meet the boat, and then cutting back to the boat which is now in the process of docking. Viewers understand what has happened because they understand film language. Someone watching this sequence of shots who had never before seen a film would probably find it confusing and might even wonder if the boat docking is the same one that was out in the river just a second ago.

If the cut-away to the person walking were not used, the boat would be seen in one shot in the middle of the river and then would appear to jump magically to the dock. Viewers would not accept such a "jump cut." With the cut-away, the action appears smooth and logical.

Cut-aways are used in film because they are used in real life. This reduplicating of reality is also why there is a basic shot sequence in putting together films. The basic shot order is long shot, medium shot, close-up, and reestablishing shot. This order of shots was used in the "Charley's Arrest" sequence.

The long shot, also called the "establishing shot" (when it is used to establish where the action takes place), shows the main character or object in its general surroundings. The medium shot shows the main character or object in its immediate surroundings. A close-up includes only the main character or object or maybe even only a part of it. A reestablishing shot reminds the viewer of what surrounds the main character (or object). This technique is easy to see in this opening scene for a Western, which could even be used while the credits are being shown:

LONG SHOT—

Sunset over wide-open prairie land. The figure of a horse and rider trailing a cloud of dust can be seen in the distance heading toward a small town.

MEDIUM SHOT—

The man on horse rides along a crude trail.

CLOSE-UP—

Now the man's face reveals a grim look of determination, with tightly clenched teeth; we see a sheriff's badge on his vest.

LONG SHOT—

(Reestablishing)—Another long shot reveals that the sheriff has reached the city limits just as the sun sets.

If this basic script were given to five different directors, each would film it in a slightly different way. Long, medium, and close-ups are only approximate terms for these shots. Some long shots are longer than others, just as some close-ups are closer than others.

This basic order of shots makes psychological sense because this is the way we see things in reality. Imagine entering a classroom on the first day of school. First you look around the room to establish where you are—a long shot. Then you begin to look around at who is in the room and to scan faces—your medium shot. Third, you see someone you know and narrow in on an empty desk nearby—close-up. After you sit down you go back to examining the entire room again—reestablishing shot.

This basic order of shots is widely used, and you should be able to spot it easily in almost any film. You will also be able to spot many exceptions to this basic order, just as there are exceptions in reality. If your main concern as you enter the classroom is the rumor that your favorite teacher is teaching the course, you might look first to see who is standing in front of the room. In a film in which the person entering is concerned about the teacher, the first shot would then be an extreme close-up of the smiling (or scowling) teacher instead of a long shot of the room. A film director has to be part technician, part artist, and part psychologist to select the right shots.

In film there are as many "general rules" as there are exceptions to the rules. This basic shot order can even be completely reversed. Most often this is done for a shock effect. For example: An extreme close-up of a spider crawling; cut to a medium shot revealing that the spider is crawling on a person (shock number one); and finally a shocking long shot showing a cobweb-covered dead body complete with dagger. If this sequence were shot in normal order, the shock effect would be much less.

You can't say as much as you can in writing, but you can say what you say with great conviction.

—ROBERT FLAHERTY,
Documentary filmmaker

EDiTiNG

Every art form has some kind of "editing"—the process of selecting the best words, colors, lines, building materials, or sounds and rejecting those that are less good.

When a film is finally shot, all the bits and pieces must be put together skillfully so the viewing audience will follow the story and be entertained. Putting together the bits and selecting the best is called editing. Editing in film can be done with a scissors and tape, but special editing machines make the job easier and faster.

The person editing the film works with a copy of all the footage shot, while the original is safely stored until the final steps of the editing process. (In making your own movies, you probably won't want to spend the extra money to have a copy of your film made.) The editor joins the shots into scenes, the scenes into sequences, and the sequences into a film. He or

she rejects film that is not exposed correctly, scenes that are poorly acted, or shots that contain too much or too little information. For professionally made films, ten to twenty times as much footage as is needed will be shot. To edit a one-hour film, the editor may have ten to twenty hours of film from which to select.

Just as the sentences and paragraphs of a book must be linked together by transitional devices, so a film must fit together according to the logic of its story. A film must be put together so the audience is involved rather than confused. For example, an editor putting together the scenes from our "Goal Line Stand" sequence could thoroughly confuse the viewers by changing the order of the shots. If the shot of the center snapping the ball were followed immediately by one of the pass receiver running after the ball, a confused audience would conclude that the center had somehow snapped the ball to the receiver.

Editing is the magic of film by which places hundreds of miles apart can be made to appear on the same street. Take a piece of film of a person looking out a window, join to that a two-second shot of ocean surf, and the viewer will conclude the person is looking out the window at the ocean. In reality, the person is in a Hollywood studio where there is nothing outside but a parking lot. The shot of the ocean probably shows a beach in Hawaii and was made three weeks later. Through the magic of editing, an audience will be led to believe the person is on the ocean's shore.

There must be some logic to splicing one piece of film to another. If you were making a home movie of a baby and you first showed it crying into the camera, then followed with a shot of a huge black spider, the audience wouldn't know what connection there was between the spider and the baby. If, however, you showed the baby sitting next to a small tree and smiling into the camera; then looking toward the righthand side of the picture frame (where the tree is) and starting to cry; and then spliced on a shot of a spider crawling on a tree branch toward the left side of the frame (a shot you may have made years ago), the audience would assume the baby was being attacked by the spider. The act of looking toward the edge of the frame leads the audience to expect the next shot will be what that person sees.

A good many years ago, a Russian director took a strip of silent film that showed an actor's face staring down. The director spliced this same shot in between a shot of a steaming bowl of soup, one of a dead woman in a coffin, and another of a child at play. His finished film was (1) face, (2) soup, (3) face same as in shot 1, (4) coffin, (5) face same as in shot 1, (6) child, (7) face same as in shot 1. Pretending it was a screen test for the actor, he screened the film for a small audience. The audience praised the unknown actor, commenting on his subtle expressions of hunger at the sight of the soup, grief at seeing the coffin, and amusement as he watched the child play.

This experiment illustrates the power of editing as well as its ability to make film acting much easier than stage acting. Even the world's worst actor can turn in an acceptable performance in a film if the editing makes it so. If a scene requires an expression of fright, our non-actor is told to look to the right and register an expression such as a person would have if there were a 20-foot-tall rabbit outside the window about to eat the house. The director would have the actor (or non-actor) simply look to the right and express fright. If the actor cannot do even that, perhaps a well-timed and unexpected firecracker from a stagehand would accomplish the task. As edited, the actor's fright at the noise of the firecracker would be followed by a shot of the giant rabbit, and the audience would conclude that the actor is reacting to the sight of the rabbit.

When the editor works with the copy of the film, he or she cements together the bits and pieces of film that will eventually make a finished product. This glued-together film is then copied in a film lab into one complete piece of film. The magic of the movies has again been created out of skill, hard work, and patience.

Shown here is an editing machine. Notice the digital counter to help find single frames, the small size of the screen, and the presence of two screens to aid in matching shots.

MEDIALAB

The Grammar of Film

1. While filming, you (a) shot a few seconds of a friend standing against a wall; (b) stopped filming but left the camera absolutely still, mounted on a tripod; (c) told your friend to walk away while the camera was not running; (d) began filming again without moving the camera. Describe the resulting film.

2. What would happen if, while filming, you did these steps? (a) You again pointed the camera at your friend standing against the wall. This time you ran the camera for as short a time as possible—ideally, advancing the film only one frame. (b) You stopped filming and left the camera absolutely still. (c) While the camera was not running, you told your friend to move four inches to the left. (d) You again ran the camera for one frame or as little as possible. (e) You stopped and had your friend move four inches to the left again. (f) Repeat this process until your friend is out of view of the camera. What would the resulting film show?

3. You are assigned to film a sequence in a railroad station. The script calls for the star to kiss the co-star, get on the train, and wave from the window as the train leaves. You arrive at the railroad station only to find that no engineer is available to move the train. No one else is able to drive the train and you cannot change the script. How would you solve this problem?

4. An editor can arrange the following three shots in ways that will give the audience an impression of either cool courage or cowardice. Do you see how?

Face Filled with Fear

Gun Pointed

Face with Confident Smile

5. Using either a short film or a TV program, find clear examples of:

an establishing shot

a scene

a sequence

a shot

a scene or portion of a scene in which a long shot is followed by a medium shot, followed by a close-up.

6. Carefully study one scene or sequence in a film and see how it was made and put together.

7. What would happen if a director arranged the following events? An actor located at A shoots an arrow as indicated in the sketch. The camera begins to film as the actor shoots the arrow and then quickly pans around and stops so actor B is in view. Actor B already has an arrow lodged in balsa wood underneath his shirt back. As the camera stops on him, he staggers forward and falls to the ground. How would this appear on the screen?

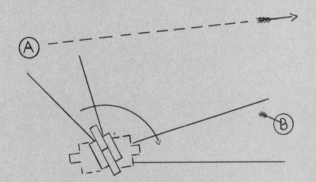

8. Write a shooting script (no longer than one page) for the following action: A person approaches your house at night while you are asleep, leans a ladder against the house and begins to climb it. Halfway up his foot breaks through a rung on the ladder and awakens you suddenly from a deep sleep. Make your shooting script clear enough so that a director and actors could take it and actually make the scene from your directions. Number each shot and indicate about how long each should last. The entire scene should last no longer than 45 seconds.

9. What effect on the meaning of the film would the elimination of shot 114 have in the example that began this section? Shot 114 was a long shot of the bank building on a busy street.

10. In the editing process, one of the critical decisions to be made about each shot is how long it should be left on the screen. How would a shot that lasts too long affect an audience? A shot that is not shown long enough? Be aware that a shot left on the screen too long will have a different audience reaction than a shot left on the screen for too short a time.

11. Watch at least a few minutes of any kind of sport televised within the next week. While you watch, note to yourself the beginning of each new shot. Look for cut-ins and cut-aways. Be aware of the use of close-ups, medium shots, and long shots.

12. Prepare a rough draft of a shooting script (no longer than one-half page) that condenses time. Take any action that would normally take several minutes and condense it down to a few seconds. Your script should be clear enough for a director to use in making a film and should leave no doubt about what has happened.

13. Do you think the experiment of the Russian director involving the actor's face and the soup/coffin/child shots would work today? Remember that the people who viewed his experiment were very unfamiliar with film.

How the Camera Gives Meaning

CAMERA MOVEMENT

Movies move. Give a beginning filmmaker a camera, and he or she will move the camera back and forth, up and down, and play with the zoom lens like a new toy. An experienced photographer moves the camera only when necessary and only after careful thought about how the movement will affect the viewer.

You should be able to recognize the most commonly used camera movements.

PAN

The tripod remains in place, but the camera swivels from left to right or right to left. The resulting shot duplicates a person surveying a situation by standing in one place and turning his or her head. A pan (short for ''panorama'') is used in film, as in reality, to survey a scene or to follow a moving object.

Tilt

A tilt shot is a vertical (up and down) pan. The tripod again remains in place while the camera pivots up or down. This seldom-used movement gives viewers a trip up or down a building, a person, or other tall object.

DOLLY

The camera rolls smoothly toward or away from the subject. In professional films the heavy camera is mounted on a special cart called a dolly. In amateur filmmaking the same effect can be obtained by moving the camera on a wagon, skateboard, or any wheeled platform. The ground must be smooth for this shot to work.

Tracking Shot

Also called a traveling shot or a follow shot. This is a variation of the dolly. If you want to move the camera parallel to a fast-moving car, the camera can be mounted on a second car and moved alongside the car that is being filmed. If the camera is to move smoothly along rough or sandy ground (to follow two people walking on a beach, for example), a special wooden track is laid down and the dolly ''tracks'' along it for a smooth shot.

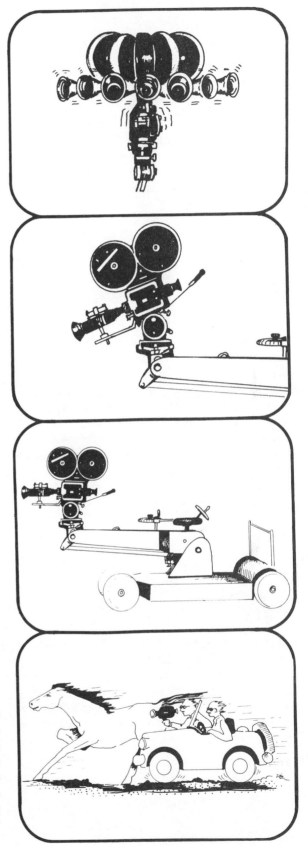

BOOM

This shot involves mounting the camera on a special and very expensive crane on the end of a hydraulic arm. The camera mounted on this "boom" can be moved very fluidly in almost any direction.

zOOM

This shot is used for a dramatic or shocking effect. A zoom lens is manipulated while the camera remains stationary. The effect created is similar to looking through a telescope or binoculars and moving from the least to the greatest magnification (zoom-in) or the reverse (zoom-out). A zoom can be very fast or gradual. A zoom lens is available for home movie cameras and is much overused by amateurs. It is seldom used in professional films because there is no comparison to this kind of "seeing" in reality. Our eyes are not equipped with zoom eyeballs.

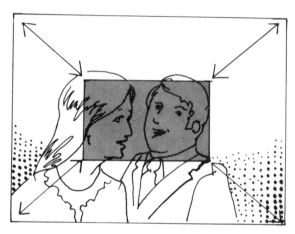

Hand-Held

All the previous techniques of camera movement depend on the fact that cameras are usually mounted on a tripod. But newer cameras are light enough to be carried by hand so that a film can be made by picking up a camera and walking around with it. This is most often done in documentary films and in filming for news.

CAMERA ANGLE

A basic problem in any filming is where to place the camera. Part of that problem is solved by deciding what you want to appear on the screen. But the question remains, from what angle will you film?

Let's say you need a shot of a fighter standing alone in a boxing ring in an empty auditorium where tomorrow he will face the champ. Do you place the camera in one corner of the ring and look the boxer in the eye? Do you place the camera below the ring and look up at him, or perhaps even go into the rafters and look down on him? Each of these choices will produce a different emotional effect on the viewer. Your final choice will depend on the story line and on what you know about camera angle.

There are three basic camera angles:

1. You can place a camera rather normally so that you are looking at people or things from eye level.

2. You can place the camera below the person, looking up. This "low angle" shot is used when you want the viewer to "look up" to someone. A low angle shot will make a person appear strong and superior, even superhuman.

3. A "high angle" shot involves placing the camera so that it looks down on the subject being filmed. When we are above someone, looking down, we tend to feel superior to that person. So a high angle shot is used to make a person appear small, inferior, lonely, or looked down on.

If, in filming the boxer, we want to emphasize the fact that the boxer is small and alone in the face of the champ, the best camera angle would be in the rafters looking down. If the script calls for showing the boxer as superior and confident, then it would be best to place the camera below the ring, looking up at him.

There is a simple law governing the filming of novels: if it is worth doing it can't be done, if it can be done, it isn't worth it.

—JOHN SIMON, film critic

An awareness of how different camera angles make pictures look different is necessary to solve one of the basic problems of movies. Reality is three-dimensional, but the movie screen has only length and width. The problem is to give an appearance of depth to flat pictures. A movie camera is like a one-eyed person unable to see depth. If you close one eye and try to touch various objects a few feet from you, you will have difficulty because you can no longer see in three dimensions.

Camera operators rely on angles to give the illusion of depth. Consider these two pictures of the same face.

The picture below has more "depth" to it, because we see two sides of the face. The picture on top is "flat" and dull because it shows no depth. If you look at the faces in the ads in magazines, you will notice that rarely is a face shown straight on. A slight angle off to the side reveals more of the head and adds depth to the picture.

A movie screen, a TV picture tube, and a photograph all have only two dimensions and yet are called on to represent three-dimensional reality. Let's say your assignment is to take a picture of an automobile so that a person looking at it will have a good idea of what the car looks like from the outside. Where would you place the camera to take such a picture?

To give three-dimensional reality to static objects, you would use an angle-on-angle camera position. To use angle-on-angle positions, you take the film or picture from both an angle other than straight on *and* an angle other than eye level. If you look at pictures of products in ads, you will see that angle-on-angle shots are common indeed.

People go to the movies for the various ways they express the experiences of our lives, and as a means of avoiding and postponing the pressures we feel. This latter function of art—generally referred to disparagingly as escapism—may also be considered as refreshment, and in terms of modern big city life and small town boredom, it may be a major factor in keeping us sane.

*—*Pauline Kael, *American film critic*

Straight On

Angle

Angle-On-Angle

Camera Movement and Angles

1. If there is at least one movie camera available for class use, make a film in the classroom with as many people participating as possible. The purpose of the film is to illustrate the various camera movements and angles discussed in this section. The film should contain examples of the following:

Pan from right to left

Pan from left to right

Tilt from bottom to top

Tilt from top to bottom

Dolly shot toward an object

Dolly shot away from an object

Tracking shot

Hand-held following a person or moving object

High angle shot

Low angle shot

Zoom—slow zoom *in* on an object

Zoom—slow zoom *out* from an object

Zoom—fast zoom *in* on an object

Zoom—fast zoom *out* from an object

These last four shots are possible only if the camera is equipped with a zoom lens.

Make no attempt to have the film tell a story. Simply illustrate the above shots without making any attempt to connect one shot with the next. Use a film that needs no special lights.

2. When the illustration film is developed, watch it as a class. Discuss the different effects of each shot. For example, does the pan from right to left feel any different than the pan from left to right? Does the "dolly in" toward a subject feel any different than a "dolly away" from a subject? What feeling does a zoom shot give? Judging from your own film, why do you think professional filmmakers seldom use a zoom shot?

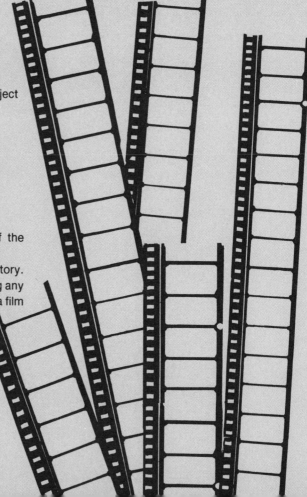

Meaning through Composition, Color, and Sound

COMPOSITION

A painter, a photographer, and a filmmaker all share a concern for the composition of a picture. Composition is how the parts of the picture are arranged, or "composed," within the frame. A poorly composed picture will look somehow "wrong" and will be distracting to the viewer. Seeing good composition in pictures takes a trained and knowledgeable eye. But even a beginner can quickly learn a few basic ideas of composition.

The kinds of lines in a picture is important. If the film calls for a shot of the office of a strict male army sergeant, the director will know that straight, angular lines should be part of the picture. Straight lines are considered masculine, curved lines feminine. The army sergeant would not have a round desk or rug or a chair with a curved back. But if the film calls for a shot of the bedroom of a female character presented as traditionally "feminine," the lines will be curved—oval rugs, paintings with curves, a vase. The choice of the kinds of lines in each room communicates to the viewer something about the kind of person who lives or works there.

If the director wants a quiet, peaceful sequence, he or she will compose using long horizontal lines. The horizontal line is restful, perhaps because it suggests the line of the body at sleep or rest.

Vertical lines inspire awe. The sight of a skyscraper as seen looking up from its base, the majestic vertical height of a distant mountain, or even the imposing vertical of a six-foot-tall adult as seen by a three-year-old are all awesome. If a group of people are to be filmed sitting around a table and one of the people is supposed to be strong and determined, the director might have that person stand up, thus creating a vertical line.

Diagonal lines suggest action and dynamism. If the script calls for a long shot of a racing car, the director will often make sure the camera is placed so that the car moves across the screen diagonally.

In this still from the film *Up the Down Staircase*, the boy's leather jacket forms a massive dark shape filling nearly half the screen His right arm extends directly across the other half of the frame suggesting a barrier. If the camera were placed where the three spectators are, the idea of the huge dark shape blocking the way of the actress would be missing. The boy with the jacket is not actually blocking the sidewalk, but the careful use of shapes suggests that idea. The boy's head is also carefully placed in relation to the background. If the white wall with the graffiti were not placed where it is, the picture would be much less effective.

The boy in this film still from *400 Blows* is trapped. The picture is composed in such a way that his head has little room to move within the frame. The fence also acts as a visual barrier adding to the feeling of imprisonment.

The angle of the raft makes this picture more exciting than if it were positioned parallel to the base of the photo. (*Rapids of the Colorado*, Pyramid Films.)

A picture of a girl skipping rope sounds like quite an ordinary shot. But to make the picture more intriguing in this frame from the visual poem documentary *Jumprope*, the cameraperson used an extremely low angle. (*Jumprope*, Pyramid Films.)

Low angle gives this character an added dignity and impressiveness. The contrast between the white face and darkness of the rest of the picture also adds interest. (*Legend*, Pyramid Films.)

COLOR

Most of the film *Fiddler on the Roof* was shot through a camera lens covered by a piece of brown nylon stocking bought at a local department store. Director Norman Jewison wanted the film to be filled with a warm and earthy feeling, befitting the peasant people and earthy location of the story. He found that a very sharp focus and bright colors gave a slick, too contemporary look. He also realized that "modern life is perceived sharply, but the moment you move into a period (of the past) it becomes, somehow, faded and a bit hazy. Your references to it are through old photographs and books and things. You don't see it quite as clearly as you see life today." To give the film the earthy look and to establish the mood of its taking place in the remembered past, the best solution was to shoot it through some kind of filter. The best results were obtained with a stocking that gave the film a subtle tint and softened the focus very slightly.

In addition to the unusual filter, nearly all primary colors were taken out of the sets used in the film. There are few pure reds, blues, or yellows in *Fiddler on the Roof.* The film gives the "feeling" of black and white, although it was filmed in color.

Does the average viewer notice that certain colors are missing or call out to the projectionist to get that stocking off the projector? Of course not, but the techniques give the film a subtle reality it would not have had under more conventional shooting conditions. The careful use of color, composition, angles, camera movement, and other film techniques should not be so obvious that they are noticed by the viewer, but they should *influence*

the viewer. Film techniques work best when the audience is not aware they are working.

The Godfather is carefully colored, and many shots are composed to resemble Italian chiaroscuro painting. This served to link this story of the Mafia with its origins and to give the picture a properly historical look.

Film directors do not take whatever color comes along. They realize that color, like composition and movement, influences the feeling the film creates in the audience. Often the color of a costume, an automobile, a room, or even an entire stage set is changed for a scene of a few seconds.

A film about a joyless future world that is run by a dictator and allows no personal freedom would not look right shot in "living" color complete with bright, gaudy splashes of color. Such a film would very likely be shot in a very subdued, almost colorless style, perhaps tending toward an overall bluish cast.

In the 1939 version of *Jesse James,* the James gang holds up a railroad train near sunset. Jesse leaps atop the train and runs along the top while it is still moving. The camera is alongside the train and shows James silhouetted against the darkening sky; below him the train windows glow with an orangish lamplight. Such care in filming was not done to make a "pretty" picture, but to point out through color the difference between the dangerous, cold world of the criminal and the comfortable, warm world of the law-abiding citizens.

A film director must be sensitive to colors and their effects on the mood of the audience.

sound

Silent films always had sound—piano, organ, or orchestra accompaniment, along with the cheers and boos of the audience. Since the first sound pictures in 1927, talkies have always had silence. The audio experience in any film is composed of these two elements—sound and silence. A creative filmmaker uses silence as much as sound. An amateur filmmaker looks with horror at holes in the sound track and fills them with noise or music.

Silence is what makes sound meaningful. Music can be considered a period of silence rhythmically interrupted. Without silence, or at least a large variation in sound level, there can be no "beat," no rhythm. If notes never faded away into silence, music as we know it would not exist. Most musicians realize that most of their time "playing" is spent in silence, changing from one note to another.

Film sound can be either *synchronous* or *nonsynchronous.* Synchronous sound is the most common; the sound track includes the sounds that are being made by the people or things on the screen at that time. Two people talking, a gun being fired, the sound of marching as a military parade passes are all examples of synchronous sound. Background music is nonsynchronous sound; the viewer doesn't see the orchestra playing the music. Often scenes

will contain a combination (or "mix") of both kinds of sound.

Some sound is recorded "live" on the location where the film is made. The camera is placed in a soundproof blimp so viewers will not hear the motor running. In documentary films when a hand-held camera is used, the blimp is sometimes discarded to increase portability. In these films, viewers can hear the sound of the camera running if they listen closely.

Much sound is dubbed into the film after the original shooting. In a fistfight, the appropriate crack of a fist hitting a jaw is added in a recording studio. In reality the actor probably missed, or at least pulled his punch, making it silent. If all the thousands of fistfights ever filmed were to be run with live sound, the results would be more humorous than dramatic and exciting.

Dubbing is often used to produce natural sounds that add to the atmosphere. A lightning storm, the clanging of the jailhouse door, the crash of an overturning automobile, a squeaking floorboard, or a ticking clock are all added from a library of recorded sounds prepared for such occasions. The proper "mood" sounds can add suspense and realism to any film.

MEDIA LAB

Meaning through Composition, Color, and Sound

1. Much of what is said in this chapter about composition, color, and camera angle is as true for still photography as it is for motion pictures. Find photographs or illustrations in magazines or elsewhere that illustrate each of the following:

(a) The use of a low camera angle to make a person or thing appear superior.

(b) The use of high angle to make a person or thing seem inferior or weak.

(c) A picture strengthened by verticals.

(d) A picture made restful with horizontal lines.

(e) Diagonal lines used to suggest excitement and dynamism.

(f) Curved lines and circles used to suggest femininity.

(g) Color carefully chosen to give added meaning to a picture.

2. View a number of short films and discuss them in the light of the main points that you learned in this chapter. Notice how the various techniques of editing, shot selection, camera angle and movement, color and composition are used to make the film work. Select one film and write a short paper pointing out how the filmmaker used these techniques to give the film meaning.

3. Take a short sequence from a film and then play it for the class without sound. Have volunteers bring a tape or record they think would fit as a sound track for that sequence. Play the sound tracks while watching that sequence and notice how different sounds influence the meaning or feeling of the sequence.

4. The film techniques discussed in this chapter are often used to manipulate audience feelings during a feature film. By using the proper technique, the director can create in the audience feelings of sympathy for the main character, even if he or she is a criminal. Every shot is carefully planned to produce the desired audience reaction. These same techniques can be used in television news camerawork, in documentary films designed to persuade the audience, in still photos used in magazines or newspapers, in advertising photography and TV commercials, or in educational films.

To illustrate how these techniques might be used to influence public opinion, discuss each of the following situations and how they could be presented in film to produce different audience reactions:

Situation 1: A person working on an assembly line at an automobile factory. Picture this person first as an example of the dignity and nobility of work; as the common person as hero. Then devise a way to picture the person as a slave of the assembly line, condemned to a wasted life through meaningless tasks.

Situation 2: An automobile as a magnificent example of the miracle of modern technology. Then picture the automobile as a wasteful piece of junk that pollutes the air and destroys the environment.

Situation 3: An ordinary person walking down an ordinary street. First use various film techniques to make the audience suspect that this person is a suspicious character and is very dangerous. Then present the same person and the same street in such a way that the audience will feel that this person is trustworthy and courageous.

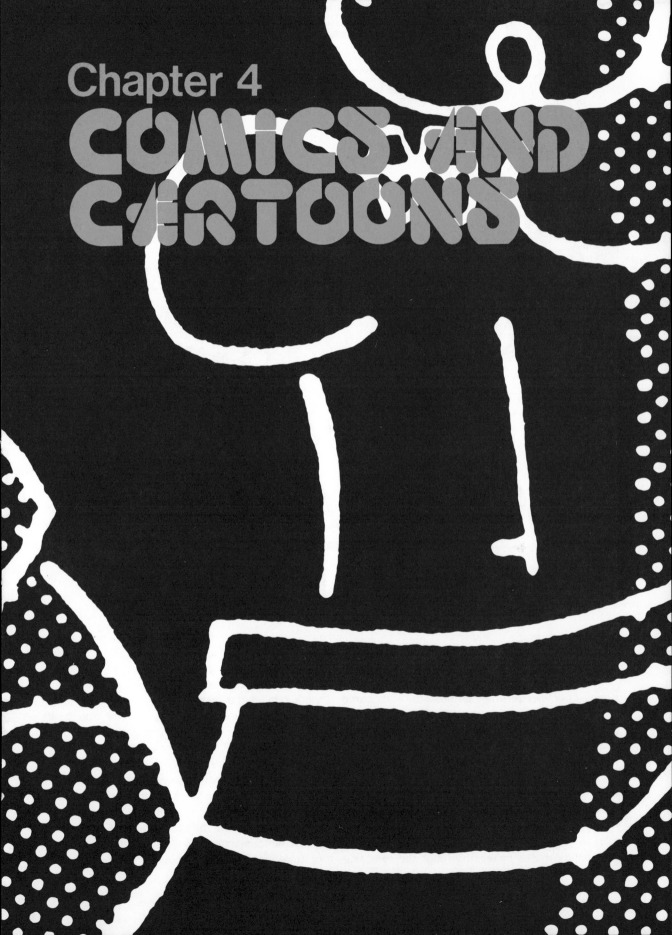

Chapter 4
COMICS AND CARTOONS

SOME CARTOONS BITE

Every year Americans purchase about 300 million comic books. Comic strips are most people's first contact with a newspaper, and every survey about newspaper readership comes to the same conclusion—the comics are the most widely read part of the daily paper. For many adults comic strips are a daily ritual, and for many youngsters comic books are their main contact with reading.

Almost all newspaper comic strips are "syndicated." That is, a cartoonist draws one cartoon or strip a day (or one a week) and sends his or her work to a newspaper syndicate. The syndicate distributes the strip to those newspapers that subscribe, and the cartoonist receives payment through the syndicate from each subscribing newspaper. Gag cartoons (one box rather than a strip) that appear in magazines are done by free-lance cartoonists who work in much the same way as free-lance magazine writers. The free-lancer works at home and sends cartoons to various magazines; the cartoonist receives from $10 to $400 for publication.

Some comic strips are purely entertainment, while others give advice, preach, or make political and social comments. Many papers feature "political cartoons." These single-frame cartoons are editorials in pictures and therefore are most often found on the editorial page. The illustrations show political or "message" cartoons from newspapers.

MEDIALAB

Newspaper Cartoons

1. What comics—comic books, comic strips, magazines with cartoons—are read by class members?

2. Find out who syndicates some of the cartoons carried in your local papers.

3. Select the comic strip or comic book that you read most often. Write a brief article about the strip or book explaining why it is fun to read, what some of the cartoonist's favorite subjects are, what the comic says about life, and what kind of person probably would not enjoy that particular comic.

4. Study the satirical cartoons on these two pages and determine what each one says.

5. Find political or "opinion" cartoons in your local papers or elsewhere and bring them to class. Collect them on a bulletin board; when there are enough gathered, discuss those that seem most effective.

6. If you have some artistic ability, draw your own opinion cartoon and add it to those on the bulletin board.

The Language of Comics

Each mass medium has its particular "language," one that most users of the medium understand but probably could not describe if asked. Film viewers know that a fade or a dissolve means a long passage of time, book readers expect a new chapter to mark a new time frame and location for the action, TV viewers know a station break does not mean the end of a program, and newspaper readers do not confuse the news with the ads. Why? Because users are familiar with each medium's "language." They have learned these languages by experience with the media rather than through schooling or formal training. An adult who for some reason first saw a film at the age of 25 would no doubt find it confusing and meaningless. The "language" of a medium is made up of the conventions, the rules, and the traditions that media creators use.

An adult who read a comic strip for the first time at the age of 25 would wonder what all those strange blobs are over the characters' heads. Of course, most comic readers learn the language when they are children. They learn that those strange blobs are dialogue balloons. Dialogue balloons show many examples of the conventional language of comics. The tail pointing to the speaker is one such example. If the balloon line is perforated, the character is

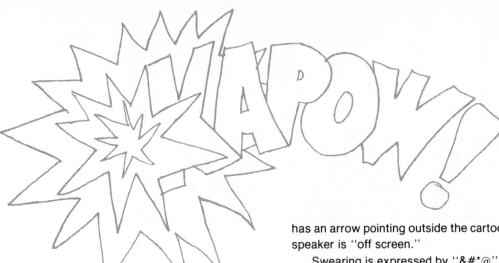

whispering—the cartoonist need not print out "this person is whispering." Tiny letters in a huge balloon show the speaker is frightened or ashamed. A cry has a jagged outline, while a telephone voice has a zig-zag shape with an arrow going into the telephone.

If a balloon has little icicles underneath it, the words or thoughts are taken to be cold and cruel or filled with hatred. If the balloon has a series of small smoke-puff circles instead of a tail pointing to the character, the contents of the balloon are thoughts or dreams rather than spoken words. If the balloon has an arrow pointing outside the cartoon frame, the speaker is "off screen."

Swearing is expressed by "&#*@" or "!!!!." A lightbulb above a character's head means a bright idea, dark clouds signify depression, and musical notes symbolize music or singing. The boldness of the letters indicates the volume of the speaker's voice.

Speed lines indicate movement and sometimes are used to hide violence. A split panel can be used to indicate the passage of time without having to write "and several hours later. . . ."

These bits of the total language of comics are only a few examples of the hundreds of details that make up the grammar of the medium of comics. They are rules, but they are not strict and can be changed and modified in a great number of ways.

1. Go through a single comic book or a variety of newspaper comic strips and find examples of at least a dozen techniques of comic strip language. Include at least three that are not mentioned in this chapter.

2. Look at several comic strips and comment on the size of the head, hands, and feet. Explain what you find.

3. Comment on the different drawing styles used in various strips. In writing, attempt to describe the style of a particular cartoonist or strip.

4. Why do you think comics are so popular? In other words, what need do they supply to the millions who read them so faithfully? Do different comic strips satisfy different needs?

5. Find characters who appear in comic books or comic strips and also in other media—television, film, records, radio.

6. Bring a comic book to class. Go through the comic and note visual techniques that are also used in films.

7. Prepare a research report on the history of comic books in the United States.

The Gag Cartoon

A "gag" cartoon is a single picture, a comic strip is a row of pictures, and a comic book is a collection of stories told through comic-style drawings. All these comic forms share the same language or drawing devices discussed earlier in this chapter. But the gag cartoonist has to use the most finely developed bag of techniques to evoke laughter. Because the whole point of the cartoon must be carried by a single printed line beneath the cartoon, nothing in the drawing must distract from the point. Sometimes the gag is done in pantomine, without a single word below the drawing. The restrictions of the form make gag cartoons the ultimate in cartoon art. The following article explains some of the subtle and finely developed techniques of the gag cartoonist.

The Techniques of the Gag Cartoonist

by John L. Hulteng and Roy Paul Nelson

How are those wonderful gag cartoon jabs at our shams and illusions carried out? Here are some of the techniques.

To the real cartoon connoisseur, gag cartoons represent the ultimate in the cartoon art. A gag cartoon is to be savored, not just looked at and read. The subtleties of the art are considerable. Note that the whole point revolves around a single line printed underneath the cartoon, and everything within the drawing must substantiate that point. The gag cartoonist keeps his cast of characters down, his setting simple. He must make it clear at once, without benefit of balloon, just who within the drawing is doing the talking.

Sometimes he can put his gag over without a single word below. He does his gag in pantomime.

Unique among the cartoonists, he has no particular axe to grind. His objects of ridicule, when they are there, are hard to pin down, because he deals less in personalities and issues, more in general statements about mankind. He's never happier than when, in the words of Stephen Becker, he is "jabbing away constantly at our shams and illusions."

Gag cartoonists come onto their gags in a number of ways. Sometimes they dream up a scene and then try to imagine a scene that will make it funny.

Most gag cartoonists buy ideas from outside sources. They pay the writer 25 percent of what the cartoon earns and keep 75 percent for themselves. Only the cartoonist signs the cartoon.

It has been said that the novelist has only a few basic plots to work with. Similarly, the gag cartoonist has only a few basic ideas. The setting, the props, the characters change; the words in the gag lines vary; but the ideas stay the same. Perhaps you will recognize them:

1. The cliché. Most journalists avoid the cliché. Not the cartoonist. He can take a cliché and let a character act it out literally and get a laugh. Virgil Partch (Vip) is a master of this kind of gag. Vip shows a man lying dead on the sidewalk while a companion, unaware of the tragedy, turns to watch a cranky woman walk by. He says: "Boy! If looks could kill, eh, Steve?" Dana Fradon makes a slight change in a cliché in a *New Yorker* cartoon dealing with deteriorating telephone service. An executive leads a caller to the door and says: "Don't try to call me. I'll try to call you."

If you'd like to be a gag writer or cartoonist, see what you can do with these cliché lines:

"Mind if I smoke."
"You'll only encourage him."
"You're putting me on!"
"Been waiting long?"
"Am I getting warm?"

2. That's life. This includes any gag that depicts life as it is, so that the reader will identify with it, and say, in effect: "Ain't it the truth!" Tom Henderson in *The Saturday Evening Post* shows a lazy, unshaven man reading the paper, the phone on a table at his side. His wife has just picked up the receiver after rushing in from in front of the house where she's parked the car. She's dropped groceries all the way in and knocked over a chair in her rush to answer the phone. She's saying: "Yes, he's here."

3. Ridiculous situation. The opposite of "That's Life." It just couldn't be that way! Jerry Marcus in *True* shows a worried woman driver with her husband sitting beside her. In back of her is a line-up of cars: a tow truck, a police car, and an ambulance. The husband says: "Relax, it's probably just a coincidence."

4. Out of character. Sweet little old ladies act like gangsters. Kids talk like grownups. Ministers sit in bars with worldly ladies. Mulligan in *The New Yorker* shows a perplexed man and wife looking at a painting of a haggard, hungry woman holding a baby with a frightened child at her side. The scene is dark, desolate. The painting is signed "Norman Rockwell." The man says: "Well, there must be more than one Norman Rockwell in the world."

5. In character. People act out their roles to the point of absurdity. B. Tobey in *The New Yorker* shows a young man smooching with a girl on a park bench. With his free hand, and without looking, he's reaching into a bag of popcorn and feeding a flock of pigeons and squirrels. An older couple is walking by, and the man says to the woman: "Now, there's a warm human being for you."

6. Understatement. This is a favorite theme for the cartoonist; and British cartoonists have no corner on it. Jim Stevenson in *The New Yorker* shows an art expert examining a fine painting while the owner looks on. The expert has rubbed his finger across the painting; his finger is wet with paint. He says: "Well, this initial test suggests that the authenticity of your Rembrandt may be questionable."

7. Exaggeration. The opposite of understatement. Chon Day in *The Saturday Evening Post* shows a tired, middle-aged man asleep on a couch. His wife, a little portly, and a lady visitor are talking. The wife says: "He's had a bad back ever since he carried me over the threshold."

8. Ingenuity. When man solves some problem in an unusual way, readers—even readers of gag cartoons—appreciate it. Rodrigues in the *Saturday Review* sets up a situation in which a father tries to tell his side of the story to the rebel generation. He's fat, balding, middle-aged, well dressed; he stands on stage at a run-down coffee house, strumming a guitar. Hippie types sit watching him, frowning. He's singing: "...Oh, my kid's twenty-three and he don't like to work/Oh he don't like to work/When I was twenty-three I worked very hard/Oh, I worked very hard ..." You could classify it as "out of character" too.

9. Stupidity. This kind of a gag especially satisfies the reader, because the cartoonist always lets the reader know something a chief character in the cartoon doesn't know. The reader feels superior. Jerry Marcus, again, this time in *The Saturday Evening Post*, shows a middle-aged couple already in bed, looking bored. Another couple, obviously visitors, stand nearby. The man, hat in hand, says, "Well, we really must be going."

10. The letdown. Some definitions of humor suggest this is the real core of humor. The reader is led to believe one thing, then finally disappointed. Jim Stevenson again, in *The New Yorker*. A guru sits in front of his high mountain cave. Around him are signs scrawled on the rock: "Smile and the world smiles with you, cry and you cry alone"; "Early to bed and early to rise makes a man healthy, wealthy and wise"; "A penny saved is a penny earned"; and so on. A disappointed, slightly hippie-ish couple has just arrived. The girl says to her male companion: "Something tells me we've come to the wrong guru." Again, classification can never be exact. This gag could serve as an example of "Understatement." ∎

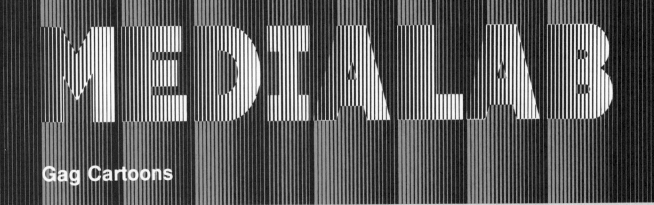

MEDIALAB

Gag Cartoons

1. What is a "gag" cartoon?

2. Make your own gag cartoon. If you do not want to draw, use existing drawings or magazine cut-outs. Or use an existing cartoon but change the "punch line."

3. Make a class collection of gag cartoons.

4. The article suggests ten types of "gags" com-

monly used in cartoons. Find examples of at least five of these techniques.

5. Are these same techniques used in other forms of humor? Find examples.

6. Provide titles or captions for the illustrations on this page. Your captions can be satire or "gag humor." Show an understanding of the techniques of the cartoonist.

a.

b.

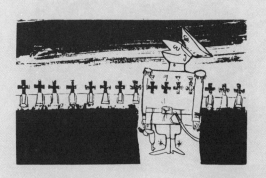

c.

d.

Cross Media Study:

Comics and Film

Learning about the techniques of any one mass medium often helps to understand other media. This is particularly true for films and comics. In a sense, comics were the first movies. Like films, they use a series of still pictures to tell a story. In film the movement is supplied by the camera and projector, while in comics the movement is supplied by the tricks of the artist.

The following article was written by Steve Gerber, who writes comics for the Marvel Comics Group and also makes his own amateur films. He is well aware of the similarities between film and comics. Since the previous chapter of this book was about film language, you should have little trouble applying film techniques to the world of the comic artist. So here, with a little help from Spider-Man, is "What Comics Can Teach You About Movies."

What Comics Can Teach You About Movies

by Steve Gerber

**"A comic book is essentially a film . . . in shorthand."
Here's a look at the techniques of comics writers and
artists as they create their stories.**

On the most basic level, the creators of comics and of cinema are faced with an identical task: *telling a story in a series of still pictures designed to give the illusion of motion.* Visual narrative and movement are at the heart of both. And the similarity doesn't end there. Even the mechanics of the creative processes are remarkably alike for the two media. Much of the terminology is the same. Indeed, the only major differences between comics and film — with regard to storytelling, at least — are technological ones.

Otherwise, a comic book is essentially a film . . . in shorthand. And what comics teach about movies is something all filmmakers, whether their interest is documentaries, sports reportage, or biblical epics, need to know: how to construct a dramatic event in pictures; how to make the pictures move.

Comics Writer as Screenwriter
A comic book begins as a typed synopsis in which the writer describes the action of the story page-by-page, often even panel-by-panel, for the artist. Every relevant detail is noted: what each character is thinking and feeling, the expression on his or her face, what they're doing with their hands, their physical appearances, and the settings, costumes, and props. Diagrams and sketches of these items may be attached to the synopsis. And snatches of dialogue are often included, along with ideas and suggestions for unusual artistic approaches and special effects. Fight scenes are choreographed. The need for an establishing shot here, a close-up there, is specified. And perhaps most importantly, the writer includes his estimation of how much space (one panel, one page, more?) each scene should require.

Thus, in form, style and content, the writer's synopsis for a comic book bears a distinct resemblance to a story treatment for a film. In the case of a silent Super-8 short, it could even suffice as a shooting script. Chances are a film will require *more* separate shots than a comic book, but consider the advantages of planning your shooting on paper as tightly as I plotted the following sequence (shown in Illustration One) for a comics story called "The Return of the Living Mummy."

Scene One: Four-panel opening page with sequence as follows: (1) A wooden crate resting on the floor of the Egyptology Room of a New York museum; the room is dark except for moonlight streaming in from a skylight in the ceiling. (2) Same shot, but a bandaged arm is smashing out from inside the crate. (3) Entire crate flies apart as Mummy breaks out. (4) Large panel; long shot of Mummy looking around him, seeing the various Egyptian art objects, etc.

Now let's look at the techniques involved in creating these

Illustration One: Comic book as shooting script for opening sequence of mystery thriller; four panels outline storytelling techniques.

panels. A picture of a wooden crate in a dark room (panel 1) is not particularly exciting in itself, but it poses a mystery immediately. And the lighting, a single shaft of cold silver from above, casting stark, shifting shadows, at once establishes a mood. Without a word of dialogue or sound effects, we've made it clear that whatever is inside the crate poses a threat.

To create the same mood in a film, you might open with a long shot of the Egyptology Room, with the crate standing upright in the center of the shot. (Actually, the panel shows you where to position the crate and your camera.) You might dolly in slowly, silently, until the crate dominates the scene. Then you halt, holding the same shot for several seconds. Next, the crate itself rocks ever so slightly, creating the first sound of the film. Suddenly, one arm smashes out, splintering the wood; then you cut to the other arm, as it comes through the opposite side of the crate; then a foot, a knee—each shown separately in a series of quick cuts. Then you take a long shot as the entire crate flies to pieces, revealing the full, fearsome figure of the Living Mummy.

The point here is that the storytelling techniques of comics are directly translatable into cinema *if* you, the screenwriter, remember that the comic book is presented in visual "shorthand." That "if" cannot be overemphasized because the image on the movie screen is constantly changing. The viewer isn't able to flip back a page or reread a panel to see if he's missed something. This means that the "information gap" between panels in comics can be much wider

than the gap between shots in film; every action need not be detailed in comics. Nevertheless, the technique of getting from "point A" to "point B" in the plot is virtually identical.

Comics Artist as Filmmaker

Working from the writer's synopsis, the comics artist draws the story in pencil, breaking down each page into an arrangement of panels, composing each individual drawing, deciding which panel, if any, should dominate the page. In so doing, the artist also contributes to the overall rhythm and continuity of the story, and performs functions similar to those of the filmmaker.

The *size* of a panel drawn by the artist, for example, is roughly analogous to the *duration* of a shot—but only roughly. In this respect, comics are somewhat more flexible than film. The artist is not bound to a rectangular frame of predetermined size for his panel; the filmmaker, obviously, is. Then too, the effect on the audience of certain approaches to a scene are different in comics. For example, a page consisting of, say, nine small panels, may either elongate a scene, if the content of those panels is calm, or produce a staccato effect, if the content is rapid-fire action. A series of short, quick shots in a film is almost always likely to produce the staccato effect, regardless of content.

Aside from these differences, though, the function of the artist is like that of the filmmaker who does all the shooting, as well as directing and editing. The artist, in effect, sets up the shots, blocks the actors' movements, and generally provides the print

equivalent of shooting and cutting. Dialogue and captions are added later by the comics writer, much the same way background music and voice-overs might be added to a silent film. As a rule, the tighter the writer's synopsis, the more likely it is that the artist will draw what the writer had in mind.

This principle can be applied to cameramen and screenwriters, too. Take, for example, the 3-panel sequence shown in Illustration Two. Matt Mudrock—the blind attorney who is secretly Daredevil—hears a voice from "off-screen." We cut immediately to the source of that voice as Matt perceives it with his radar sense, the unique power that compensates for his lack of sight. For the comics artist, Sal Buscema, each of these panels required written description down to the last detail. The direction from which the voice is heard, the "radar sense" special effect, the matched action from the "real" shot to the "radar" shot, and, of course, the urgent emotions and movements of both characters all had to be carefully written out for the artist to render the sequence correctly. For the cameraman/filmmaker the same tightly written directions are useful. If you construct your shooting scripts meticulously, the chances of making the film you set out to make are greatly enhanced.

At the same time, a certain flexibility is desirable. Just as the comic artist may visualize a shot differently than the comics writer, you-as-cameraperson may discover possibilities that you-as-screenwriter never anticipated. For example, look at Illustration Three, which shows the final comic-book sense of a

  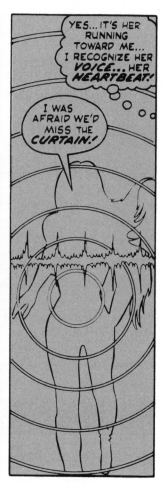

Illustration Two: Comic-book version of off-screen voice, special effects, and matched cuts.

drama about a clown who commits suicide in a swamp. The monster you see is Man-Thing, here returning to his home. The scene is composed of three panels (note the vertical dividing lines that do not completely separate the panels), and is the comic-book equivalent of a "tracking shot." The idea for this scene was entirely the creation of artist Mike Ploog. My own unimaginative little ending for the story had Man-Thing wander off into the marshy swamp in a typical "wide angle" type panel. Mike, on the other hand, created a more powerful image by depicting the monster in two stages of movement:

standing fairly straight, and then slouching deeper into his swamp.

The monster seems to lumber towards the reader. If you were filming him, he'd be moving closer to the camera even as you move it, tracking him from left to right. Meanwhile, the characters who are delivering their final lines about the clown's suicide, seem to recede in the background. Of course, this type of scene should be carefully planned *before* it is shot on location, but you should also give yourself room to maneuver once you get there. Lots of good ideas come at the last minute from unexpected sources.

Besides sharing responsibility with the writer for visualizing the overall flow of the story, the comics artist shares a concern for using a variety of panels. Nothing is duller in comics than a page made up entirely of close-ups (or long shots, or medium shots). In breaking down a page, the artist again plays the role the filmmaker and film editor play in shooting and cutting a scene—all the same rules apply. The shots must be varied, but they must come together to form an integrated whole. And just as the overuse of "trick shots" is to be avoided in film, overly fragmented layouts are shunned in comics. If the cinematic tech-

Illustration Three: Comic-book equivalent of a tracking shot; the monster is shown in two stages of movement across three panels.

nique is to be effective, it must be "invisible." It must not distract the viewer or it defeats its own purpose.

We turn to Matt Murdock again—this time in his Daredevil outfit (see Illustration Four)—for a lesson on placing diverse shots together. Gene Colan drew this fight sequence using several separate panels arranged to present a coherent picture of the action. First you see the scene from street level (low-angle shot); then from the air (vertical dolly shot); then from the points of view of the villain, the hero, and the spectators. The result is a fast-paced action sequence (it *had* to be fast paced, we ran out of pages), in which the reader alternately sees the fight as if he were a participant and an observer. Comic books are filled with sequences like this one; for the filmmaker, they are the perfect guide to new framing techniques and the provocative use of various camera angles.

Summing up, then, it seems clear that the problems to be solved by the comics artist and the filmmaker are very nearly the same. How best to tell the story? Convey the mood? Follow the action? To find answers to these questions, you can study the work of the best comics artists: Jack Kirby, John Buscema, Rich Buckler, Jim Starlin, Will Eisner, as well as those whose work is displayed here. Their names are usually listed in the credits which appear at the beginning of each comic-book story.

How Comics and Movies Differ

Despite all the parallels, comics are not movies, and understanding their dissimilarities is equally vital to learning about one from the other. First, and perhaps most crucial, even though the goals and the creative mechanics of the two media are analogous, the technologies involved are vastly different.

Given a little imagination and a sharp pencil, the comics writer-and-artist team can tackle anything from a sock hop to an intergalactic war. Most Super-8

filmmakers, it's safe to assert, will probably have to content themselves with the more mundane end of that spectrum. So it's wise not to let yourself be influenced by the subject matter of the comics, enticing though it may be. Don't attempt the sequel to "E.T." as your first film—or even your second.

But realize, too, that it would be far more difficult to portray the sock hop scene in comics than it would be in movies! The finite areas of space on the comic-book page, the limited number of pages in each book, and the relative unsophistication of the four-color printing process, make subtleties extremely difficult to achieve, both in dialogue and illustration. Generally speaking, the artist gets only one chance at each panel. The printer has a range of only thirty-two shades. If the writer writes too much copy, he covers up the picture.

The filmmaker has a far greater range of moods, textures, and colors to work with. He need not rely on archetypes and ste-

Illustration Four: Comic-book version of fight sequence; the series of panels shows how to place together different camera angles and points of view.

reotypes as substitutes for real characterization. (True, the comics are maturing, coming out of that phase, but it's still possible to tell the hero from the villain by the color of their respective longjohns.) The themes that film can explore are much richer, much more complex. And they can be dealt with, even by the novice, with a pretty fair degree of success. ■

Cross Media Study: Comics and Film

1. As a class, list ways in which comics and films are alike and ways in which they differ.

2. Could an intelligent person who has never seen a comic strip understand a Batman comic right away, or would it take some learning first? Support your answer.

3. Which do you think would be most difficult to become—an expert creator of comic books or a film director?

4. Find examples in comics that would match the following devices in films. Make a chart of examples, labeling each one and explaining why each particular technique is used.

Films	Comics
frame	
scene	
low angle	
high angle	
camera movement	
subjective camera	
color to influence feeling	
lighting to influence feeling	

THE COMICS CODE

CODE OF THE COMICS MAGAZINE ASSOCIATION OF AMERICA, INC.

Adopted on October 26, the enforcement of this Code is the basis for the comic magazine industry's program of self-regulation.

CODE FOR EDITORIAL MATTER

General Standards   Part A

1) Crimes shall never be presented in such a way as to create sympathy for the criminal, to promote distrust of the forces of la and justice, or to inspire others with a desire to imitate criminals.

2) No comics shall explicitly present the unique details and methods of a crime.

3) Policemen, judges, government officials and respected institutions shall never be presented in such a way as to create disrespect for established authority.

4) If crime is depicted it shall be as a sordid and un-pleasant activity.

5) Criminals shall not be presented so as to be rendered glamorous or to occupy a position which creates a desire for emulation.

6) In every instance good shall triumph over evil and the criminal punished for his misdeeds.

7) Scenes of excessive violence shall be prohibited. Scenes of brutal torture, excessive and unnecessary knife and gun play, physical agony, gory and gruesome crime shall be eliminated.

8) No unique or unusual methods of concealing weapons shall be shown.

9) Instances of law enforcement officers dying as a result of a criminal's activities should be discouraged.

10) The crime of kidnapping shall never be portrayed in any detail, nor shall any profit accrue to the abduc-tor or kidnapper. The criminal or the kidnapper must be punished in every case.

11) The letters of the word "crime" on a comics magazine cover shall never be appreciably greater in dimension than the other words contained in the title. The word "crime" shall never appear alone on a cover.

12) Restraint in the use of the word "crime" in titles or sub-titles shall be exercised.

General Standards Part B

1) No comic magazine shall use the word horror or terror in its title.

2) All scenes of horror, excessive bloodshed, gory or gruesome crimes, depravity, lust, sadism, masochism shall not be permitted.

3) All lurid, unsavory, gruesome illustrations shall be eliminated.

4) Inclusion of stories dealing with evil shall be used or shall be published only where the intent is to illustrate a moral issue and in no case shall evil be presented alluringly nor so as to injure the sensibilities of the reader.

5) Scenes dealing with, or instruments associated with walking dead, torture, vampires and vampirism, ghouls, cannibalism and werewolfism are prohibited.

General Standards Part C

All elements or techniques not specifically mentioned herein, but which are contrary to the spirit and intent of the Code, and are considered violations of good taste or decency, shall be prohibited.

Dialogue

1) Profanity, obscenity, smut, vulgarity, or words or symbols which have acquired undesirable meanings are forbidden.

2) Special precautions to avoid references to physical afflictions or deformities shall be taken.

3) Although slang and colloquialisms are acceptable, excessive use should be discouraged and wherever possible good grammar shall be employed.

Religion

1) Ridicule or attack on any religious or racial group is never permissible.

Costume

1) Nudity in any form is prohibited, as is indecent or undue exposure.

2) Suggestive and salacious illustration or suggestive posture is unacceptable.

3) All characters shall be depicted in dress reasonably acceptable to society.

4) Females shall be drawn realistically without ex-aggeration of any physical qualities.

NOTE: It should be recognized that all prohibitions dealing with costume, dialogue or artwork applies as specifically to the cover of a comic magazine as they do to the contents.

Marriage and Sex

1) Divorce shall not be treated humorously nor represented as desirable.

2) Illicit sex relations are neither to be hinted at or por-trayed. Violent love scenes as well as sexual abnor-malities are unacceptable.

3) Respect for parents, the moral code, and for honorable behavior shall be fostered. A sympathetic understanding of the problems of love is not a license for morbid distortion.

4) The treatment of love-romance stories shall emphasize the value of the home and the sanctity of marriage.

5) Passion or romantic interest shall never be treated in such a way as to stimulate the lower and baser emotions.

6) Seduction and rape shall never be shown or suggested.

7) Sex perversion or any inference to same is strictly forbidden.

CODE FOR ADVERTISING MATTER

These regulations are applicable to all magazines published by Members of the Comics Magazine Association of America, Inc. Good taste shall be the guiding principle in the acceptance of advertising.

1) Liquor and tobacco advertising is not acceptable.

2) Advertisement of sex or sex instruction books are unacceptable.

3) The sale of picture postcards, "pin-ups," "art studies," or any other reproduction of nude or semi-nude figures is prohibited.

4) Advertising for the sale of knives, concealable weapons, or realistic gun facsimiles is prohibited.

5) Advertising for the sale of fireworks is prohibited.

6) Advertising dealing with the sale of gambling equip-ment or printed matter dealing with gambling shall not be accepted.

7) Nudity with meretricious purpose and salacious postures shall not be permitted in the advertising of any product; clothed figures shall never be presented in such a way so to be offensive or contrary to good taste or morals.

8) To the best of his ability, each publisher shall ascer-tain that all statements made in advertisements con-form to fact and avoid misrepresentation.

9) Advertisement of medical, health, or toiletry products of questionable nature are to be rejected. Advertisements for medical, health or toiletry products endorsed by the American Medical Associa-tion, or the American Dental Association, shall be deemed acceptable if they conform with all other con-ditions of the Advertising Code.

COMICS MAGAZINE ASSOCIATION OF AMERICA, INC.

300 PARK AVENUE SOUTH

NEW YORK, N.Y. 10010

Chapter 5
NEWS MEDIA

Before you read this chapter, spend a few minutes thinking about your own definition of "news." In one or two sentences, write a definition of what you think "news" is. Do this now before reading any further.

What Is News?

If you were to ask a dozen professional news people for their definition of news, you would collect a dozen different opinions.

If you were to ask a dozen professional news people for their definition of news, you would collect a dozen different opinions. The dictionary definitions are most unsatisfactory. For example, one dictionary's first meaning for "news" is "recent events and happenings, especially those that are unusual or notable." Yet the fact that you cleaned up your room yesterday for the first time in two years would fit the definition, but would hardly make the morning paper or the evening television newscast. The dictionary proceeds, realizing perhaps that the first definition was inadequate, and describes news as "new information about anything previously unknown." Yet when you walk into math class and learn for the first time how to factor a quadratic equation, that is new and "previously unknown" information to you. But again your math class would not make the news. So what is news? Can it be defined?

For you and me, the consumers of news, news might be defined as what newspapers and newscasters decide is newsworthy. But the people who run the papers, write the stories, and edit the news have to decide what is news and what is not. They do this partly by following tradition and partly by making educated guesses about what the reading, viewing, or listening public wants to know.

If a person eats a fish, that is not news; but if a fish eats a person, that is probably news. If a fish eats a person in your town, it will certainly be news in your town. If a fish eats a famous person, it will probably be news all over the world. News favors the unusual. NBC-TV news commentator David Brinkley explained: "If an airplane departs on time and arrives on time, it isn't news. If it crashes, regrettably, it is." Walter Cronkite of CBS-TV was once asked by a college student why so much coverage of college students is devoted to misbehavior. She asked why there wasn't more coverage of the students who quietly go to class instead of the others who demonstrate, riot, or stage wild fads. That, Cronkite explained, would be "a little bit like having to report all the cats that aren't lost that day."

The desire of journalists to report the unusual (a desire encouraged by their readers' attraction to the out-of-the-ordinary and the bizarre) explains why so much news is "bad news." People often ask why newspapers and TV newscasts dwell on tragedies, accidents, crimes, and generally negative human events. Since planes are so safe, people are usually honest, buildings rarely burn, and criminals are only a small part of the population, such negative events are precisely what is *unusual*. It is normal for things to work fairly well and for people to lead their lives with a certain degree of contentment. A society in which the good news would be out of the ordinary would be a sorry place to live.

But all that is unusual is not news (cleaning your room, for example), nor is all news unusual. There are other qualities that make items newsworthy.

Timeliness

News should be new. There is no such thing as old news; only history. Instant news has become the standard.

Significance of the Event

This news value demands the most personal judgment on the part of the news editor. News events must be events that are important in some way to the audience.

Closeness to the Audience

A fire in the house next door would certainly be news in a neighborhood paper, or even a city paper. But the fire would not be news on national television since it would not be "close" enough to most viewers. A national election in Afghanistan might not even be mentioned in American papers, but the national election in America will fill several editions of most American papers.

Importance of the People Involved

If your next door neighbor is famous, the fact that his or her house burned down might make national news. A speeding ticket is rarely a newsworthy event unless the person speeding is well known.

Drama of Human Interest

The news has to be interesting (some say entertaining) or the audience will not read or watch it. Some stories are included with the news because they are particularly dramatic or have "human interest" value; this news value can make an otherwise minor event into real news. If the fire in your neighbor's house happened on Thanksgiving Day, for instance, the "human" value in the story might make it national news.

MEDIALAB

What Is News?

1. Examine each story in the first three pages of your local paper and decide which news values it embodies. By doing this, you will be answering the question "Why is this news?" Apply the five news values mentioned earlier in order to make your judgment. Do the same for the first three stories carried on local TV news.

2. Decide if each of the stories on the first three pages of the paper fits the definition of news you wrote at the beginning of this chapter. After doing this, you might want to change your definition of news.

3. Discuss the various definitions of news proposed by class members and try to find one that most of the class agrees is valid.

4. Debate or discuss the idea that news reports should place more emphasis on good news than on tragedy and violence.

5. Discuss the idea that the government could operate more efficiently without a free press.

Where Do People Get the News?

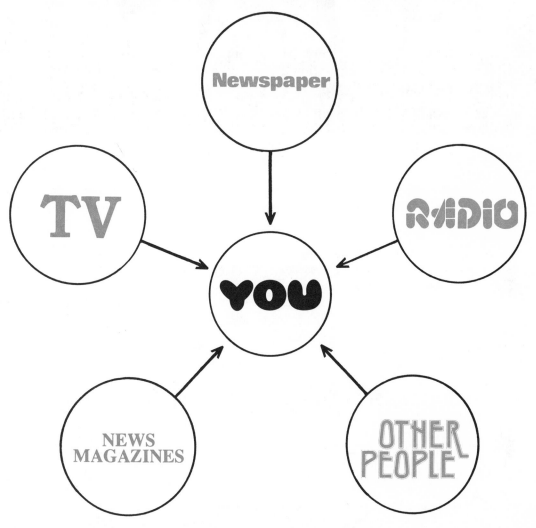

The diagram above shows the various sources of news available to most people. Conduct a study among the class, asking each person, "Where do you usually get most of your news about what is going on in the world today?" Compile the answers and determine which of the five sources is the most important to the class. Every two or three years, the Roper organization conducts such a survey across the nation asking a sampling of people the same question. Their results over recent years are:

Source of most news:	'61 %	'64 %	'68 %	'71 %	'72 %	'74 %	'76 %	'78 %	'82 %
Television	52	58	59	60	64	65	64	67	65
Newspapers	57	56	49	48	50	47	49	49	44
Radio	34	26	25	23	21	21	19	20	18
Magazines	9	8	7	5	6	4	7	5	6
People	5	5	5	4	4	4	5	5	4

MEDIALAB

Where Does Your News Come From?

1. Compare the results of your survey with that of the Roper study. Try to explain any differences you find.

2. Discuss how people's answers have changed through the years. What do you think the survey reveals about how well-informed people are about world affairs?

3. Survey the class to determine which newspapers, magazines, and television and radio newscasts provide news to the class as a whole.

4. Find out who owns the news sources in your city—television and radio stations, and newspapers. Does one owner control several sources—say, two newspapers, or a newspaper and a TV station?

How Are the Various News Media Alike?

The news media are all united by their concern for reporting the news and by their need for an audience. They all depend on advertising and the need to show a profit; they all rely on the Associated Press and United Press International as main sources of news; and all have a "gatekeeper" who controls the flow of news to the public.

News, in the United States, is a product that is sold to consumers. In some countries, news is whatever the government wants the people to believe. The fact that the United States government does not run the news media gives them a certain independence and a willingness to point out flaws and to criticize the government. This ability of the press (both print and electronic) to criticize government and industry is essential to freedom of the press. It is quite natural for governments to at least bend the truth they give out. It is the mission of the press to dig for the whole truth. For this reason many politicians, from mayors to presidents, are antagonistic toward the press. If the press were subject to the government, it would do little but print whatever the government told it to. The Watergate scandal would never have been uncovered (*Washington Post* newspaper reporters were the first to report it); mistakes made in Vietnam would still remain hidden (it was the *New York Times* who first published the "Pentagon Papers"); and scores of dishonest politicians and businesses would still be in power preying on the ignorant and uninformed.

But the press must pay a price for this freedom. Since no news medium is supported by taxpayers' money, the high cost of gathering and spreading the news is assumed by advertisers and the news-buying public.

Another little-known similarity among the news media is their reliance on the wire services of the Associated Press (AP) and United Press International (UPI). If you were to walk into the nerve center of news-gathering activity in any TV or radio station, newspaper, television network, or even news magazine, you would see teletype equipment transmitting news from all over the world.

If you look for the symbols (AP) and (UPI) on the pages of your local newspaper, you will see how important these two wire services are. The symbol at the beginning of a story indicates that the story was provided by the wire service and sent via teletype machines to the newspaper.

Newspapers and news departments of broadcast stations subscribe to or join the wire service. Each subscriber pays a fee to the wire service and also agrees to supply it with coverage of local events that might have national interest. The reports from the wire services arrive 24 hours a day. AP and UPI reporters all over the world phone or send stories to the New York headquarters. From there the stories are sent to subscribers who can print them as news, rewrite them, use them as a research source, or ignore them.

An average newspaper contains more news from the wire services than from its own reporters. The smaller the paper, the truer this is. Many small-town papers are little more than a collection of wire service reports and syndicated material. The average radio news broadcast is at least 90 percent wire service material. Edward Jay Epstein, in his five-year study of network (not local) TV news, concluded that the source for 70 percent of NBC-TV's Nightly News was wire service reports. There is no way that the news consumer can tell the source of a TV or radio news story.

A third similarity all news media share is the use of a "gatekeeper." A news medium could be pictured as a funnel. Into the wide and always open mouth of the funnel flows a steady stream of news. Since there are over 4 billion humans on earth, there are potentially billions of news stories happening every day. Someone has to make the decision as to what is worth giving out to the public and what belongs in the wastebasket or on the floor of the film-editing room. The person who performs this function has different titles in each news organization. In many places he or she is called the managing editor or simply the news editor or news director. Social scientists use the term *gatekeeper* to describe this person, since he or she acts as a kind of control for the news, deciding which items make the paper or the broadcast and which do not gain entry.

Although gatekeepers are extremely important to the news process, they are usually unknown to the general public. They do not get by-lines on newspaper stories, nor do they read the news on television. The gatekeeper is a powerful ongoing influence, but when decisions are made on important stories, the publisher of the paper or the director of the TV or radio station may step in. However, the sheer volume of news that flows into news media headquarters and the limited amount that comes out means that the gatekeeper is the one person most influential in deciding what is and is not news.

In newspapers the gatekeeper uses only about one in five stories that come in; in television and radio the number is probably closer to one in ten or twenty. On large city newspapers, news pours in so fast that only one in ten items scanned by the gatekeeper makes the paper. The gatekeeper is given a certain amount of air time or magazine space or newspaper pages to fill. This number is determined by the amount of advertising available. A large amount of advertising means less news; less advertising gives the consumer more news. Because ad space has already been committed, it is figured first, and the news must fit in the space that is left over.

All the news media have a "gatekeeper" who controls the flow of news to the public

MEDIALAB

How Are News Media Alike?

1. This section suggested only a few similarities among the news media. List several other qualities they all share.

2. How do you think news in the United States would be different if it were government controlled and paid for from tax money?

3. Find some current examples showing the news media and the government in conflict.

4. Do you think it is dishonest for a government agency, a corporation, or an individual to release news about itself that presents it in the best possible light? Support your answer.

5. How much advertising does each news medium generally contain? Use a single issue or broadcast as an example. Express all answers in terms of

percentage. For example, time a 30-minute TV newscast; use a stopwatch to count the exact number of minutes and seconds of news. Count the number of minutes and seconds of ads during that half hour. If there are 20 minutes of news and 2 minutes of advertising, then you can say that 10 percent of the news time is devoted to advertising. For newspapers, measure in terms of column inches.

6. Draw two conclusions from the statistics on the amount of advertising in each news medium.

7. Do you think the need to show a profit and to sell advertising influences the kind of news the various media will report? Explain your answer.

8. Determine what percentage of all the news in your local papers is provided by AP and UPI.

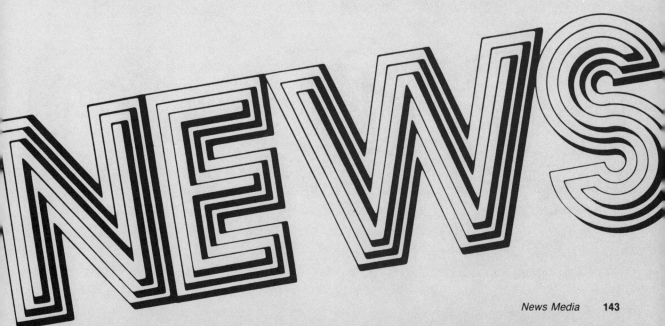

MEDIALAB

9. Prepare a written or oral report on the Associated Press or United Press International (or any other wire service).

10. Does anyone serve as "gatekeeper" for the school paper? If so, what does this person do?

11. Compare the major national news magazines for the amount and quality of their news coverage. Compare the opinions or biases you find in their coverage.

12. Draw up a list of "Some things I would like to see in newspapers that are not there now."

13. After comparing and judging the local newspapers, do the same with the *local* newscasts of all the TV stations in your area. Arrange a class project to compare and rate the local newscasts. One way to do this is to time exactly how many minutes and seconds of a nightly 30-minute local newscast is news, how much is advertising, how much is sports

and weather, how much is chatter among the announcers. Find out which station gives the most news. Which station uses news film best? Which station gives the most detailed coverage of local events?

14. If you have the chance to attend some event that is covered by the media, be sure to read, watch, and listen to all the media reports on that event you can. Compare them with the experience you had at the actual event.

15. Report on a comparison of the three major news weeklies—*Time, Newsweek,* and *U.S. News and World Report.* You may wish to work in small groups.

16. Form a small group to find examples of the same news item reported in the local papers, papers in other cities, news magazines, radio, and TV. Compare the treatment each medium gives the story.

How Do News Media Differ?

Each news medium may report the same news, but the words, the images, and their effects on the news consumer are different. Let us consider how the four major news media (TV, radio, newspapers, news magazines) differ in their presentation of the news.

TELEVISION

Television, and to some extent radio, have one or two individuals who present the news. The television viewer sees a person who is regarded as trustworthy or hears a radio announcer with a voice that rings with authority. Newspapers and news magazines lack this element of personality and instead must depend on the printed word. Television news commentators are often highly paid public celebrities. Some TV newscasters are not reporters at all; they are announcers with a favorable public image. Newspaper editors are seldom recognized on the street and rarely become celebrities.

Television can present a strong visual image. A written news story about poverty will probably make less of an impression on a reader than a powerfully filmed story of a starving family. A live telecast of some important happening is far more memorable and emotionally powerful than a series of printed words in the newspaper. Television news is at its best when it can show what is happening as it happens—the space walks, Congressional hearings, wars, disasters, and sports news. But the national networks require events of great national interest before they will preempt regularly scheduled programs for a live telecast.

Another form of network news presentation that is almost as powerful as the live events is the documentary. These 30- or 60-minute network "specials" have included in-depth programs on topics such as poverty, the law, the Pentagon, migrant workers, pollution, football injuries, and hundreds of other subjects. Such documentaries are usually about topics of national interest and are probably produced by one of the three networks for nationwide broadcast rather than by a local station about topics of local concern. Documentaries are expensive to produce and invariably lose hundreds of thousands of dollars for the networks. Although they do rather poorly in the ratings, they are still seen by millions of people and sometimes have a noticeable effect on government agencies and future legislation. It is in these documentaries that television is at its best in providing in-depth news coverage. In 30 or 60 minutes, a documentary can give the depth lacking in the evening news as well as present powerful visual images to influence opinions.

For the majority of viewers, TV news *is* the evening network news. A television newscast allows viewers less selectivity than a newspaper allows its readers. A newspaper reader scans the headlines first and reads complete stories only if the headline promises a story of particular interest. Television news is usually watched in its entirety. The TV viewer is not as free to select which items he or she will watch. NBC reporter John Chancellor explains: "Many middle-aged people who are opposed to television news are people who had not been subjected to serious news, seriously presented, until they got a television set and until television in the mid-fifties began to develop serious news programs. Before that, people read daily newspapers. They read the sports page, the comics page; they glanced at the front page. If people didn't want to read about an ax murder, they didn't have to read about it. If they didn't want to read about the race problem, they didn't have to read about the race problem. Then came television, and the problem with television is that to see any news you pretty much have to see it all. It's a very brutal way to get the news. You can either accept the news that comes off the tube or turn it off completely. You can't pick and choose."

Another unique quality of television is that the presence of film or TV cameras at an event can change what happens there. In the presence of a camera, we all become actors; and the TV news is then a stage on which we can act out our viewpoint. Some members of Congress objected to the idea of television for Congressional hearings (during the Watergate hearings, for example) on the grounds that the presence of TV cameras would create a "circus" atmosphere. Such fears turned out to be groundless, but the TV camera does have far more effect than a newspaper reporter with a notepad or even a radio reporter with a small tape recorder and microphone.

Still another aspect of television news not shared by the other media is that a person who looks and sounds believable can influence viewers' opinions. The same person's statement in printed form might be far less convincing. However, the opposite can also be true. This importance of the "image" a person can project over television has become an important factor in political campaigns.

RADIO

For the most up-to-the-minute, quickest, and most frequent news, no medium currently does better than radio. Many stations carry news every 30 minutes; most, every hour. Radio is available anywhere in the country, thanks to transistors and radios which have become almost standard equipment in automobiles. Using a telephone, a radio station can present news almost as it happens. A newspaper has to wait at least until the next edition, and television has to wait (with the exception of special bulletins) until the next evening news broadcast. Radio serves the nation more as a headline service. Many radio news broadcasts are what is called "rip and read." The disc jockey (the same one who announces songs and reads commercials) is given paper news reports ripped off the wire service teletype machines and reads them for five minutes.

Better radio stations, usually in large cities, have news departments and reporters out looking for stories. But radio news today functions best as a headline service, as a first alert for important news, and as the best source for recent weather information. There are a few stations in the country that broadcast only news, but they have yet to make a serious contribution to the advancement of news broadcasting.

NEWSPAPERS AND NEWS MAGAZINES

The physical problems associated with publishing a newspaper make the news at least a few hours old by the time the paper hits the street. But of all the

THE SAME NEWS... RE

news media, newspapers offer the reader the greatest variety and the greatest personal choice. Each newspaper reader is his or her own editor, selecting the news that he or she thinks important and ignoring what is not. Newspapers have been in the news business far longer than any of the electronic media and have the most people working on gathering and writing the news.

Newspapers and news magazines provide the most in-depth reporting, while radio and television (with the exception of documentaries) go into comparatively little detail. The news magazines often provide the most detail about national stories but are a few days or a week behind the newspaper in getting the news to the readers.

There are currently three national news weeklies with a large circulation—*Time* with over 4½ million readers; *Newsweek* with about 3 million; and *U.S. News and World Report* with about 2 million circulation. The news magazines report the news with a more entertaining and lively writing style than the newspapers. They have more time to prepare in-depth stories since they are not under the pressure of putting out a daily publication. However, both *Time* and *Newsweek,* which are printed on a Sunday, can publish a story about an important event that happened on Saturday in time for the newsstand copies available Monday morning. *Time* is printed in a number of printing plants around the world and begins selling each edition on Sunday night and Monday morning in more than 150 countries.

The news magazines provide the most retrievable form of news. Radio and TV news is gone once the show has ended. A listener or viewer cannot go back and check what was said or find the text of the news broadcast at a public library. A newspaper is more retrievable, but its size and inexpensive paper make it hard to store without the inconvenience and expense of microfilm. News magazines are readily checkable in any library or in the basement piles of back issues in thousands of homes. A news magazine also is on sale for at least a week, while a newspaper disappears from newsstands within twelve hours. Because of this longer sales period and the relative permanence of the news magazine, magazines have developed a policy of stressing facts and checking their accuracy.

News magazines (as well as other magazines that use factual articles) have full-time "checkers" whose only job is to verify the facts reporters mention in their stories. The checkers also are charged with filling in facts that reporters leave out. A story might come to a checker with a line such as "The 00-person Sudanese army . . ." It will be up to the checker to fill in the "00." Other news media are careful about reporting facts accurately, but none treat even the least important facts with the passion of news magazines. The presence of insignificant, but often colorful, facts is one of the aspects of news magazine writing that distinguishes it from newspapers. A news magazine story might begin: "Flowers were in bloom on the crumbling towers of St. Hilarion, and hawks turned soundlessly high above Kyrenia." A newspaper story, on the other hand, would begin simply by noting: "Strife-torn Cyprus was reported quiet today with only sporadic outbreaks of shooting."

News magazines present the news in the form of dramatic stories. Unlike newspapers, they have no tradition of reporting unbiased news and restricting opinions to columns and editorials. They often present opinionated news and interpretations of events, sometimes in articles signed by the writer. News magazines present their opinions as part of the news; newspapers keep opinion pieces separate; television editorials are clearly labeled on the local level, while interpretive documentaries are presented on the national level. The presentation of news in a TV documentary is somewhat similar to that in a news magazine.

PORTED DIFFERENTLY

MEDIALAB

How Do News Media Differ?

1. Construct a news media comparison chart using the general form given here. Before filling in the chart, discuss exactly how the questions should be answered, the amount of detail desired, the time spans to be used for comparison, and any other points of possible confusion about the chart. Either individuals or small groups can fill in the charts.

2. Compare charts with others in the class (or other groups) and discuss reasons for your answers. Draw the chart on the blackboard or a transparency for an overhead projector and fill in the boxes with answers that reflect general agreement (where possible) among the class members.

3. Draw two general conclusions from the charts.

	RADIO	TELEVISION	NEWSPAPER	NEWS MAGAZINE
1. How much time or space does each medium devote to actual news?				
2. How much detail does each medium provide?				
3. How fast does each provide the news? Which is fastest and which slowest?				
4. Which media depend on advertising to make a profit and thus stay in business?				
5. Is the news part of the medium economically profitable?				
6. Which are the best known nationwide suppliers of news in each medium?				
7. Which are the local news suppliers in each medium?				
8. Which do you think has the strongest emotional effect on the audience?				
9. Which do you think most influences people's opinions?				
10. What is the strongest point of each?				
11. What is the weakest point of each?				
12. Which covers each of the following best: sports events at your school / local politics tragedy / human interest weather / in-depth news stories financial news / world events				

MAKING NEWS

Most of what appears on televised news is not really the "news"; it is people reacting to the news. How can you gain television time on the news other than by committing a crime or hitting a home run to win the World Series? Easy. Represent a special interest group (political party, police, union, corporation, entertainer, etc.) and stage an event to which the "press" is invited.

Once television time is gained, you either prepare a favorable statement or stage an event with visual interest that makes your point. If you are interviewed by a local reporter, you try to control the interview to create the impression of yourself as the "good guy."

Joe Saltzman is a former journalist and now a journalism professor and media consultant. Here are his reflections on media control and the fine art of controlling interviews.

How to Manage TV News

by Joe Saltzman

All the world's a stage, at least if you know how to manipulate local television reporters.

It is a blunt fact of life that the local television news we see every night — the only news source for more than 60 percent of the American people — has been staged for television by outside special interests.

Consider the following cases and use them as a guide when watching tonight's local news programs:

A politician wants to get publicity for legislation he is sponsoring. He calls a news conference. Reporters from every television station show up. Viewers will see the news conference on the evening news but probably little else. What they won't hear about is any political wheeling and dealing out of the glare of the television lights. . . .

A major company holds a news conference to issue its year-end report. The figures are glowing, the cameras are rolling, everyone is smiling. If the reporter works harder than most do, the viewers might hear figures questioned and policies doubted when the story gets on

the air, but that kind of information can't be dug up in the course of a press conference. No one will call in cameras and reporters to reveal economic reverses, mishandling of funds or worse. And if reporters find out something suspicious on their own, they probably won't even get to talk to the company president, much less record an interview with that person.

A picket line goes up around a market to protest higher prices. A spokesperson is there when the television reporters arrive. For the next hour or so, the cameras cover the staged event. The reporters thank the spokesperson and leave. Five minutes later, the picket line disappears.

The list is endless. Politicians, police, the military, entertainers, government agencies, corporations, businesspersons, individuals and groups all stage news "events" for their own benefit. And those with money to hire a savvy public relations firm can get their news—and usually their version of the news—broadcast into living rooms with sports

and the daily weather.

"Any sharp public relations person can get the story covered by television," says Robert Irvine, a former news director of the Eyewitness News team at KABC-TV in Los Angeles. "He knows how to schedule a story for maximum exposure, how to alert the news media and make sure they show up, how to get the inexperienced reporter to put his PR release on film, how to make sure it will get on the evening news. Most of what you see on television news is stuff handed to . . . assignment desks who then feed it to reporters who are usually guided in their coverage by the public relations person involved. . . ."

A local television news reporter who has worked for 25 years for several stations shares Irvine's opinions. He says news executives like well-organized stories that don't leave unanswered questions. "Investigative reports or stories that take a lot of time and effort never look as smooth or polished as the simple PR story," he explains. "Nobody is very happy about partially finished, dull or nonvisual stories. So eventually you either give up or keep fighting until you get fired or change jobs."

Thousands of stories from special interests make the air only slightly altered from their staged creation. It takes money to cover stories well and most local television stations don't have the funds. Assignment desks, faced with limited budgets and a handful of inexperienced personnel, look for stories they can film fast—and most of the time those are staged for the media by outside sources. ABC producer and former NBC reporter Mike Gavin explains: "Every demonstration, every scheduled interview, every news conference, every notification of a planned story, every time a person wants to get his or her point across—it's 'staged.' "...

Most editors and reporters insist that the bulk of these staged events is not inherently bad. They often provide information the public should have. The danger is that this is the *only* news the public usually gets while enterprising, investigative television reporting is becoming a thing of the past.

Couple that with television management that is entertainment-oriented and wants short, snappy stories with no loose ends, all packaged neatly into less than two minutes, and it is easy to see why most local news shows are filled with stories that are the easiest to get....

In the past, reporters were more expert than special-interest group representatives in creating and fleshing out stories for the media. No longer. Major corporations and other special-interest

groups are training their people in how to deal with the media in specific and formalized ways.

A prototype for this new sophistication is the Standard Oil Company television training seminar, a two-day, intensive education program for top company executives on how to handle the broadcast media. Executives are brought to a rented television studio, interviewed by a hired reporter then, "critiqued."... By the time executives "graduate," they are ready to handle any radio or television reporter in any local news market in the country. More and more companies have copied the Standard Oil television seminar, which itself was modeled after the very successful program pioneered by J. Walter Thompson Company in the early 1970s.

As one of the university specialists brought in on several occasions by Standard Oil for its "Television Training Seminar," I came to understand that we were preparing Standard Oil executives to cope easily with reporters who have never received such comprehensive briefings....

We would teach these managers and administrators, these top representatives of Standard Oil how to overcome nervousness (before being introduced "take a deep breath, hold it for about three seconds and then let out slowly ..."); how to stand and relax ("Stand naturally with your feet about shoulder-width apart; let your hands hang naturally. Relax your fingers. Then start vibrating your fingers and wrists as fast as you can. Then let that vibration flow through your body to free your muscles of tension").

We would teach them how to get rid of butterflies in the stomach and how to wet a "dry mouth": "A dry mouth can make speaking uncomfortable. Just before you go on, work up a quantity of saliva in your mouth and swallow. It will moisten your mouth and throat and speaking will be easier."

What to do if, under stress, the voice becomes shrill: "Don't talk from the throat, talk from the diaphragm. Use your lungs and entire chest as a sound-source resonator. That way you won't have to shout. It improves the sound of authority in your voice."

We emphasized that the executives must speak clearly, not mumble; they must be aggressive, not passive. After various other voice-training procedures, we showed them how to project a good image through the eyes and we emphasized the importance of good grooming: Dress comfortably; wear solid colors; avoid sharp, flashy clothes; avoid large cuff links or gaudy jewelry.... Shave before an appearance, TV accentuates the beard....Wear knee-length hose; avoid short socks, garters, argyles; if they don't have high socks, wear boots....

Those were just the preliminaries. The main event was how to deal with reporters on television. The first part of the lesson was how to prepare for the interview. By Sunday afternoon, after an intensive weekend, the executives would go home feeling confident, knowing a good deal more about interview techniques than the majority of broadcast reporters they would run into.

We put the executives

through a rigorous interview schedule. Thrown cold into a television studio, they were interviewed by a seasoned reporter specially paid to make the guest feel uncomfortable. Every ploy was used, from argumentative and personal questions to cheap shots and dropping film cans off-camera. The tape was later played back while two media experts—in a carefully rehearsed piece of criticism—ripped it apart. After that, the executive was interviewed again, and those tapes were evaluated.

Avoiding "question traps" and learning how to control an interview were the most important parts of the lesson. We insisted that the executives be prepared, that they have specific objectives in mind when being interviewed and be ready to talk about them whenever possible by taking charge of the interview. The most important single technique is called "bridging." Months later, I happened to see one of our executives use it. He responded to a question by saying, "That is not my area of expertise, — (reporter's first name). I came here to talk about oil and that reminds me of . . ." Before the reporter knew what was happening, the executive was into a two-minute summary of what he wanted people to know about Standard Oil. The answer had nothing to do with the question, but the confused reporter thanked him and that was that.

Besides bridging, we demonstrated to the executives how to handle all types of questions. One was "the loaded preface question" that "stacks the deck and colors any answer." It implies charges and guilt and "puts you in a corner before you even get a chance to open your mouth." An example goes something like this: "You're a representative of a company that polluted the Bay of San Francisco with its tanker collision, ruined the shrimp and oyster business in the gulf with an oil well blowout, and foisted a phony gasoline hike on the public. In light of that track record, what is the new management of your company doing to mend the error of its ways?" How should they handle this? First, as the interviewer sets out this laundry list of charges, we taught the executive not to try to remember all the charges and not to try to answer them all. We instructed him to zero in on one he was sure he could respond to and by implication discredit the rest. The executive was taught to say, "Hey, wait a minute. That's quite a laundry list of accusations, — (reporter's first name), and I doubt that we have enough time on this program to answer them all. I can assure you that you're way off base on all those charges. For example, let me deal with just one of those. That well blowout in the gulf had no effect whatsoever on the shrimps and oysters. A study by the University of Texas biology department proved this, and the courts dismissed all suits that were brought against us alleging harm to marine life."

Executives were also made to understand that they could not have personal opinions. "Everything you say on radio or television or to a reporter will come across as a statement of a representative of the Standard Oil Company. It will be interpreted as an official statement. Even if you say, 'Well, I can't speak for my company, but I think personally that . . . it will come out as 'a representative of Standard Oil says this and that.'" The executive was warned: "You cannot have a personal opinion. Only an official opinion. Do not give your private feelings."

We warned executives against falling for questions that pose "either/or" choices. They were also cautioned against "A-B-C ranking" questions: "Sir, list the four most important problems the industry faces today and tell us how to deal with them." They were taught not to make a list but to pick out one point, deal with it, then bridge to their own point. A sample answer: "Well, — (reporter's first name), with the kind of problems facing our whole economy today, I don't think we could cover any industry's total problems in 30 seconds. But I'd like to say this . . ." then bridge; it's just like dancing: one, two, three, bridge.

On occasion, the executive was told, there would be reporters who cut off answers, interrupt the most carefully plotted bridges, make snide comments and be downright rude. "If this happens, ride it out and try to capture audience sympathy with facial expressions and body language. If you engage in verbal battle with the interviewer, you will lose. He's on his home turf and is familiar with the techniques of broadcasting. He will win the battle. There is no way you, an amateur, can win over a professional."...

We told the executives always to keep their cool, always to be friendly and gentlemanly. No personal battles. "If you get hostile, you'll probably lose

audience sympathy and end up in a bad situation." Other tips offered were to always listen carefully to the questions, never let accusations stand, only answer questions with which they were familiar and not concerning any controversial subjects, and bridge often to what they wanted to say, not what the reporter wanted said. . . .

There may be occasions when the executive would not want to answer a question, but he was urged to avoid saying, "No comment," at all costs. That sounds evasive, as if he has something to hide. If the executive can't or won't answer a question, he was urged to say so and explain why.

Executives soon learned one way to avoid answering the question was to ask another question they liked better. Example: "Why haven't the oil companies reduced their gasoline prices and their earnings a little instead of making such obscene profits?" Answer: "You know, — (reporter's first name),

what we should be asking ourselves is why you and other people seem to think the idea of profits is in any way obscene. We ought to be asking ourselves if we're providing enough incentive for the economy to generate the level of profits we need to expand energy supplies." And the executive kept going, bridging to another little speech.

We warned the executives never to lie—never to make up anything, shade or distort facts. "It is a good probability that sooner or later you'll be found out if you do not tell the truth. It will blow your credibility. There is no chance to recover. No more believability. Never play games with the truth."

They were taught how important it was to keep their answers brief. "Twenty to 30 seconds is a target time; make it lucid and brief." A nice 20- to 30-second speech would make the editor's work easy and improve the chances that the executive's statement would be used. They were told to avoid the use of

jargon, to give support to generalizations, to use an authority— an expert who holds the same view—to use statistics to illustrate a point, to use analogies to support answers: "Raising taxes on our industry would be like buckling a lead belt on a long-distance swimmer.". . .

It is small wonder that much of what we see on local television news is created by special interests who only want their version of a story told. In many stories, two special-interest groups collide, and sometimes the public gets enough facts to make an educated decision. . . .

The danger that special-interest groups' staged news is becoming TV's primary news has already been realized. Individual reporting enterprise is becoming less and less the norm as special-interest groups become more and more sophisticated. Only when newspapers and magazines do the leg work, does television discover that there are stories not being regularly supplied to it. . . . ■

MEDIALAB

Making News

1. Why are so many of the stories on local news provided by special interest groups or individuals with a product or viewpoint to sell?

2. Watch the local news on television tonight. If you have more than one local television station, be sure someone is watching each newscast. Note each local story carried and determine which are examples of some person or group using television to present a favorable impression. Discuss your findings the next day in class.

3. Station managers defend the use of "staged" or "managed" news items on the grounds that they still provide the public with useful information. The danger is that because such news is so easy to report, it might become the only news. Is this true in your city? How much investigative reporting is done by local television and radio stations?

4. Interviews on local TV newscasts usually fall into one of two categories: an interview with an ordinary person who has just become a victim/hero/witness, or an interview with a professional person (corporate spokesperson, politician, public official) who is defending a viewpoint. In the first category, the reporter is not looking for information as much as for emotion. People being emotional on camera attract attention. So you will see interviews with victims of tragedy as well as heroes and lottery winners. Such

interviews are televised to add emotional content to the news broadcast; sometimes this is called human interest.

What is your opinion of this first kind of interview? How valuable is it in terms of news? How would you react if your house just burned down and a reporter asked you, "How did it happen?" or "What are you going to do now?"

5. The article deals with training for the second kind of interview. What techniques were taught to help the executives "control" an interview?

6. Watch news interviews of corporate executives, government officials, or politicians. Study how and if the person being interviewed controlled the interview. Look for examples of the techniques discussed in this section.

7. Work in groups and demonstrate one or more of the interview techniques illustrated in the article. Volunteers should play the roles of reporters and of interviewees. Illustrate how to:

- avoid question traps
- take charge of a possible hostile interviewer
- control an interview by bridging
- survive a "loaded" or "biased" question
- avoid the "either/or" trap
- avoid answering a question

How Has Mass Media Changed Politics?

Television has changed the concept of news more than any invention since the printing press. Television "invented" the idea of national news. Radio had the potential to unite the nation and create national news, but its impact was limited. Radio required the listener to use imagination. It did not show angry mobs, extremes of poverty or wealth, or the grittiness of war.

Only one politician used radio to strengthen the image of the presidency—Franklin D. Roosevelt. Roosevelt's fireside chats were a perfect match of the man to the medium. He might not have been able to survive the television news camera. Voters would have been constantly reminded that he could not walk and spent most of his time in a wheelchair.

Before televised national news, a presidential candidate could hope to get away with making a special promise in one part of the country that would go unnoticed elsewhere. But today, a promise made to factory workers in Ohio is seen on the evening news by farmers in Mississippi. So candidates avoid local issues in favor of national or even global concerns.

Presidents use television to communicate with the entire country, taking time on all three major networks for policy statements and even press conferences. Compare that to pre-television days in which a president had to travel around the country on arduous speaking tours. Woodrow Wilson defended his idea to establish a League of Nations with a cross-country speaking tour. Some historians believe the strain of the trip led to the stroke that ended his presidency.

Presidents once delivered the annual "State of the Union" address to Congress at noon. Today it is done at nine at night on the East Coast. True, this time is less convenient for the people in attendance, but the time is best for a national TV audience. Nine o'clock is prime time in the East and Midwest and still late enough to garner a large audience on the West Coast. Every trip a president (or a presidential candidate) makes is carefully planned to give the maximum television coverage. A president can now afford to address a small gathering—even a high school assembly or a local meeting of auto workers. The real crowd for such speeches is the millions who will see a few seconds of the speech on the evening news. Meetings are timed and planned for maximum television coverage. The live audience is more a stage prop provided to cheer and applaud. The audience communicates a sense of support and excitement to the millions watching at home.

Television gives a president a powerful tool to earn the nation's support and to unite the country in time of crisis.

MEDIALAB

News and Politics

1. Imagine that television ceased to exist. How would that fact change a presidential campaign and election?

2. How does the current president use television to gain public support of ideas and policies?

3. Make a note of any politician who appears on a newscast. Why is the politician gaining television time? Is the "live" audience important or merely a prop for this occasion?

4. When a president makes a policy statement or conducts a news conference, it is often carried in prime time on all three television networks. Do you think this is (a) important for the good of the nation, (b) government domination of media, (c) a shame since you sometimes miss a favorite program, or (d) not needed since it could be covered by newspapers and one network instead of all three? Support your answer.

THE NEWS BUSINESS

Reporting the news is a high-speed business involving many layers of information and people. Just exactly how is it done? Here is the story of a story: a look behind the scenes of news gathering. An early morning school bus accident in a Midwestern town is reported on the network news from New York the same day. How do the information and the pictures get to the producer in New York? How does the producer decide which stories will be shown on television? Step-by-step the process is explained in the following article.

THE ACCIDENT

A Cross-Media Study

by John Chancellor and Walter Mears

How does a school bus crash in the Midwest turn into a news story on national television and in newspapers around the country the next morning?

The break in the wooden guard rail is hard to see in the gray morning, as the rain slants across the ravine. Several cars pass over the bridge before a farmer in a pickup truck notices the broken rail and stops to look down.

The school bus is on its side, bright yellow against the green slope, its headlights on, its warning lights blinking. The farmer can hear the sound of children crying.

He passes the message to the state police on his citizens' band radio. It goes from there, by telephone, to hospitals. In a few minutes, the red lights of ambulances and police cars flash across the stubble of the harvested cornfields.

And so begins a news story. The school bus accident will join thousands of other events and occurrences on that day, part of a great river of information, carried by satellite links, high-speed teletypes and computerized word processors. The high-speed machines of the Associated Press transmit about 400,000 words a day, 1,000 stories every 24 hours.

Thirty miles from the scene of the school bus crash, a reporter

at the city desk of a small Midwestern paper learns of the event while making his routine morning check with the state police. At the radio station across town, a broadcast reporter hears the news on the police radio frequency. Their reflexes are the same: find out what happened. At this point, they don't know much, only that a school bus has crashed and that children have died.

The radio station interrupts its disc jockey with a bulletin saying just that. Essential but cruel—no one knows yet who has survived and who has not. The newspaper reporter tells his editor. Reporters and photographers head for the scene and the hospital.

It is wrenching catastrophe for the town—and a story across the country. For those initial reporters relay word of the crash to the organizations that will tell the world of it. The newspaperman telephones the Associated Press bureau in Kansas City. The radio man calls United Press International. They are stringers, paid space rates to cover local stories for the wire services.

The story is developing. AP and UPI send their first, sketchy stories across the nation. Then come advisory notes:

"Editors: A reporter and photographer are en route to the scene of the school bus crash. There is as yet no word on the number of casualties."

At NBC News in New York, a copy clerk tears the copy from the printer and takes it to the editors. The producer in charge of national stories for *Nightly News* has just had his first sip of office coffee. The program is nine hours away, but there is

work to be done right now. This is a story that will be prominent on the evening news; and he knows it.

He pulls out a map, looks for the closest NBC television affiliate, picks up the phone and calls the news director there. Crews are on the way, he's told, and some of the videotape they will shoot will be available in time for *Nightly News*. Next step: Call NBC Chicago, and order a network reporter and camera crew to the site of the crash. They'll charter a plane and be there in a couple of hours.

By now, the wire services have their own reporters and photographers on the road. They will be the first out-of-town reporters to get there; their bureaus are widely deployed, and there's one close to almost any place a story breaks. There are more than 120 Associated Press bureaus in the United States.

They'll check with the local stringers, get to the scene, talk to the police, get the casualty list, telephone the details to the bureau in Kansas City. The story is put together by editors there, relayed to New York, then transmitted to newspapers and broadcast stations that take the service.

When journalists talk about this, it is in a language as old as the first telegraph lines. A story "moves" on the "wire." It may be transmitted by way of a satellite, but the language of the business is rooted in the days when telegraphers wearing green eyeshades tapped out stories in Morse code, on wires that ran along the railroad tracks.

Today the wire services, the great engines of newsgathering and distribution, are at the center of the news business. The

wires provide both the text and the context of the news. In the editor's office, on the telephone or in the conference room, every daily news organization sorts and sifts the day's events to decide what will be published or broadcast, how much space or time it will get, and whether it belongs on the front page or back with the classified ads.

AP and UPI are central to the process of decision. They are the basic wire services. They deliver news, photos and radio reports, at the local, state, national and international levels. They cover the state governments and distribute stock market tables and weather reports. The objective is to deliver everything an editor needs to put out a daily newspaper.

The Associated Press is the oldest and biggest, a cooperative that serves about 1,350 daily newspapers and more than 5,700 radio and television stations in the United States. It is a nonprofit organization, owned by the newspapers it serves. They aren't customers; they are members. . . .

United Press International is a privately owned company, with a news and photo staff of about 1,000. UPI says it has more than 1,000 newspaper clients. After losing money for years and changing ownership in 1982, it faces an uncertain future.

Each television news department—at NBC, ABC, and CBS—employs over 1,000 news people, including technicians, and can call on help from several hundred radio affiliates and more than 200 television affiliates.

Although Reuters, the British news agency, has expanded its

operations in the United States, and competes with the American wire services, it is strongest abroad and in international financial reporting.

New York wire supervisors control the wire. On the story of a school bus crash in the Midwest, they would be in frequent telephone contact with Kansas City as the story developed. It would belong on the daily news digest, the menu of major stories each wire service transmits to advise newspapers what is coming. There's a late-morning digest for newspapers that will be published the following morning, a midnight digest for afternoon newspapers.

In the trade, those are the "cycles." AMs and PMs. The evening news on television is, in effect, an AM operation, with access to the same stories that will be in the morning papers. The PMs' news cycle is comparable to that of breakfast time television programs.

The process of deciding what stories will be shown on television on any evening and published in AM newspapers the next day is one that begins at midmorning, Eastern time.

At 10:30 A.M., about a dozen people sit down in a fourth-floor conference room at the Associated Press Building, overlooking Rockefeller Plaza in New York, to talk about the day's news.

Across Manhattan at UPI headquarters, the process is more informal; no set meeting, but a series of discussions and telephone calls.

In Rockefeller Center, the staff of *NBC Nightly News,* about ten people, meets at 11:45 A.M.

There, and at like meetings in newsrooms across the country, editors have been assessing the day's events, the wire copy, the staff reporting, the stories assigned but yet to come. Now they begin planning the product, deciding what's important, what to do about it, and where to play it.

Editors must decide long before deadline which national and international stories belong on the front page, and at what length. The decision is subject to change, because the news doesn't stop, and what seems most important at noon may be forced further back in the paper by what happens at night.

The story of a school bus crash in the Midwest would be a subject of those conferences. It is a cold, impersonal process—the mathematics of the news business. If that crash killed two children, it would be a small story nationally. If it were twenty-two, it would be a major one.

Were that the case, the story would be at or near the top of AMs news digests moved by the wire services. It happened early in the day, on PMs time. But few afternoon papers in the East would be able to print more than the first sparse reports, scant on detail that would come later, after their deadlines.

News digests are agendas, and they are a factor in the decisions made in all newsrooms. The digests are brief summaries of the most important stories of the day—twelve, sometimes fourteen of them. They deliver the lead paragraph, and an editor can write a headline from them before the story arrives.

These digests are put together by editors who have been writing, editing and judging stories for years, and much of what they do is instinctive. Former Supreme Court Justice Potter Stewart once said that he could not define pornography, but knew it when he saw it. That's sometimes the way it is with news. The pros know it when they see it.

The story lineups assembled by the two wire services, and the story decisions at the networks and the newspapers, usually are similar and sometimes are almost identical.

That is the case simply because good, seasoned editors looking at the same set of events will come to many of the same conclusions. Some of those decisions are automatic. If the President is going to make an announcement on foreign policy at 3 P.M., that belongs on the digest, and the story about it belongs in the paper and on the air. If there is a major flood in the South, a government shake-up in the Middle East, those stories do too.

The more difficult calls come on another kind of story: the piece that is not of compelling importance today, but may be next month; or the investigative story; or the complex but potentially significant science story; or the politician who announces he wants to be President but nobody knows his name. . . .

At a morning newspaper and in network television, the pace accelerates as the day goes on. By 2 P.M., in New York, Europe is beginning to shut down, and Asia has been fast asleep for hours. Washington is generating its stories, at the midday briefings by White House and State Department spokesmen, in the debates and votes of a Congress that does much of its work late in the day or at night. The dynamics of public relations are at work too. Across the country, press agents have timed their releases, their client's speeches, their staged happenings, to take place in time for the evening TV news and the morning papers. In the age of television, presidential campaigns are shaped by the deadlines of the networks. Candidates want to be on the air.

That can work in reverse. Public relations people in a government agency or a corporation that has to acknowledge bad news know that an announcement made at 5:30 on a Friday afternoon produces little coverage on television, and fewer newspapers are sold on Saturday than on other days. Federal government announcements that will affect financial markets are issued after Wall Street has shut down at 4 P.M. White House press agents choose the time of announcements according to the way they hope to see the story played. If it makes the President look good, it comes early, in time to be seen on television. If it makes him look bad, it comes late. . . .

By 3 P.M., it is decision time at *Nightly News.* There's another conference, but this time it is limited to the executive producer, his three deputies and the anchorman. It is a time for blunt talk about the importance and quality of the stories available for the evening's program. There are going to be some stories that will be broadcast without pictures, written by the anchorman. Anchormen usually argue for those stories, and producers press to get their videotape on the air. . . .

At 3:30 P.M., there's a final meeting at *Nightly News.* The lineup is set, and the executive producer announces it to his staff. It includes the stories that are going to be covered, the order in which they will be presented, and the exact amount of air time the anchormen and the correspondents will get to tell them. They'll have to edit their own copy to fit the assigned time.

The school bus crash is going to be high in the program. Eleven children are dead; the driver and seven others are gravely injured. It will be covered in exactly one minute and forty-five seconds.

Not long after that last formal meeting at *Nightly News,* the editors of the New York *Times* hold their first formal meeting of the day. They've been at work on tomorrow's paper since midmorning. The foreign desk, the metropolitan desk, the national desk and the other departments have been preparing and updating "skeds," short for "schedule," meaning the stories they see coming. They make their cases for space for those stories. They get a hearing, no decisions yet.

There, as everywhere, the process involves some internal competition. At any newspaper, the city editor wants a piece by one of his reporters at the top of the front page. The editor who handles foreign copy argues that there is a better piece coming from Moscow, and it ought to be the lead. The editor who handles features wants front-page space for a story about the zoo.

By 5:15, when the newsroom at NBC is hectic, and getting more so, the senior editors of the *Times* are meeting to plan their front page.

The executive editor, the managing editor and their departmental editors discuss the stories ready or coming for tomorrow's *Times.* The *Times* man in Washington listens on a telephone hookup. When he has something to say, his words issue from a speaker in the ceiling in New York. *Times* voices often seem that way.

After about fifteen minutes, the discussion is done. The department editors go back to their desks, and the top editors decide what the front page is going to look like and what will be relegated to pages of lesser prominence. They do it by themselves because they want no further debate. They decide what will be out front in the *Times,* and they make a sketch of Page 1. In journalism, a page sketch like that is a "dummy."

So the decisions that shape the news most people read the next morning or see that evening are made within a few hours in the afternoon and early evening. The process is repeated, time zone to time zone, Boston *Globe* to Los Angeles *Times.* . . . ∎

MEDIALAB

The Accident: A Cross Media Study

1. In the school bus accident example, which medium reported the story first? Is this medium usually the first with the news?

2. Sometimes a citizen will report a story (usually a crime or accident) to a newspaper or radio/TV station. What other means are used by news organizations to learn of the news? (The answer to this question is not "reporters." Reporters are sent to cover the event once the news organization learns of its existence.)

3. How did NBC news learn of the bus accident? What action did the producer in charge of national stories for *Nightly News* take when he learned of the bus accident? How would this differ from the action taken by a producer of a local newscast in some other part of the country? How would it differ from the action of a producer in the city where the accident took place?

4. What role do "stringers" play in news gathering?

5. AP, UPI, and the British Reuters are commonly called "wire services." Where do you think the name came from? What would be a more accurate name?

6. What is the main source of news for local papers, radio newscasts, and local televised news programs?

7. From what you have learned about news gathering so far in this chapter, how would you go about setting up a one-person newspaper without hiring reporters?

8. What are the AMs and PMs? If the school bus accident happened after school instead of before, how would its coverage on TV and in newspapers differ?

9. Imagine a spectacular fire or accident. Would that event be most likely to receive national coverage if it happened in the morning, around noon, or late at night?

10. Timing is important in controlling news. Imagine you are public relations director for a corporation that is very important to the local economy. When and how would you alert the local press about the fact that your company just received a multi-million dollar government contract? When and how would you alert the press about the fact that your company is about to fire ten percent of its workers?

11. Editors face tough decisions in selecting the news. The article points out "it is a cold, impersonal business . . . If that crash killed two children, it would be a small story nationally. If it were twenty-two, it would be a major one." Why does the "mathematics of tragedy" play such an important role in selecting the news?

12. What role does timing play in "staged news" such as press conferences, press releases, and announcements of economic indicators?

13. The decisions about what you will read in the morning paper and what you will see on the national evening news are made (barring major last-second emergencies) around what time of day?

14. The availability of pictures can influence news decisions. Explain how the presence or absence of pictures might influence a TV news producer and a newspaper editor.

15. From which medium—television or the newspaper—would you learn most about the bus accident? Which medium might present the most emotional coverage?

Chapter 6
NEWSPAPERS

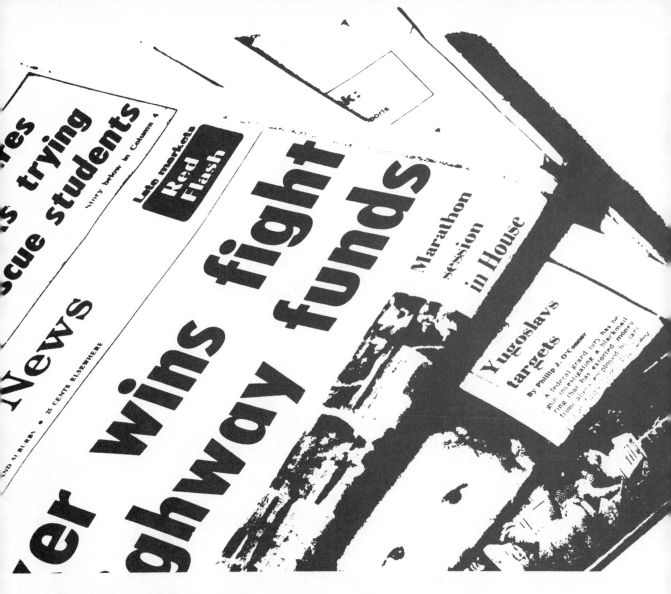

Who Owns the Newspapers?

To publish a newspaper, a machine is needed that will print large quantities of words at a relatively low cost. Such a machine could not exist until the 15th century when Johann Gutenberg invented a system of setting type that used movable, reusable type. But one hundred years after the invention, newspapers were still almost unknown. Why the long delay between the invention and its application?

Two major obstacles existed for the would-be newspaper publisher—most people couldn't read, and the local king or ruler controlled the flow of information. Although the necessary technology was available, two "social" inventions were needed in

order to establish newspapers as a mass medium—democracy and literacy.

Democracy was necessary because a free press is a threat to a king or dictator. Knowledge is power, and to give everyone the knowledge of news is to give everyone a share of the power. Literacy was needed so that there would be enough people willing to buy and read papers, and it is only in the past four generations that literacy has become common in the United States. It was only natural that the first popular democracy—the United States—would be the birthplace of the popular free press. Today, one out of every five newspapers printed is published in the United States, and about 20 percent of the world's news readers are in the U.S., even though the United States has less than 6 percent of the world's population.

American newspapers began with bulletins hung on tavern walls or printed sheets from the local postmaster or printer. Anyone could start a newspaper, and this fact was important in the development of a free press. Most schools have small newspapers that cover only events in school, but there is no legal reason why these papers could not be expanded to become neighborhood newspapers. On the other hand, a school radio or TV station cannot broadcast to the public without a government license. New, inexpensive offset printing systems make it possible for anyone with a few hundred dollars to produce a small newspaper with a circulation in the thousands.

In spite of the ease of producing a paper, very few new newspapers founded in recent years have successfully competed with already established dailies. Underground papers and papers for minority groups have performed an extremely valuable community service, but these have not been papers for the majority.

Today there are about 1,700 daily newspapers in the United States, about the same number as existed in 1920 and actually fewer than in the late 19th century. At the end of 1984 the number of TV stations caught up with the number of daily newspapers.

Newspaper ownership has recently become increasingly concentrated, with a smaller and smaller group of people owning the nation's newspapers. All the owners of newspapers in the country could assemble in an average-size high school gymnasium or auditorium. This increasing concentration of owners means there is less competition between papers. Competition among papers, as in any business, helps ensure the news consumer that the papers will try to do the best possible job of finding and reporting the news.

Without local competition, a single paper can establish a news monopoly in a city and can succumb to the temptation to turn out a paper that is a collection of wire service items, press releases, and syndicated material. Such a paper will give a certain amount of news and information to the people. But it will not ask the newsmakers hard questions, send reporters to dig around for the truth behind the press releases, attempt to expose corruption in local government or business, or spend large sums of money for investigative reporting. Very likely it will not attract the best possible talent in reporters and editors.

A paper with a local monopoly can make a substantial profit from advertising without making any effort to actively pursue local news. The people in that city then have lost freedom of the press for all practical purposes, even without censorship or government restrictions. A local monopoly does not always lead to this situation, but it is all too common, especially in small American cities.

Journalism Quarterly studied a city in which a news monopoly was established and then looked at how it changed when a strong competitor started business. The study found that the original monopoly paper gave 41 percent of its nonadvertising space to local news (local news is the most expensive to obtain since it requires reporters, travel, and time). When the competing paper began operation, the percentage increased to 51 percent—the people in the town got more news, thanks to the competitor. But when the competitor failed and went out of business, the amount of local news slipped back to 43 percent.

How common are newspaper monopolies? In 1880, 61 percent of all newspaper towns had competing dailies. By 1930 that figure had dropped to only 21 percent; in 1940 it was only 13 percent; and today fewer than 3 percent of newspaper towns have competing dailies. There are only 15 cities left with competing papers published at the same time of the day (for example, competing morning or evening papers). Some cities have two papers but one is sold to those who prefer a paper in the late afternoon and the other to those who prefer a paper in the morning. Some cities have two papers owned by the same person or company; such papers do not really compete.

About half of the nation's daily papers are owned by "chains," companies that own more than one paper. The largest chains include the Chicago Tribune, Scripps-Howard, Hearst, Newhouse, Knight, Gannett, and Ridder papers.

The decreasing amount of competition and the increase of concentrated ownership is not necessarily a bad influence on news, but the tendency in such situations is that both the quality of the news and the variety of opinions available to the public will decrease.

MEDIALAB

Who Owns Your News?

1. Try to find some foreign newspapers and compare them with American papers. Even if the paper is not written in English, it can be compared in terms of appearance and advertising. Some libraries and large newsstands carry foreign papers.

2. Find out which local paper most of the families of class members subscribe to.

3. Take a survey of class newspaper reading that will show how many people in the class read a paper daily, which sections they read most, and how much time each day they spend reading a newspaper. Expand the survey to include the families of everyone in the class.

4. Find copies of "national" papers such as *The Wall Street Journal, Christian Science Monitor, USA*

Today, and *National Observer.* Have a class member report on them, or make the papers available for class reading.

5. Find out if your area has competing papers or a newspaper monopoly. Who owns the local paper or papers? Find out what other communications businesses the owners run (for example, do they own any other papers as part of a "chain," or do they own radio or TV stations).

6. Who are the "gatekeepers" at your local paper or papers? Find out the names of all the local publishers, too.

7. Make a careful study of your local papers and discuss various opinions about them. Do they do a good job of providing news?

How News Is Published (The Process)

The basic function of a newspaper is to report the news. How is this fundamental purpose carried out? Local news stories must be covered by reporters who follow leads, conduct interviews, make innumerable phone calls, and write their stories—all under deadlines. The reporter and the city desk (the managing editor) work together to bring a story into being. The reporter may be working at top speed to assemble facts and possibly locate an angle to the story. Supporting the reporter and making sure that stories are accurate and presented clearly is the copy editor. The copy editor smooths out the writing, checks the spelling of names, reminds the reporter that a crucial fact is missing, and in many ways helps get the story into print. The following article follows a story (a large theft of uncut diamonds) from the first police report to the printed page.

From

More Language That Needs Watching

by Theodore M. Bernstein

The following story, told by a former copy editor of the *New York Times,* shows how one local news story moves from the event to the printed page.

It is mid-afternoon and the office of the morning newspaper is quiet except for the typewriters or computer keyboards of a few rewrite men tapping out short stories of routine events. The man covering police headquarters phones the city desk to report a rather large theft of uncut diamonds from a dealer's office—"Looks like a pretty fair story." Should he cover it or does the city desk want to assign another reporter to the story? He is instructed to remain on his beat. Arnold Dittenhouse draws the assignment.

He is told the nature of the story and goes to work.

From the headquarters man Arnold picks up the basic facts by phone. A diamond merchant, Gregory Lee, has reported the loss of $100,000 worth of uncut stones from the safe in his office at 1661 Sixth Avenue. Lee says the stones were there the previous afternoon but were gone this morning. The police have questioned everyone in the office except a clerk ("Haven't got his name, but the precinct cops can give it to you"). The clerk has not been questioned because he left on a two-week vacation last night and no one seems to know where he is.

Arnold next travels to the precinct station house and buttonholes a detective on the case. He learns that the clerk is Julius Feinguy, 22 years old, who rooms with a family named Fickett in Queens Village. He also discovers that the F.B.I. is investigating because of a suspicion that the diamonds may have been transported across state lines. Do the police suspect anything phony about the case— a staged theft to collect insurance

come in.

Back at his desk, Arnold knows there are still one or two angles to be explored. There is also one piece of routine that he senses he must still perform, but for the life of him he can't recall what it is. He phones the F.B.I. press officer, but, as he expected, learns nothing except that the investigators would like to question Feinguy. No, they cannot say where they are looking for him.

Next he searches through the phone book for the Ficketts. (What is that piece of routine he has overlooked?) Mrs. Fickett tells him what she knows about her roomer, Feinguy, which is not much. No, she doesn't know his home town or where he went on vacation.

Ah, yes, that piece of routine. Send to the newspaper morgue to see if there are any clippings on Feinguy. Not very hopeful, but you never can tell. While he is waiting, he organizes his notes. At last the copy boy hands him the slim folder from the morgue. It contains a single small clipping: A five-year-old dispatch from St. Louis relates that Julius Feinguy, 17, won a city-wide essay contest. St. Louis? An angle, perhaps.

It is getting late, but Arnold now has a couple of more phone calls to make. First he checks back to headquarters. Are the police looking for Feinguy in St. Louis? The police won't say. Arnold drags out a St. Louis phone book. There's a chance. Feinguy is an unusual name. He finds a number and puts through a call. Yes, this is Julius Feinguy's mother. No, Julius hasn't been there. No one else has phoned, but a detective did visit her to ask the same question.

or anything like that? No, they do not. Was the safe jimmied open or blown open? No, there were no signs that it had been tampered with in any way. Then it looks like an inside job, doesn't it? The police are offering no theory about it just yet.

A visit to Lee's office seems to be in order so that Arnold can at least get some idea of the physical layout. At the Sixth Avenue address the reporter is fortunate enough to find Lee in his office. He thus is able, in addition, to gather a few details about the personal appearance of the distraught, bespectacled, round little man who has sud-

denly found himself a figure in the news. Arnold is curious about how the safe was opened. Lee suggests the possibility that he may have left it open and unwatched very briefly the previous afternoon when he stepped into another room to answer a phone call. He has nothing else to add to what Arnold already knows.

At this point the reporter phones the city desk to report how the story shapes up and to see whether the office has any further information that would require outside checking before he returns. Time is getting shorter now, and he is told to

What is it all about? Thanks, Mrs. Feinguy.

Arnold decides to let his paper's resident correspondent approach the St. Louis police and puts in a call for him. Meanwhile, he has a story and probably an exclusive angle. It is time to begin writing. He checks with the city desk to inform the editors about the story and to get instructions about how much to write. He returns to his desk, feeds some paper into his typewriter [or accesses his computer terminal] and begins. He must hurry, he knows. The deadline is an hour and a half away. But it will take him perhaps an hour to write the story. And it has been drummed into him that every story that is to appear in the paper cannot go to the composition room at the deadline, because if that happened the paper would never be printed. So he writes as rapidly as he can, sending the story to the desk in short sections, or "takes." He pauses only to consult his notes and to take a call from the St. Louis correspondent. Out rolls the story, take after take.

What has happened up to this point is the exercise of the creative faculty of newspapering. The city desk and the reporter combine to bring the story into being. The reporter, now working at top speed, is almost completely preoccupied with his subject matter. Many fine points of writing, of presentation, even of accuracy may escape him. But he is backstopped. The critical faculty is now brought into play on the copy desk. His story is passed to a copy editor. Except for the news editor and his assistants, who oversee in a general way everything that goes into the newspaper but obviously cannot read closely all the thousands and thousands of words, the copy editor exercises final responsibility.

Let's call him Harold Aufseher. The diamond story is now in his hands. He has been told by the city desk how long the story is to be. As a practiced editor, Hal knows that Arnold probably will exceed his limit (most reporters understandably do that) and so he is on the alert to trim out the soft spots as he proceeds. In addition he will try to tighten the wording wherever he can to save precious space. When the reporter writes, "one of the employees," Hal will condense it to "an employee"; when the reporter writes that the police "rushed to the scene," Hal will strike out the phrase as an unnecessary and self-evident detail. In the second paragraph he discovers an involved fifty-word sentence; he breaks it into two short, clear sentences. When he reads that "the tray with its little bags and boxes of stones were missing from the safe," he almost automatically corrects the grammatical error. He sends the lead to the composing room and picks up the next take.

Here he finds that Arnold has inadvertently begun to refer to Gregory Lee as "Mr. Gregory." Rather than interrupt the reporter he checks in the phone book to make sure of the man's name. However, when he notes that there has been no elaboration of the statement in the lead about $100,000 worth of uncut diamonds, ranging up to nine carats in weight," he decides he will have to interrupt the reporter. "Who made the evaluation—the dealer, the police, the insurance company?" He returns to his desk and in-serts the necessary information.

Next he deletes a quotation from Mr. Lee: "I always thought there was something a little shady about Feinguy." Libelous. He also deletes a quotation from Mrs. Fickett: "He was careless personally—fingernails always dirty and that sort of thing." Poor taste and irrelevant.

Smoothly and swiftly, his critical faculties always on the alert, Hal makes his way through the story. As he goes, he writes subheads in the copy—those little headings of boldface type that are inserted to break up long stretches of gray type. And as he goes, he is trying to resolve in his mind what the headline should say. When the story is finished, he tackles the head. His job here is to condense the main news of Arnold's 600-word story into half a dozen words.

Arnold has been writing under pressure; Hal has been editing under pressure. Each has a multitude of things to keep in mind. The story, as it presently appears in the paper, is as accurate as they can make it; it is a smooth, lucid job of narrative and exposition, and it may even have some literary quality. Both have worked hard, if hastily, to make it a finished piece of news writing. For Hal, incidentally, it is only one of a dozen or more stories he has processed before deadline. He has had to switch his attention rapidly from robbery to rocketry, from budgets to bullets, from grand slams to great slums, from racket busters to filibusters. Is it extraordinary, then, that something has eluded him, that he has allowed a mistake to slip into print? It is perhaps not excusable, but it is at least understandable. ■

Newspaper Chain of Command

Owner
Sometimes the owner and publisher is one person.

Publisher
Publisher usually stays out of day-to-day production of the paper, but is responsible for all aspects of the paper.

Editor-In-Chief
Sometimes called executive editor or simply ''The Editor.'' Responsible for only nonadvertising content.

Business Manager
Has a staff who takes care of:

Advertising	Classified
Circulation	Section
Delivery	Production
Pay Bills and	(Printing,
Collect Money	Typesetting)

Editor of Editorial Page
Takes care of editorials, letters to editor, political cartoons, and syndicated columns.

Managing Editor
Coordinates the news gathering of various department editors

Copy Editor
Checks language style, writing, headlines.

News Editor
Selects and edits national and world news.

Editors of Various Sections — Sports, Home, Food, etc.

City Editor
Responsible for local news. Some papers will have a state editor also.

Layout Editor
Makes it all fit.

Wire Service Editor

Stringers
Part-time reporters usually paid on the basis of stories published.

Local Reporters and Photographers
A reporter's story has to pass through the critical eyes of City Editor, News Editor, Copy Editor. Editors determine what is news, reporters are assigned to stories of the Editor's choosing. Some reporters regularly cover certain ''beats''—city hall, the police, etc.

As you can tell from the chart, a newspaper has many editors. The people most associated in the public mind with a newspaper are the reporters, yet their job is at the bottom of the totem pole of the news process.

Each person along the line of the news process makes decisions about the news, and each is subject to possible veto by the boss. The owner of a paper is the most removed from the paper's daily operation, perhaps visiting the paper only occasionally. Yet the owner can influence the kind of news the paper prints by making the basic policies it follows.

1. In Bernstein's story, what is the main force that prevents the reporter from doing a thorough report on the crime?

2. Would your local paper rely on the police report of the gem theft or would it assign a reporter to dig up the facts? Support your answer.

3. What is the newspaper "morgue"?

4. What does *libelous* mean?

5. In the chapter on the news media, the word *gatekeeper* was explained. Who, on the newspaper chart, acts in any way as a gatekeeper?

6. Who are the publisher, the editor, and the managing editor of your local papers?

7. What could be some of the bad effects on the news if the business manager (on the chart) were the boss of the news editor?

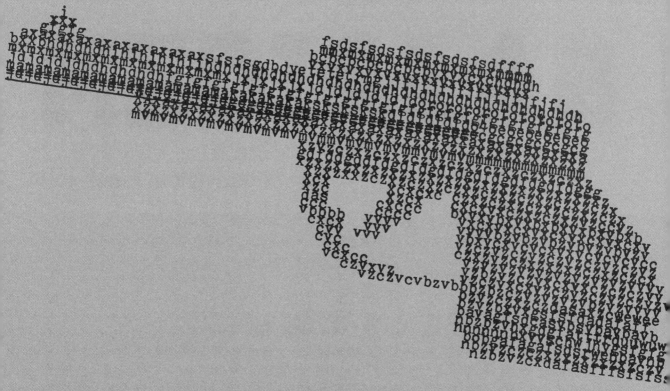

What News Is Published: (The Contents)

Unless you live in an area with a number of competing papers and have compared them carefully, you may not know whether your local paper does a good or a mediocre job of reporting the news. To make such a judgment, you must be able to compare it with other papers in cities the same size as yours, and you must be able to tell where the news comes from and have some idea of the bias of the paper and the values on which it makes news judgments. In order to make a news judgment on your local paper, or on any paper, it helps to know what is inside the paper and where it comes from. Let's take a close look at the contents of a newspaper.

The "masthead" gives the name of the paper and other details such as the date, number of pages, etc. Often the name of the paper will be printed in an old style type simply because that style used to be the darkest kind available; often it has become a kind of "trademark" for the paper. Many papers have redesigned their front pages to look more modern.

The edition of the paper is usually listed in the upper right-hand corner. Editions are called "three star final," "suburban," "market final," etc. Large papers publish a number of editions during the day, each basically the same but with more recent news and details than the preceding edition. Small papers publish only one edition a day.

The edition's most important story or "lead story" is the one with the largest headline. It usually starts in the upper right-hand part of the front page.

Newspaper headlines are traditionally written in the present tense, even if the story happened in the past.

Since newspapers are folded in half for sale on newsstands and in boxes on the street, the top half of the front page is often designed with the most attractive, dramatic, or saleable parts on it.

Headlines in newspapers are written to fill a certain amount of space. (In magazines a headline or title is written first, and then editors decide how much space to give it.) Newspapers are partly responsible for nicknames applied to public figures such as the president. Since space is so limited, a newspaper headline will often use shortened forms like Ike (for former President Eisenhower), JFK, or LBJ. Any president with a long last name will be renamed to fit the headlines.

A second and smaller headline (usually one column wide) below the story's main headline is called a "deck."

Photographs are often referred to in the newspaper business as "cuts" from the days when illustrations were made from woodcuts. The description or explanation given with a newspaper photo is called a cutline. In the magazine or book business it is called a caption.

od morning

Baseball's heirlooms

une sports writer Bob Logan se-
on old ballparks continues with a
at Chicago's own, 71-year-old
utiful Wrigley Field." In Sports.

w stadium plans—yet

resident Dallas Green says the deci-
move from Wrigley Field hinges on
g the bans on night games. In Sports.

show Mets old power

by Ryne Sandberg, Billy Hatcher
on Durham back pitcher Rick Sutcliffe
victory over New York. In Sports.

t wins at Wimbledon

ded Chris Evert Lloyd gets off to a
t with a 6-1, 6-0 victory over Mary
tek of Munster, Ind. In Sports.

ide

kman sounds alarm

stockman, President Reagan's budget
warns that a big tax increase might
only way to "fiscal sanity." Page 2.

rance tax proposed

ames Thompson says he is con-
a new tax on insurance companies
school reform. Sec. 2, pg. 1.

er taste
e Taste

of Chicago is
than ever
ear—more
ore entertain-
an extra day
se. A guide
t to expect
here to find
. In Friday.

Friday

voice for hiring quotas

coalition files a friend of the court
ing a halt to attempts to end Police
ent hiring quotas. Sec. 2, pg. 1.

t strikes unions' grip

preme Court rules that unions may
workers for quitting the union and
picket lines in a strike. Page 11.

siness

ks soar, records fall

rices climb, erasing some key market
cords. The Dow industrials rise 8.40
at a record 1332.21. Sec. 3, pg. 1.

er still after American

Travenol strengthens and extends its
llion takeover offer for neighboring
n Hospital Supply. Sec. 3, pg. 1.

eather

GO AND VICINITY: Friday: Partly to
cloudy, chance of rain late; high

Hostage transfer hits a snag

Israel frets over mood of America

By Terry Atlas
Chicago Tribune

WASHINGTON—On radio call-
in shows, in newspaper letters to
the editor and in private conver-
sations, Americans angry and
frustrated by the events in Beirut are aiming criticism at Israel for policies they believe helped
provoke Arab terrorists to hijack
the TWA jetliner and hold its
passengers hostage.

These voices may be just
straws in the wind, but they are
a sign that the hijacking has
created new tension in the usually intimate U.S.-Israeli relationship, which worries Israel and
its supporters in the United
States.

A CBS News poll, conducted
Wednesday and released Thursday, found that 57 percent of
those polled thought Israel was
not doing enough to help free the
hostages. Earlier, a Washington
Post-ABC News poll found a
marked increase in the number
of Americans who said the United States should distance itself
from Israel to minimize the danger of terrorist acts against the
nation and its citizens.

For Israel, a country dependent not only on U.S. moral and
diplomatic support but also for
billions of dollars annually in
military and economic aid, such
signs of a rift are never taken
lightly.

"There is concern here about
the trend," said an Israeli
diplomat, adding that a quick
end to the hostage ordeal would
limit "the potential for damage"
to Israel's close relations with its
most important ally.

There is a feeling even among
some of Israel's strongest supporters in Washington that Jeru-
salem in the opening days of the
hostage drama handled its role

Continued on page 7

A Shiite hijacker at the door of the hijacked TWA jetliner in Beirut gives a victory sign Thursday.

AP Laserphoto

Full coverage

● A hostage sees sympathy for his captors' cause.
Page 4

● U.S. insists 'the forgotten 7' also must be freed.
Page 5
● U.S. outlines plan to fight terrorism in the skies.
● Pilots' group wary of using armed air marshals.
Page 6

Embassies won't hold Americans

From Chicago Tribune wires

Diplomatic snags developed
Thursday in the search for a
solution to the Beirut hostage
crisis as both France and Switzerland imposed tough conditions
on their willingness to assume
custody of the 39 captive Americans.

One U.S. official said there
were "too many variables" to
predict whether the crisis would
end soon.

The United States raised the
stakes by demanding freedom
not only for the remaining 39
hostages from TWA Flight 847
seized June 14 but also for 7
Americans kidnaped in Lebanon
over the last 16 months.

Continuing a tight news
blackout imposed without explanation Wednesday, the White
House and the State Department
declined to comment on a prediction Thursday by Shiite
Moslem leader Nabih Berri that
the crisis was nearing an end.

"I think in 72 hours it will be
the exit for this affair—for the
Americans held," Berri told
NBC News. But he declined to
give the reasoning behind his
prediction.

He said only that he believed
his proposal to transfer the TWA
hostages to a Western embassy
in Beirut or to Syria had made
him "more optimistic" about
possiblities for a quick solution.

Berri had announced Wednesday that he would be willing to
turn the hostages over to a Western embassy or to Syria on condition that they remain captive
until Israel frees 735 Lebanese
prisoners it is holding.

But France and Switzerland,
two countries in contact with
Berri, made clear Thursday that
they would accept the Americans, but with no strings attached. Berri said late Thursday that

Continued on page 6

Reagan's nominee rejected

By Glen Elsasser
Chicago Tribune

WASHINGTON—The Reagan
administration suffered a
damaging setback Thursday
when the Senate Judiciary Committee rejected the nomination
of William Bradford Reynolds,
the Justice Department's controversial civil-rights chief, as associate attorney general.

During a stormy session in
which tempers flared, the Re-
publican-dominated committee
failed to muster enough votes to
send the nomination to the Senate floor for a final vote. Unless
a Senate majority approves a
discharge motion, a seldom-used
procedure, the Reynolds nomination is dead.

At the White House, President
Reagan reacted angrily. "That
some members of the committee
chose to use the confirmation
process to conduct an ideological
assault on so superbly qualified
a candidate was unjust and
deeply wrong," Reagan said.

"Let me emphasize that Mr.
Reynolds' civil-rights views reflect my own," he said. "The
policies he pursued are the policies of this administration, and
they remain our policies as long
as I am President."

Earlier, White House

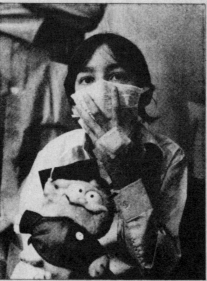

Graduation day for heart recipient

In a mask to prevent infections, heart recipient Brian Tomayer, 14, is
joined by classmates at Loyola Hospital Medical Center to celebrate
his graduation from eighth grade. Story, Sec. 2, pg 3.

Tribune photo by Ovie Carter

Defense bill passes House with strings

By Lea Donosky
Chicago Tribune

WASHINGTON—The House
approved a fiscal 1986 defense-
authorization bill of $292 billion
Thursday, night after voting to
bar the President from sending
U.S. troops to Nicaragua unless
conditions met a long list of exceptions that would leave him
free to do so without consultation
with Congress.

The modified ban was attached
to the Defense Authorization Act,
approved by a 278-106 vote after
two weeks of debate. The bill
would freeze defense spending at
1985 levels, approximately $292
billion, which is $10 billion less
than approved by the Senate.

Supporters of the Nicaraguan
provision say it established the
principle of prior consultation
and would prevent President
Reagan from waging war with
Nicaragua for "ideological or political" reasons.

Opponents called it an attempt
to encroach on the President's
constitutional powers as commander in chief, but they also
claimed victory Thursday in saying they had succeeded in "de-
fanging" the measure with exceptions.

The measure was approved
312-111 and attached to the De-

● House Democrats back away
from a plan to hike taxes on
Social Security benefits. Page 2.

fense Authorization Act after a
heated debate resurrected the
specter of Vietnam and invoked
the current Middle East hostage
situation and other acts of terrorism.

According to the amendment,
Reagan could take military action against Nicaragua without
first consulting Congress if there
were a "clear and present danger" to the United States, its
allies or the U.S. Embassy; if
nuclear weapons or Soviet-made
MiGS were stationed in Nicaragua; or if the action was taken
as a response to a hijacking,
kidnaping or other act of terrorism involving U.S. citizens or
U.S. allies.

By a 235-186 vote, the House
rejected a proposal by Rep. Dan
Burton [R., Ind.] to allow
Reagan to send in troops to Nicaragua if it found that nation
directly or indirectly involved in
supporting terrorist and guerrilla
actions against other Central
American countries, something
the administration contends the
Sandinista government already

Continued on page 2

Newspaper Advertising

Few people would answer the question "Why do you watch television or listen to the radio?" with the reply "For the advertising." But many people do buy and read newspapers because of the advertising. Only in newspaper advertising is the potential consumer told exact prices and places to shop. Only newspapers carry ads for neighborhood stores and tell what is on sale tomorrow. Magazine and television advertising is concerned more with motivation and persuasion; newspaper advertising gives information. The classified section contains almost pure information, with little of the psychological techniques and trick-working of the kinds of ads discussed in the advertising chapter. Newspaper advertising is most often cited by people as being useful and reliable.

Not only is advertising a service to the public, but it is also the way the paper makes a profit. The subscription or delivery price of a newspaper helps to pay expenses but is not sufficient to make an attractive profit. A full page of advertising space will cost from a few hundred to many thousands of dollars, depending on the paper's circulation. Space in the paper is sold by pages, half pages, column inches or, as in the classified section, by the column line. Sixty percent of the average paper is advertising; this helps account for the fact that newspapers as a business enterprise are among the most profitable in the nation.

In this chapter we will consider over a dozen different kinds of "news" items that are printed in a paper. But from the viewpoint of the publisher and editor, there are only two kinds of space—advertising space and the "newshole." The "newshole" is the amount of space left to fill once all the advertising is accounted for. Still, not everything that goes into the "newshole" is "news."

Wire Service Material

The newshole in the average paper is 40 percent of its total number of pages. About 37 percent of that space is filled by wire service material. Such material is clearly marked:

Storms renew fury on West Coast

United Press International

Pacific storms, which have been pounding the West Coast with wind, rain and snow for nearly a week, struck with renewed fury Tuesday, touching off more floods, mudslides and power failures. A tornado caused heavy damage to an air terminal in central California.

The tornado raked the Fresno, Calif., Air Terminal, shattering plate-glass windows and ruining sections of a roof on a hotel-restaurant. Cars were overturned and utility poles snapped in half, but authorities reported no injuries.

THE TWISTER, spawned by a string of valley thunderstorms, left a layer of hail three to five inches deep on fields around the air terminal. After spinning away from the facility, it touched down two more times near the neighboring community of Clovis.

Thunderstorm after thunderstorm hit California after midnight. Winds hit 50 knots. Commuter traffic was snarled with freeways and streets covered with water up to five feet in depth. Mudslides closed many arteries. Power was knocked out at the San Jose, Calif., Police Dept., causing communications problems for headquarters.

Traffic officers said many cars became stalled in water during the morning rush hour, putting a heavy strain on tow trucks.

Sometimes the wire service report is rewritten, sometimes it is published as it is received.

More rain pounds California

Los Angeles (UPI)—Heavy rains pounded the Southern California coast Wednesday with a wind-driven intensity which guaranteed new flooding and destruction in a region saturated by week-long storms, which have killed 22 people and have wrecked scores of homes.

The new storm, powered by 40 mph winds, was the latest in a series of savage Pacific onslaughts blamed for millions of dollars in property losses—mostly from uncontrollable mudslides.

Associated Press sports writer at work in his New York office. He simultaneously receives information from a teletype machine (on his left), types the story on his computerized word processor, and verifies last-minute facts by telephone.

Syndicated Material

Syndicates are another source of material for newspapers. Feature syndicates supply comic strips, cartoons, columns on topics from cooking to politics, and longer "feature" stories. Syndicates do not supply "hard" news. The material arrives by mail at the newspaper ready for printing or typesetting. Papers pay for what they use on the basis of circulation—the larger the paper's readership, the higher the fee for using the item. Some of the larger syndicates include King Features, Midcontinent Features, Religious News Service, and United Feature Syndicate. Some syndicated material is marked with the name of the syndicate for copyright purposes. About 10 percent of the entire average paper (about one-fourth of the newshole) is taken up with syndicated material.

Most newspapers feature one or more syndicated columnists. A good paper will serve its readers a varied diet of columnists with different viewpoints. Since columnists can write about whatever they please, they are usually very opinionated and biased. It is their purpose to argue strongly for their viewpoint rather than to present straight news reporting. Many columns are political, but others are about religion, bird watching, gossip, or almost any conceivable subject.

A newspaper editor can select only very conservative or very liberal columnists or only those he or she personally agrees with. But such a limited selection does not serve the needs of the readers. One way to evaluate the slant or bias of any paper is to study the viewpoints of its regular columnists and other syndicated material.

Sections and Departments

Almost every daily paper has a sports section and many have either pages or separate sections for society news, food, family features, entertainment (movies, theater, music, etc.), books, business and finance, real estate, and travel.

On larger papers each of these sections might have a full-time editor and staff. Such sections can provide readers with news, valuable how-to information, consumer advice, and features. In cities with competitive papers, these sections have great influence on which paper people will buy.

Unfortunately, there is a tendency to allow these sections to become little more than disguised advertising. A real estate section, instead of giving news about real estate trends in the city, will be filled with articles written by realtors advising people to buy a house now or by developers extolling the beauties of their latest suburban housing tract. A food section or department can provide, for instance, economical and creative recipes, shopping advice, articles on how to tell and select quality meat, advice on which foods are good buys and which are not. A good section could report on sanitation conditions at local food stores and restaurants and even give comparative prices. On the other hand, a food section can print recipes supplied by advertisers (using brands advertised a few pages later) or ads disguised as articles from public relations groups for butter producers (or prunes or coffee or frozen food or whatever) telling how healthful and inexpensive their product is.

The temptation for the paper is to keep the advertisers contented. An article in a real estate section about the shoddy building at a local housing project is hardly likely to make that builder spend money to advertise in the paper. An article warning consumers that a certain supermarket has a confusing labeling system for meats might be uncomfortable for the supermarket—which spends thousands of dollars a year for newspaper advertising.

Filling special sections and departments with press releases is tempting because they are free and already written, and they pour into the newspaper office by the thousands. The New York Times, the nation's largest newspaper, throws away 168 bushels of wastepaper every day, according to one of its associate editors. And much of the wastepaper is press releases.

The Editorial Page

One section of the newspaper where editors can exercise some influence on the city is the editorial page. It is on this page that the paper, or its editors or owners, can speak its mind. On page one the newspaper has the obligation to present the facts, but on the editorial page it can indulge in argument and opinion. On this page it also often prints letters from readers. The editorial page should offer a variety of opinions and a fair sampling of the mail it receives.

Press Releases

Every large corporation—as well as government agencies, large institutions (such as universities), and other groups—has a public relations ("PR") department, whose aim is to tell the community about the good things the organization does and to create a favorable public image.

One of the jobs of the PR director or department is to send "press releases" to newspapers, radio, and TV stations. The press release is usually written so that it can be reprinted almost word for word in a newspaper or magazine. Such press releases, or slightly rewritten versions of them, form the basis for many items in newspapers. This news item is an example of a story based on a press release:

Here is an example of news by press release:

NEWS

TEXAS MOBILE HOME ASSOCIATION

Release Date: Immediate

Contact: Les Bears

Grover Mitchell

MOBILE HOMES TO BE ANCHORED

AUSTIN, (TX), July 6—Texas Mobile Home Owners will soon have the responsibility and expense of properly blocking and anchoring their homes as a result of an act recently signed into law by Texas Governor Dolph Briscoe, according to E.L. Murray of Corpus Christi who is Chairman of the Board of Directors for the Texas Mobile Home Association.

The law becomes effective 180 days following the effective date of the minimum standards which are to be established by the Texas Performance Certification Board, the policy-making body for the Mobile Homes Division of the Texas Department of Labor and Standards. Only mobile homes purchased after this effective date will be required to be blocked and anchored in accordance with this law. Exempted are mobile homes located more than 300 feet from any other occupied or inhabited building or structure.

Actually, two sets of standards will be in effect: Mobile home dwellers within the first two tiers of coastal counties in Texas will be required to block and anchor their homes to withstand hurricane force winds.

(more)

New Shopping Center to be Constructed on Northwest Side

J.D. Bosch, Inc., today announced plans for a new three-million-dollar shopping center to be constructed on the city's northwest side near Newburg Park. It is scheduled to open for business next April with nearly 85 stores.

The new complex will be designed by R.G. O'Brian and Company and built by the Atlas Construction Company of Rochelle. Mr. Gerald Bosch, chairman of the board of J.D. Bosch, Inc., proclaimed the new shopping center a welcome addition to the northwest side community. He said the new center will enable area residents to shop without the long trip downtown and will provide about 900 parking spaces.

Bosch promised that the new center will be the most modern shopping facility in the entire area.

The problem with press releases is that they are a form of "managed news." They are usually truthful, but most often the "truths" are carefully selected to give a favorable impression of the company, government agency, or other organization responsible for the release.

An average large city newspaper receives about one hundred press releases daily. They are either thrown out, rewritten and used, used as is, or used as a lead for a reporter to investigate and supply more objective details.

AUSTIN, Texas—Mobile home owners will soon have the responsibility and expense of properly blocking and anchoring their homes as a result of an act recently signed into law by Texas Governor Dolph Briscoe, according to E.L. Murray of Corpus Christi, chairman of the board of directors for the Texas Mobile Home Association.

The law becomes effective 180 days following the effective date of the minimum standards which are to be established by the Texas Performance Certification Board, for the policy-making body for the Mobile Homes Division of the Texas Department of Labor and Standards. Only mobile homes purchased after this effective date will be required to be blocked and anchored in accordance with this law. Exempted are mobile homes located more than 300 feet from any other occupied or inhabited build-

The Houston Post
Columbia Journalism Review

MEDIALAB

What News Is Published?

1. Find out how much your local paper or papers charge for advertising space. This information can be obtained from the newspaper or the library.

2. What percentage of your local paper(s) is advertising? The national average is 60 percent—compare your paper(s) to this average.

3. Which local advertisers pay the newspaper the most money for advertising? Your answer will probably have to be an educated guess based on an examination of as many editions as possible. In some cities, a few large stores contribute half or more of a newspaper's advertising revenue.

4. What percentage of your local paper's average edition is the "newshole"? To measure it, subtract the answer to Item 2 above from 100 percent. (The average paper comes in with 40 percent news.)

5. Which wire service does your local paper(s) use the most? What percentage of its newshole is filled by wire service material? How does this compare with the national average?

6. Find examples in your paper of syndicated material other than comics or cartoons.

7. Which syndicated columnists are available in your local newspapers? What is the subject matter and viewpoint of each?

8. Does each local newspaper offer a variety of syndicated columnists or does it favor those with a particular political viewpoint? Support your answer with specific examples.

9. Work alone or in small groups to evaluate various sections and departments of local papers—sports, finance, real estate, etc. Report the findings to the class. Be sure to determine whether much of the material in the sections is "puffery"—press release material praising certain products or companies.

10. Does your local paper have an editorial page? If so, does it express a consistent viewpoint? Does the editor tackle important local and national issues?

11. Does your local paper print letters to the editor? If so, do they represent a fair cross section of opinion or are they limited to those who agree with the editor?

12. Find one or two examples in your paper of what seems to be a press release. Discuss the pros and cons of printing press releases. Does your school send out press releases?

13. Using the sample newspaper page found on page 175, identify the following parts:

a) lead story   d) edition title
b) headlines   e) decks
c) masthead   f) cutlines

What Fills the News Hole

LOCAL NEWS

Each newspaper needs its own reporters, especially to handle local events that the national news services will not cover. Reporters are either part of a general reporters' "pool" assigned to stories as they break, or are given regular beats such as city hall, the police, the state legislature, etc. A small paper, of course, will have only a few reporters to cover everything.

Reporters write their own stories, which are then subject to rewrite by various editors. For a last-minute important story, a reporter may phone the information directly to the paper, where a rewrite editor takes it down and hurries it into an acceptable form for the paper.

A reporter covering a story never knows whether the event will be considered newsworthy enough to make the paper or how much space it will be given. For this reason, news reporters write in what is called "pyramid style." They arrange the news item so that the essential details are all in the opening paragraph. Each paragraph thereafter is more general and less important. A good reporter writing in the pyramid style will answer the questions *who, what, where, when, how,* and *why* in the first paragraph. This done, the news editor can fit the story into any available amount of space. A reporter might write 1,000 words on a story and have only 100 used in the paper. You can see the difference between the pyramid style and other writing styles by reading a front page newspaper story and stopping after any paragraph—the story still seems complete. If you try this with a magazine article, the item will not seem complete and will very likely lack some essential information.

A by-lined story carries the reporter's name. Most reporters are unknown to the general public and receive few by-lines. The reporter's job is sometimes exciting but involves many long hours of boring meetings, writing and rewriting, and simply waiting.

NEWSMAKERS

One common reporting assignment is to cover a speech, airport arrival, dedication or whatever, by a famous person—a newsmaker. This is more common in large cities than in small towns where few newsmakers put in an appearance.

"Newsmakers" are people who make news when they talk, marry or divorce, date, write, or do

almost anything. They are politicians, celebrities, media heroes, people in the public eye. What they do often is not terribly important or newsworthy, yet it somehow ranks as "news." Some newsmakers, such as the president of the country, do things that are really news. But they can also make news by doing ordinary things such as walking the dog, talking to people on a street corner, or attending church services.

You are probably not a newsmaker. If a newsmaker were caught shoplifting a typewriter from your local department store, the event would be news. The more important the newsmaker, the bigger the story. If you were caught trying to steal a typewriter, the story would not be news unless you live in a very small town.

PSEUDO-EVENTS

The term *pseudo-event* has been coined to describe a certain kind of event that often receives space in newspapers and in radio and television news broadcasts.

Pseudo-events are events designed to produce news favorable to the person or persons planning the event. The success of a pseudo-event is measured by the amount of space it succeeds in capturing in the news media. Such events are planned with the convenience of the news media in mind and would often be meaningless without news media coverage.

Press releases are one special form of pseudo-events. Other, more ordinary pseudo-events include anniversary celebrations of companies or institutions; dedications or ground-breaking ceremonies or ribbon-cuttings; press conferences, interviews, "leaks" and trial balloons, prepared statements, and speeches; demonstrations and picket lines; hunger strikes; symbolic actions of various sorts; banquets; some law suits (filed only to gain publicity); tree plantings or parades.

The news item that follows could well have begun at a meeting of the board of directors of Crandall Brothers Department Store. The board perhaps noticed a decline in sales and so called in a public relations consultant to boost sales. The PR consultant suggested that the store stage a celebration of 40 years of existence. The event is, in actuality, no more newsworthy than the store's 39th or 38th year of business, neither of which was reported in the local press. All the newspapers and radio and TV news departments were invited to the ribbon-cutting, which was scheduled in the morning to allow plenty of time for pictures in the evening paper and film on the 5:30 local news. At the ribbon-cutting, a press release was given to all media people there. That evening the following story appeared in the paper:

Crandall Brothers Mark Forty Years of Service

Crandall Brothers Department Store in downtown Rochelle today began its week-long celebration of 40 years of service. In a ribbon-cutting ceremony dedicating the newly remodeled store, William Crandall, son of founder Malcolm Crandall, pledged better service and continued efforts to serve the needs of Rochelle. Events planned for the week include the distribution of free candy to all children who enter the store, a vacation sweepstakes, reduced prices, and a two-day Downtown Days Sale in which all auto traffic will be stopped, turning the street into a pleasant mall for pedestrians. A circus will be held in the evening of Downtown Days on State Street, with admission free to all.

CRIME AND DISASTER

Another common kind of local reporting covers the disaster or crime story. The story of a deadly accident, a fire, or a crime is the staple of the newspaper. Why these tragedies are so important as news is hard to understand. But they remain important to papers because people like to read them. The same subjects—crimes, fires, disasters—are important in novels, movies, and television programs as well as in news reporting.

Some sociologists claim that people like to read about the tragedies of other people to gain assurance that their own lives aren't so bad after all—things could be worse. Others guess that people like to read about crime and tragedy because they are exciting, something to break the ordinary and sometimes dull routine of daily life.

INVESTIGATIVE REPORTING

There are many papers whose pages have not seen an investigative news report in twenty years. Even the best papers can manage only a few a year. An investigative report is one that looks deeply into

other dishonest practices in grocery stores; unsanitary conditions at restaurants and hamburger stands; housing conditions among the poor of the city; or political influences in the city school system. Such reporting takes time, money, and courage.

Investigative reporting in the early 1900s eventually resulted in the passage of the Pure Food and Drug Act when reformers and writers like Upton Sinclair described unsanitary packing houses and meats filled with waste and dirt. Ida Tarbell's investigative reporting on the Standard Oil Company led to its break-up into a group of smaller companies. Such reporting was once called "muckraking" and is still called that by some newspeople today.

Investigative reporting takes a great deal of time to do well, and many papers unfortunately consider it a luxury. It is true that investigative reporting sometimes leads to lawsuits, political pressure, threats, and loss of advertising revenues.

HUMAN INTEREST STORIES

A newspaper that reported only the facts, only the world's most important events, only the actions and ploys of world leaders and criminals, might soon find itself without the large number of readers it needs to stay in business.

Most newspapers include what are called "human interest" stories. Sometimes these are local stories written by staff reporters; other times they are provided by the wire services. Human interest stories are about non-newsmakers, about the troubles or heroics of the ordinary person. Whether tragic or humorous, they are often moving and dramatic.

some situation and reveals facts not previously known. Often investigative reports reveal corruption in government or business. A newspaper might investigate the local ambulance services, for example, to look for corrupt practices, kickbacks, hidden charges, and the like. Or it can check on city workers to see if the taxpayers are receiving a full day's work for a day's pay from those employees paid by tax money. A paper can investigate short-weighting and

MEDIALAB

Local News

1. If possible, have a reporter from a local paper talk to the class. Be ready with questions to ask about the newspaper business and reporting.

2. Look at the front page of any newspaper and notice the pyramid style of writing. Take one of the following events (make up your own details) and write a four-paragraph news report about it:

    A fire at the school

    Your teacher has won a state lottery of one million dollars

    A student at school has broken the world record for sleeping without waking

The first (lead) paragraph should contain the who, what, where, when, how, and why of the event. Each following paragraph should be more general and contain less important information. The story must be complete whether the editor decides to use one, two, three, or all four paragraphs in the paper.

3. Check to see how often your local paper uses reporters' by-lines—never, sometimes, or usually. What kind of stories are usually by-lined?

4. Find a story in the paper either on the local or national level that involves a newsmaker other than a politician. Discuss the value of such news in the paper.

5. List the currently best-known newsmakers. Are there some qualities that most of these people have in common? Why do you think the news media and their readers are so fascinated with these people?

6. Find examples of pseudo-events in newspapers.

7. Think of some kind of pseudo-event that would (a) give your school favorable publicity; (b) call the attention of the people in your city to some local problem; (c) call the attention of the country to some problem or event that the class agrees on.

8. As an ambitious class project and an experience in obtaining the news media's attention, attempt to gain news space or time on TV or radio by staging a worthwhile pseudo-event. Make the event an attempt to gain media coverage for some cause the class believes deserves attention.

9. A fairly large percentage of news that makes up the main section of a newspaper is crime: murders, robberies, arson, riots, etc. What do you think is the effect on readers of the news decision that "crime is front page news"? Do you think crime should be so important? What kinds of crimes are rarely reported?

10. Why do you think people read stories like this one about a murder victim? Do they enjoy it? How do they feel after reading it? One way of looking at this kind of news story is that it is included as a sort of violent form of entertainment. Certainly no paper would be justified in keeping such a story secret. Do you approve or disapprove of the way the details of the murder and the finding of the body are presented? Are they necessary? What purpose do they serve? How else could the story have been written?

Murder Victim
Found in
Garbage Can

The body of an unidentified 28-year-old woman was found last night, stuffed in an alley garbage can on the 1300 block of West Front Street on the city's east side.

The partially clad body was discovered by James Hanson, a resident of the block, after he had parked his car in a nearby garage. "I saw a leg sticking out of the garbage can," Hanson told police, "and looked in and saw the body. I rushed home and called the police."

The victim had been stabbed repeatedly and had a cord tied around her neck, according to police. The body has not yet been identified, and police have no suspects in custody.

11. Where does most of the information about crimes come from? How does the source influence the story?

12. If you live in a large metropolitan area, your newspaper probably does not report all crimes. Certainly it does not give the same amount of space to each crime. What do you think determines how much space is given to a local crime story?

13. Judging from the "human interest" stories you have read, what qualities does an editor look for in such an item?

14. A human interest story is featured on this page: "Steve's a stand-up type." Speculate why the story was interesting enough to warrant AP attention and to be used by many newspapers. Rewrite the "Steve's a stand-up type" story so that it is an editorial. You do not have to use all the details in the story, but do use the item as a basis for some kind of expression of opinion.

Steve's a
stand-up type

PHILADELPHIA (AP)—Stephen Tolvish has the only residence on the block with a folding door.

He lives in a telephone booth in northeast Philadelphia.

"It's nice and it's warm and I keep it clean," said the former mailer for a printing firm.

Tolvish, who is 54 and mostly unemployed and has never been married, said he has been living in the telephone booth "off and on for a year."

He stores his suitcase and clothes atop the booth. Tolvish does odd jobs for people in the neighborhood, and the "boys on the corner" take him home sometimes so he can get a bath.

He dines out, when he has the money. He sleeps standing up for obvious reasons, and getting a good night's sleep is often difficult.

"When people want to use the phone," Tolvish said, "they knock on the door. I wake up and get out."

15. Find out what kind of investigative reporting your local paper(s) have done recently. If they have done none, write a letter to the editor and ask why.

Opinion VS. Objectivity

THE DILEMMA

To be objective means to eliminate personal opinion and prejudice from reporting. Some say that a completely "objective" story is not humanly possible; individuals can only express their viewpoints. They feel that each reporter expresses personal opinion as well as possible and that if people read these various viewpoints, they will then be able to reach their own decisions. Others say that this gives the reporter too much power; only the facts should be presented, and opinions left up to the reader.

Newspeople themselves are undecided about the problem of objectivity. David Brinkley, well-known NBC-TV newscaster and commentator, said this: "A person presumably is expected to go on the air and to have no likes, no dislikes, no feelings, no views, no values, no standards—to be a machine. If I were objective, I would have to be put away somewhere in an institution, because I'd be some sort of vegetable. I make no pretense of being objective. Objectivity is impossible to a normal human being. Fairness, however, is attainable, and that's what we strive for."

A. M. Rosenthal, who was managing editor of the most powerful and well-known newspaper in the United States, the *New York Times,* has said that objectivity is ". . .the determination to write and edit with the elimination of as much personal bias as humanly possible, to present facts and situations as close to reality as possible, to avoid our own pejorative phrases or comments, to give accused people or institutions the right of immediate reply, to present all shadings of opinion and counter argument, and most of all, to keep examining ourselves day by day and story by story to see if we are being as objective as we can."

HEADLINES

Headlines serve a number of purposes. They are a convenient way for a newspaper reader with only a few minutes to learn what has happened in the world. Sometimes the headlines are written to entice readers to purchase a newsstand copy. When this practice of using headlines to sell papers is carried to an extreme, it is called sensationalism. A paper might report a murder with a huge headline reading, "Mad Murderer Rampages Through City." Few papers practice such outright dishonest sensationalism any more, mainly because it is poor journalism and because most readers have the paper delivered to their homes rather than purchasing a copy from the newsstand. A more responsible headline for the

The Lower case

Fish & Game To Hold Annual Elections

Berkshire Courier
Great Barrington,
Massachusetts

Between 9:00 and 5:00, the noise was audible even over the daily street din, though apparently not enough to rankle the day people, who could only have heard it during brief forays from their insulated office buildings. Just we full-timers rang our hands in despair, for at night the roar was all ours.

New Times

The breaking down of most prejudices and discriminations has lifted women from mental work to important management and top professional positions.

The Scranton Tribune

A favorite piece by Tchaikovsky is highlighted as Andre Kostelanetz conducts the National Symphony Orchestra IN PERFORMANCE AT WOLF TRAP Monday, Dec. 23 at 8:00 p.m. on PTV. IN PERFORMANCE AT WOLF TRAP is made possible by a grant from Atlantic Richfield Company.

Aroostook Hepublican, Caribou, Maine

No Permit Needed For Accidents

The Times Argus
(Barre-Montpelier, Vt.)

Two innings later, Jefferson was beaned in the back of the head by a line drive off the red-hot bat of Mariner all-star Bruce Bochte. Jefferson was not injured on the play; the baseball, which ricocheted all the way to right field, was taken to hospital for X-rays.

Toronto Globe and Mail

CIA Reportedly Sought to Destroy Domestic Flies

San Francisco Chronicle

Only a third of state's voters went to polls on Nov. 5

One-third of the registered voters in Massachusetts stayed home Nov. 5, nearly a record for absence at polls.

The Boston Globe

Stolen Painting Found by Tree

The (Philadelphia) Evening Bulletin

The license fee for altered dogs with a certificate will be $3 and for pets owned by senior citizens who are altered the fee will be $1.50.

Santa Barbara News-Press

Bland Music Contest Set For Feb. 23

Page News and Courier, Luray, Virginia

462C UNIPRESSERS:

TO ALL OF YOU AND YOUR FAMILIES, MAY THIS BE A MOST PLEASANT HOLIDAY AND MAY THE NEW YEAR BE BRIGHT AND PROSPEROUS.

UPI 12-25 02:09 PPS

EDITORS: PLEASE DISREGARD 462C UNIPRESSERS. IT WAS INADVERTENTLY TRANSMITTED ON THIS CIRCUIT.

UPI 12-25 02:21 PPS

Tuna Biting Off Washington Coast

Seattle Post-Intelligencer

same story might read, ''Man Found Murdered in Hotel.''

Headlines summarize the news. Some newspapers employ one or more people whose only job is to write headlines. They must be accurate, must contain the most important facts of even complex stories, and must fit into a certain number of spaces.

A headline can be written so that it summarizes a story accurately and clearly, or it can be written to express a ''slant'' or ''bias''—an opinion about the story.

For example, a gathering of a large number of people in Washington, D.C., for the purpose of encouraging Congress to pass legislation favoring a ban on nuclear weapons could receive either of the following headlines: ''7,000 Gather to Urge Ban on Nuclear Weapons'' or ''Mob Invades Washington to Push Weapons Ban.'' The use of a ''loaded'' word like *mob* in the second headline would tend to influence readers against the gathering. The use of the word *urge* in the first headline could be taken as a word loaded in favor of the action. A more neutral headline would be ''7,000 Demonstrate for Ban on Nuclear Weapons.''

The two headlines below appeared in two Chicago newspapers, both referring to the same event. Both headlines are true; the man was both a veteran and a gang member. But the second calls the dead person by a negative term while the first uses a more favorable label. Each headline has a different effect on the reader.

Newspapers can be quite objective and present a wide variety of viewpoints or they can consistently give readers slanted or biased news. Newspapers often are labeled conservative or liberal, or are known as pro-business or pro-labor, or have certain viewpoints they stress constantly. For example, a newspaper editor who favored gun controls might use every story possible in which innocent people were killed because of the careless use of guns. A newspaper can present opinions in many ways:

Editorials or items clearly labeled ''opinion''

Slanted headlines

''Loaded'' words in stories

Careful selection of what to print and what to omit

Selection within each news item of details

Placement of the stories (placing an item on the front page says it is more important than if it appears in the back pages of the paper).

Veteran Shot in School

Gang Member Shot By Police

MEDIA LAB

Bias and Opinion

1. Examine your local paper or papers to see if you can find any particular bias. Usually you will need to study more than one issue to make the bias clear. Ask adults who have been reading a certain paper for many years if they have found any viewpoint or bias. Do they object to it, or is it one reason they read that paper? Do you think newspapers should try to be objective or should they allow their own opinions to show in their news coverage?

2. Rewrite some headlines in your local paper so they are biased. Then rewrite the same headlines with a different bias.

3. If you find any examples of biased or slanted headlines, bring them to class—start a bulletin board of them if enough are found.

4. The following "news item" and speaker is fictional, but it is based on an actual event. Read it and then go on to the questions.

Tax Dollars Used To Pay For Anti-American Talk

Richard Owen, who apparently has switched from music to militancy, delivered a lashing lecture Tuesday against almost everything. He spoke at Lakeland Community College.

Over 1,000 listeners, most of them young college students, crowded the lecture hall to hear Owen attack America as a "sick, degenerate country run by a bunch of insane fool maniacs."

Owen was paid $1,500 for his ninety-minute scolding. The money was taken from the college's public affairs budget. He was invited to speak by the Culture Committee of the college.

Owens attacked the ". . . rich get richer system of the United States," and then flew back by private jet to his comfortable Palm Beach home.

This "news story" not only presents news, namely the fact that Richard Owen spoke to students at the Community College, but it also reveals the opinions of the newspaper or, at least, of the writer of the story.

Find specific words, phrases, and selection of details that reveal the writer's opinion about Owen and the talk.

Rewrite the news item (you can make up additional details) to show how it might have been written by (a) someone who wrote a fair and objective news story without revealing his or her personal opinion; and (b) someone who agreed very much with Owen's opinions and expressed that agreement in the news item. Your rewrite should also include a new headline.

MEDIALAB

Chapter Summary

1. The contents of a typical American daily newspaper are as follows:

Advertising	60%
Wire service material	15%
Syndicated columns and items	10%
Sports, society, and special departments and sections	10%
Local news from reporters	5%

Compare your paper with these statistics and draw some conclusions.

2. If there are competing local papers in your area, obtain copies of each for the same day. Examine them carefully and decide which gives the most news, which is the most objective, and which the most interesting. Which one would you subscribe to and why?

3. Newspapers today are a mix of the tragic and the humorous, the historical and the insignificant. An axe murder is placed next to the weather map, and both are followed by an ad for bananas and grapefruit. In a talk to newspaper editors, Robert Hutchins told them that newspapers "should do as well as they can the things they can do best, and should leave to others the responsibility of entertaining the public." Do you agree with Hutchins or do you find other factors at work that make it necessary for a newspaper both to entertain and to inform? Support your answer.

4. Suppose you are the travel editor for a newspaper. A large international hotel chain offers you and your family or a friend a week's free vacation (including air travel) to the Bahamas along with 300 other reporters. Do you accept the offer? Justify your position as an unbiased reporter of the news. You should be aware that such press "junkets" are quite common. Some newspapers have a policy forbidding the acceptance of such offers, while other papers allow reporters to accept. Such junkets usually include a press packet complete with prewritten stories and photos.

5. What are the policies of your local papers on identifying juveniles who are arrested? Some papers treat juveniles as adults, while others refuse to print their names. Is it more important to publish such names to alert the larger community or to protect a young person from being given a possibly undeserved bad reputation?

MEDIALAB

6. Using a crayon or marking pen and the main section from a local daily paper, label the following according to the letters here:

a. Wire service story
b. Syndicated material
c. Pseudo-event
d. Press release item
e. "Newsmaker" story that is included only because a newsmaker was involved
f. Loaded headline
g. Adjectives in news stories that convey bias or opinion
h. Editorials
i. A photo with a message

7. Some newspapers perform valuable service to their community while others survive nicely by printing a minimum of news and a maximum of advertising. Every year *Time* magazine compiles a list of "The Ten Best American Dailies." Recently that list was as follows (in alphabetical order):

The Boston Globe
Chicago Tribune
The Des Moines Register
Los Angeles Times
The Miami Herald

The Philadelphia Inquirer
The New York Times
St. Petersburg Times
The Wall Street Journal
The Washington Post

In order to compile this list, *Time* evaluated 1,760 dailies according to this standard: "They [the ten] make a conscientious effort to cover national and international news as well as to monitor their own communities. They can be brash and entertaining as well as informative. They are willing to risk money, time, and manpower on extended investigations. Through 'Op-Ed' [opinions and editorial] pages and dissenting columns they offer a range of disparate opinions."

You might be lucky enough to find your own paper on this list. Obtain as many of these papers as you can (from a newsstand, or by writing to the papers and purchasing a copy through the mail) and examine them to see why they are considered superior. Remember that the list would be different if made up by a different group of people and that it reflects subjective judgments and opinion.

8. Using all you have learned in this chapter, make an evaluation of your local paper or papers.

9. Is your local newspaper providing more or less news now than a few years ago? A way to measure this is to count the total number of columns devoted to advertising for six days, Monday through Saturday. Then count the total number of columns of nonadvertising material (the "newshole") for that same six-day period. This measuring task could be divided among several class groups. This will give you a ratio of news to advertising—50/50, or 60/40, or whatever. Then, using either your library or the back issues of the paper at the office of the newspaper itself, compare the recent count with that of a similar week, three, five, and ten years ago. If you find that there is less news today and more advertising than in the past, chances are you are not getting all the news you should. If your paper provides about 100 columns of newshole per day or less, it ranks low in comparative news space. If it provides 140 columns or more a day, it is giving a good amount of news. This column count is based on an 8-column paper (each page has 8 columns across). If your paper is four columns wide, cut the numbers in half; if six wide, divide by three-fourths.

Since this measurement with the past is time-consuming, divide the work among the class and reach a conclusion about the recent history of news coverage in your area.

10. Spend at least one day of class time examining some newspapers other than dailies. These would include papers such as the *National Enquirer* sold in grocery stores, newspapers for ethnic groups and racial minorities, *USA Today,* neighborhood weeklies, and other special interest publications. Collect as many of these papers as possible and pass them around for reading and discussion.

11. A commission of 22 national authorities in law, education, and journalism studied high school newspapers throughout the country and concluded that most are "house organs" or public relations tools for the school administration. The commission found that "Censorship and the systematic lack of freedom to engage in open, responsible journalism . . . is a matter of school policy—stated or implied— in all areas of the country." Discuss your own school paper as an exercise in learning about the news. Should school papers be public relations instruments or a chance for students to exercise freedom of the press?

Chapter 7
MAGAZINES

A Short History of

Perhaps more than any of the other mass media, magazines offer a wide choice of subjects that appeal to small groups of people with special interests. The thousands of magazines published today offer something for almost everyone from comic book fans to crossword puzzle lovers to classical scholars. Many magazines, in fact, are so specialized that it is hard to think of them as *mass* media. Yet even these can exert strong influences on their readers, who in turn influence others.

Benjamin Franklin is credited with starting the first American magazine, a monthly with the ponderous title of *The General Magazine and Historical Chronicle for all the British Plantations in America.* His first issue, in February 1741, made media history and gave many others the idea of publishing a magazine. Franklin's magazine and its early competitors were almost solid print and would be unlikely to receive a second glance from today's reader, who is accustomed to attractive magazines that depend heavily on the modern inventions of photography and four-color printing.

Within fifty years of Franklin's venture, there were almost one hundred magazines in the United States, including *The American Magazine* published by Noah Webster (better known today for his dictionary than his magazine). Webster and Franklin and their colleagues were among early magazine publishers in the United States. The *publisher* is the person who starts the magazine—the person (or group of people) with the idea and the money needed to make the magazine work. The publisher hires an *editor,* who finds articles for the magazine and has the general responsibility for the content of the magazine. The actual writing in the magazine is not usually done by the publisher or by the editor but by writers, both free-lancers who write for a number of publications and full-time staff writers, employees of the magazine.

In the mid-nineteenth century, magazines were read mainly by the educated elite. During this time magazines such as *Atlantic Monthly* and *Harper's* were started as intellectual journals. But even as early as 1840 there were signs of what we today would call mass circulation magazines. One of the most popular, *Godey's Lady's Book,* was edited by Sarah Hale to instruct women about manners, proper housekeeping, and fashion. Even during the Civil War, *Godey's Lady's Book* distributed 100,000 copies and was probably read by four times that many people. Included in its pages were stories and poetry by writers now found in today's textbooks of American literature—Edgar Allan Poe, Nathaniel Hawthorne, and Henry Wadsworth Longfellow.

Many new magazines were started around 1880, after Congress passed a bill granting magazines special mailing privileges. Magazines were given a kind of government subsidy because they were "published for the dissemination of information . . . or devoted to literature, the sciences, arts or some

SMALL GROUPS....

the American Magazine

special industry." This mailing privilege still exists, in modified form. Five to ten magazines can be mailed for the cost of a single first class letter.

The completion of the first railroad line across the entire United States in 1869 made the national magazine practical. Also, as education spread, more and more Americans were able to read, and the potential audience for a magazine was greatly increased. In the 1880s and 1890s, *Ladies' Home Journal, Good Housekeeping, McCall's,* and *Cosmopolitan* began. *The Saturday Evening Post,* founded in 1821, became the most influential and powerful magazine in the nation after it was bought by Cyrus Curtis, who also published *Ladies' Home Journal.* Curtis made the *Post* a reflection of American life and presented in it the image of pro-business, "America for Americans." The *Post* published writers such as P. G. Wodehouse, Sinclair Lewis, F. Scott Fitzgerald, William Faulkner, and Ring Lardner.

The Saturday Evening Post had no serious competition as the largest magazine until 1932, when a small black-and-white magazine was issued from a Greenwich Village basement. It was *The Reader's Digest.* The *Digest* promised an article for every day of the month and caught the public's fancy almost immediately. Today that magazine, founded by Lila and DeWitt Wallace, has the second largest circulation in the world with over 18 million readers in dozens of different languages.

In 1923 Henry Luce published the first issue of a weekly news magazine called *Time.* The magazine helped the news make sense; it provided clear summaries of the succession of confusing events called "news." *Time* was a success and gave rise to later successful imitators such as *Newsweek* and *U.S. News and World Report.* In 1936 Luce started *Life* magazine, a magazine that brought vivid pictures of World War II into the homes of Americans in that pretelevision era. *Look,* with a similar slant, began publication the next year, and both thrived on superb, vivid photography.

From the end of World War II until the late 1960s, magazines attempted to be a truly mass medium, appealing to everyone. But then well-known and successful general circulation magazines, such as *Saturday Evening Post, Life,* and *Look* shocked their readers by announcing they were going out of business. Magazines that attempted to appeal to everyone found it increasingly difficult to compete with television as a general entertainment media. The great circulation race slackened to a slow walk. Instead of a few gigantic magazines reaching tens of millions, the current trend in magazine publishing is the specialized magazine for a small but interested audience. Increases in the cost of paper, printing, and postage have made magazines too expensive for advertisers who want to reach most of the nation with their sales message.

SPECIAL INTERESTS

MAGAZINES

So many magazines are published in the United States that no one knows exactly how many exist. Every day at least one new publication is born and another dies. There are currently at least 20,000 different magazines published, ranging from *The Biscuit and Cracker Baker* and *Auto and Flat Glass Journal* to *Reader's Digest* and *Sports Illustrated.*

Most magazines are sold by subscription and/or through newsstands. Neither the subscription rate nor the newsstand price is sufficient alone to enable a magazine to survive and show a fair profit. Magazines make much more money from advertising than they do from what the readers pay for each copy. A few publications, usually intended for very specialized audiences such as doctors or teachers, are actually given away. These "controlled circulation" magazines assure potential advertisers that their message will be delivered to a guaranteed number of doctors or history teachers in the country. At the other extreme are specialized magazines and newsletters that contain no advertising and are supported completely by subscription prices that run to more than $100 yearly.

The majority of magazines contain both advertising and editorial content such as articles, columns, and cartoons. In this way, magazines resemble newspapers, television, and radio. All these media have some kind of "content" (shows, news, music) mixed with and economically supported by advertising.

The editorial content of magazines is created by their own full-time staff, by free-lance writers, or by both. Some of the publications written by a full-time staff are *Time, Newsweek,* and *Mad.*

However, a completely staff-written mass circulation magazine is the exception. Most magazine

---

Tips to Writers

SEVENTEEN, 850 3rd Ave., New York NY 10022. Executive Editor: Ray Robinson. Monthly. Circ. 1,500,000. Buys first rights for nonfiction, features and poetry. Buys first rights on fiction. Pays 25% kill fee. Byline given. Pays on acceptance. Computer printout submissions OK; prefers letter quality to dot matrix printouts. SASE.

Nonfiction and Photos: Articles and features of general interest to young women who are concerned with the development of their own lives and the problems of the world around them; strong emphasis on topicality and helpfulness. Send brief outline and query, including a typical lead paragraph, summing up basic idea of article. Also like to receive articles and features on speculation. Length: 2,000-3,000 words. Pays $50-500 for articles written by teenagers but more to established adult freelancers. Articles are commissioned after outlines are submitted and approved. Fees for commissioned articles generally range from $350-1,500. Photos usually by assignment only. Vicky Peslak, art director.

Fiction: Dawn Raffel, fiction editor. Top-quality stories featuring teenagers—the problems, concerns and preoccupations of adolescence, which will have recognition and identification value for readers. Does not want "typical teenage" stories, but high literary quality. Avoid oversophisticated material; unhappy endings acceptable if emotional impact is sufficient. Humorous stories that do not condescend to or caricature young people are welcome. Best lengths are 2,500-3,000 words. "We publish a novelette every July (not to exceed 30 double-spaced manuscript pages)—sometimes with a suspenseful plot." Conducts an annual short story contest.

TODAY AT LEAST 20,000 OF THEM

articles are written by free-lance writers. Publications receive thousands of manuscripts through the mail; their writers range from professional, often-published authors to students who submit school assignments that a teacher considers worthy of publication. In one year *Playboy* received over 12,000 unsolicited and unagented fiction stories as well as thousands of additional nonfiction manuscripts. Of these 12,000 stories, *Playboy* published only four. The odds are always against the free-lancer, yet thousands of free-lance articles are published each year. (*Unsolicited* means that no one at the magazine asked for the article—it simply arrived in the mail. On many occasions a magazine will originate an article idea and "solicit" an author to write it. *Unagented* means that no literary agent was involved. Professional writers often use a literary agent—a person, usually located in New York, who knows the best markets for articles. Agents sell manuscripts to publishers and receive for their services 10 percent of whatever the author is paid.)

Anyone can submit an article or an idea to any magazine and hope for publication. If the article or story is published, the writer will be paid anywhere from $20 to $2,000, depending on the circulation of the magazine and its payment policies.

Most writers who send in unsolicited articles receive a standard form letter called a rejection slip; sometimes an editor will send a letter with the rejection. Rejection by one magazine does not mean that the idea or manuscript is unpublishable. There are many other reasons for an editor's rejecting it. Many articles have been successfully published after having been rejected by dozens of magazines.

from Writer's Market

Poetry: By teenagers only. Pays $5-25. Submissions are nonreturnable unless accompanied by SASE.

Tips: "The best way for beginning teenage writers to crack the *Seventeen* lineup is for them to contribute suggestions and short pieces to the Free-For-All column, a literary format which lends itself to just about every kind of writing: profiles, puzzles, essays, exposes, reportage, and book reviews."

STOCK CAR RACING MAGAZINE, Box 715, Ipswich MA 01938. Editor: Dick Berggren. For stock car racing fans and competitors. Monthly magazine; 100 pages. Circ. 120,000. Pays on publication. Buys all rights. Byline given. No computer printout or disk submissions. SASE. Reports in 6 weeks.

Nonfiction: "Uses nonfiction on stock car drivers, cars, and races. We are interested in the story behind the story in stock car and sprint car racing. We want interesting profiles and colorful, nationally interesting features." Query. Buys 50-60 mss/year. Length: 100-6,000 words. Pays $10-350.

Photos: State availability of photos. Pays $20 for 8×10 b&w photos; $50-250 for 35mm or larger color transparencies. Captions required.

Tips: "We get more queries than stories. We just don't get as much material as we want to buy. We have more room for stories than ever before. We are an excellent market with 18 issues per year."

Publishing an Article

If you have an idea for a story or an article for a magazine, how can you go about getting it published?

The first step is to decide which magazine is best for the idea. If you have an idea for an article about horseback riding, for instance, you certainly would not submit it to *Popular Mechanics,* any more than you would submit an idea about your custom car conversion to *Horsemen's Journal.*

The best way to select the proper magazine is to read that magazine frequently and become familiar with the kind of articles it publishes. Another helpful guide to finding the best magazine market for an article idea is a book called *Writer's Market,* revised yearly and available at most libraries. This book lists magazines and their addresses, and tells what kinds of articles the magazine needs and how much it will pay per word or per article.

Once the writer has picked a magazine, the typed manuscript can be sent along with a ''cover letter'' explaining that the article is being submitted for possible publication. (If you want your article back, also send along an envelope addressed to yourself, plus the postage needed.) Another approach is to send a ''query'' letter. A query letter explains the article idea, presents an outline, and perhaps includes a sample of a portion of the article. If the magazine responds positively, the writer completes the article and then submits it to the editor. Very

often the editor will return the manuscript, suggesting minor or major changes before it is finally accepted for publication. Once accepted, the article will probably be published anywhere from one to eight months later.

After you have spent many hours of writing your great magazine article, and weeks or months of waiting for a reply, the answer might come back clipped to your manuscript and looking like this.

Please include return postage, or manuscripts will not be returned if rejected.

Health Magazine

212 East Ohio Street

Chicago, Illinois 60611

Thank you for letting us read your manuscript. We regret that it does not meet our current needs, but we express our continuing interest in quality contributions in the field of health education. The Editors

---

MEDIALAB

Magazine Content

1. Prepare a query letter to some magazine with which you are familiar and propose an article suitable for its audience. Select one or two alternatives that would also be suitable.

2. Either as part of this media course or in connection with a writing course, send query letters and/or manuscripts of high quality to magazines in an attempt to have some student writing published. Through some kind of screening process, make sure that only the class's best efforts are sent out to magazines. Avoid the major magazines and concentrate your efforts on the smaller, more specialized publications. High school students can and have published magazine articles, and many classes have been successful in this project.

3. Using either *Writer's Market* or another reference source, find the name and address of a magazine that interests you. The magazine should be one you have not read before, perhaps one that is not readily available in your town. Write for a sample copy—be sure to send the amount listed for a single copy price. Keep the magazines in a classroom collection for the duration of this course so others can see the variety of magazines that is available.

4. Find out if any magazines are published in your area (use the *Yellow Pages*). If so, find out what kind of magazines they are. If possible, invite someone from a magazine to talk to the class or arrange a tour of the editorial offices.

5. The *Readers' Guide to Periodical Literature* is a handy index to magazine articles published in hundreds of popular magazines. It is a valuable research tool but does not index even 20 percent of all the articles written each year. Many other periodical indexes exist to cover more specialized fields. There is an index for magazines in the arts and humanities, one for film magazines, and dozens of others. Find out which indexes are available at the largest public library in your area and examine them. For each one, describe the kind of magazine included and the kind of articles indexed.

6. *Debate:* Magazines should or should not have special mailing privileges.

7. *Debate:* Magazines are more valuable or less valuable and useful than newspapers.

Magazines and the Marketplace

Advertisers often choose magazines rather than other media because of the specific "demographics" that magazines can provide. "Demographics" is the measurement of the kinds of people who read the publication—their age, income, interests, and the like.

If, for example, you wanted to sell a kit that could be used to chrome-plate an automobile engine, the best place to advertise would probably be in a special-interest magazine. You could select from the many magazines read by people interested in cars—for example, *Hot Rod, Motor Trend,* or *Car & Driver.*

If you advertised on television or radio or even in a general magazine such as *Time* or *Reader's Digest,* your money would be spent to reach millions of people who wouldn't want to chrome-plate their engines even if you supplied the kit free. Magazines, by limiting their audiences to specialized interests, create the best possible "market segments" for advertisers.

Mass circulation magazines used to engage in circulation wars to obtain as many readers as possible. The more readers a magazine had, the more it could charge for each advertising page. But magazines with millions of readers, such as *The Saturday Evening Post, Look,* and *Life,* went out of business because, with their general appeal, they couldn't offer advertisers the specific kind of audience they wanted. Each of these was revived later, as a monthly magazine with smaller circulation. On the other hand, magazines could not compete with television in the "numbers game"—the millions of viewers who might see one commercial. These magazines, then, did not stop publication for lack of readers or because of poor quality in the editorial content, but because of too little income from advertising. While mass circulation magazines aimed at "everybody" have been going out of business or struggling to survive, specialized publications have prospered.

In order to fill as many pages as practical with

advertising, magazines themselves advertise to the business community. Some of these ads give an idea of the aims of magazines that relate to both the editorial content and the advertising.

The ads shown on the following pages, for *Rolling Stone* and *Scientific American,* are typical of those that most large magazines use to attract new advertisers.

The box in the lower left-hand corner of the *Scientific American* ad is an example of the findings of demographic research. Such research is very important to advertisers. *Reader's Digest,* for example, knows that men influence 49 percent of the purchases of salad dressing and 46 percent of the purchases of frozen orange juice. *Reader's Digest* also knows and boasts that about one-third of all purchases of goods in the nation are made by *RD* readers. *Architectural Record* magazine knows its readers are responsible for over 90 percent of the total dollar volume spent on architect-planned buildings. In order to attract its yearly $100 million in advertising, *TV Guide* knows that it must maintain its current position of being looked at each week by about 30 percent of the American population.

The magazines young people read are equally well researched. *Rolling Stone* knows that it can offer a prospective advertiser (willing to pay $14,000 for a full black-and-white page or $21,000 for a full color page) 800,000 readers with an average age of 22. They know that the average *Rolling Stone* reader buys $72 worth of books and 57 LP record albums a year and goes to the movies 22 times; 74 percent of *Rolling Stone* readers have camped overnight in the past year, 26 percent own electric guitars, 11 percent own motorcycles, and 78 percent are male. Such specific demographics are crucial to the magazine business.

"ATOM" SMITH.

Or How Corporate Ads Can Capitalize on Our Unique Chemistry.

The venerable prophet of profits never foresaw what's going down today.

Economics used to be as stately as the Emperor's Waltz. The workers toiled, and the mills of profit ground predictably. Often they ground exceedingly large.

No more.

Today, more of us work with our heads than our hands; we produce services (60% of the GNP), rather than products.

Today, it's knowledge that raises the bread. Organized, systematized knowledge.

The fuel for our trillion dollar service economy. And that's where we come in.

SCIENTIFIC AMERICAN.

Our readers and writers are the do-ers, the need-to-know-ers, the avantists and the knowledge organizers who lead this revolution, a revolution producing a new kind of society.

Social scientists call it a knowledge society. It's a society of education, affluence, new lifestyles and new headstyles, where net income often runs second to psychic income. The environment. Consumerism. Job enrichment. Quality of Life. It's a society of new media, new formats, new audiences.

That's why calling corporate media plays the old way is like quarterbacking in Pudge Hefflefinger's leather helmet.

The Leadership Game.

We've all been taught to file leaders

Adam Smith

under professional/managerial.

Today's leaders are filed under another address: pro/tech. They are the men and women who discover knowledge, who invent it. They take these discoveries and turn them into new products. New markets. New solutions to old problems.

	Business Week	Smith-sonian	Fortune	Time	SCIENTIFIC AMERICAN	S/A Rank
Age: 18-34	40.2	34.2	38.9	45.4	51.7	1
Education: Graduated from college	35.9	43.1	52.6	34.4	53.5	1
Occupation:						
Managers/Professionals	36.3	31.7	43.4	28.1	44.1	1
Professional/Technical	19.5	23.5	26.2	19.2	38.4	1
Individual Employment Income: $20,000+	16.2	10.5	20.7	7.7	11.7	3
Ever written to an elected official	25.4	24.0	28.6	21.6	28.7	1

How our leaders stack up against their leaders as corporate prospects

They're the real opinion leaders.

The energy crisis, the environment, resources, population, health care. With those issues who else *could be* the opinion leaders?

They see problems coming decades before anyone else, so they are "the experts" the media interview. They give the testimony that shapes legislation. And they supply the Federal Government with administrators, regulators, advisers—as well as opinions and attitudes. (Want a for-instance? Look in our May issue at an article "Nuclear Strategy and Nuclear Weapons", written by a lawyer and former DOD analyst. He reports that two *very* top cabinet officers...oh, you know who we mean... had their noses in it almost before it was off the press. Aides of one called the author for more dope, and senators used the piece for some verbal nukes of their own in floor debate.)

A convenient label for such leaders is pro/tech.

Scientific American has the highest concentration of them of any TGI-measured

medium.

Small wonder.

We're not a mirror magazine that tells its audience what they already know.

We're the discovery monthly—a magazine of new ideas and original information.

This is where our leaders read and write about issues *before* they become issues.

So it's where you can talk to these influentials *before* problems—and opinions—go public.

Get The Kiddies Off "The Street."

But putting our advertisers in touch with the opinion leaders isn't the only way we protect their futures from future shock.

We help them on "The Street". It's changed too. No place for amateurs. Big money going after big earners.

Where do we fit in?

As Wall Street's early warning system for the profitable technologies that keep these giants big.

What better place to tell corporate prospects a dynamic growth story than in the pages of Scientific American, where the financial world shops for future profits.

Corporate advertising in Scientific American. The formula for communications synergy.

You can bank on that.

SCIENTIFIC AMERICAN

THE HUMAN POPULATION $1.25

THE KNOWLEDGE SOCIETY

The Rolling Stone Cult.
How about you? Do you qualify for membership?

Rolling Stone readers are a very special crowd. Loyal? Hell, they're *fanatics* about their favorite magazine. What are they like? Well, in 10 words or less, they're surprisingly well educated, well rounded, well heeled.

Why don't you run through the questions below and see how *you* compare with "the typical Rolling Stone reader."

YES NO
- ☐ ☐ **Do you see** at least 22 movies a year?
- ☐ ☐ **Do you own** at least one camera? An expensive one?
- ☐ ☐ **Do you go** camping at least once a year?
- ☐ ☐ **Do you like** to travel? Have you traveled out of the U.S. in the last 3 years?
- ☐ ☐ **In her heart,** does your mother wish you'd get a haircut?
- ☐ ☐ **Are you now** in college or have you recently attended college?
- ☐ ☐ **Do you own** your own wheels (car, camper, truck, motorcycle)?
- ☐ ☐ **Do you like** good wine?
- ☐ ☐ **Have you** recently discovered tequila?
- ☐ ☐ **Do you like** to read?
- ☐ ☐ **Do you listen** to a lot of FM?
- ☐ ☐ **Do you find** that having the TV set jawing at you hour after hour gets to be an awful drag?

YES NO
- ☐ ☐ **Do you like** to be up to date about music, the arts, politics, people in the news?
- ☐ ☐ **Do you own** a sophisticated stereo system?
- ☐ ☐ **Do you buy** 61 record albums or more a year?
- ☐ ☐ **Do you own** a musical instrument?
- ☐ ☐ **Are you into** The New Journalism— exciting, honest, fearless reporting that is non-objective, deeply involved in the subject at hand?

If you answered Yes to a lot of these questions, then you and Rolling Stone aren't that far apart. Maybe you should fill out the coupon below and get better acquainted.

Adult Cult
c/o Rolling Stone
78 East 56th Street
New York, New York
10022

Dear Mr. Cult: I'm thinking about maybe joining. Only I'm not sure whether I'm (1) too old to learn any new tricks (2) too straight (3) too square (4) too stuffy. (Check one if it applies). I need more time, more facts. So why don't you mail me a FREE copy of Rolling Stone so I can see what all the hollering is about.

NAME _____

TITLE OR JOB _____ COMPANY _____

ADDRESS _____

Rolling Stone: a general interest magazine covering contemporary American culture, politics and arts, with a special interest in music.

MEDIALAB

Magazine Marketing

1. What is your reaction to the *Rolling Stone* ad?

2. Do you see any way in which advertisers might influence the content of magazines?

3. Find out which magazines are the most popular with members of the class. Why are these the most read? What kinds of ads do they contain?

4. Have each person in the class select a different magazine and do a ''profile'' of it. To ''profile'' the magazine, find out the following information by using issues of the magazine, *Writer's Market*, and the library's copy of the Standard Rate and Data Service magazine volume.

Title.

Subscription and newsstand price.

Frequency of publicaton.

Does the magazine accept free-lance articles?

If so, what is the pay?

What kind of articles are published?

Who is the intended audience?

How much does a full page of advertising cost?

How many pages are there in a typical issue?

How many ad pages are there in a typical issue? (Add up partial pages and include the cover ads in your count.)

What percentage of the total magazine is advertising?

What is the estimated yearly income of the magazine? (To estimate income, multiply the subscription price by the number of subscribers. Add to this the estimated amount spent in the magazine by advertisers.)

What kinds of products are advertised most?

What is the publishing philosophy that governs the choice of articles?

What does an advertiser pay to reach one person when a single full-page ad is bought?

Chapter 8
RADIO

A HISTORY OF RADIO

Radio was the first of the electronic mass media. Its history shaped our expectations of what a mass medium could deliver and paved the way for an incredibly fast acceptance of television.

Before 1920, most radio broadcasts were the property of either the Navy or amateur radio hobbyists. But on November 2, 1920, station KDKA in East Pittsburgh, Pennsylvania, broadcast the first nonexperimental public program. From a small transmitter housed in a shack atop a six-story building, KDKA told listeners the results of the national election that day, in which Warren Harding became the twenty-ninth president.

Only a few hundred people had the equipment needed to hear KDKA, but radio as a mass medium had been born. KDKA still exists today, serving Pittsburgh. And its owner then, Westinghouse Electric Company, is still very much in the radio business.

Within a year radio became a national craze. Some called the invention a "wireless telephone," others "radio telephone" or simply "wireless." People bought crude receivers by the tens of thousands. The earliest sets required headphones; only later did "top of the line" models include loudspeakers that would allow a whole family to hear the broadcast. Reception was poor, static ever present, and programs few and infrequent. But two years after the first KDKA broadcast, there were 1½ million radios in the U.S. and more than 500 broadcast stations.

Corporations and wealthy persons quickly obtained federal licenses to broadcast. Some of the earliest license holders included Ford Motor Company and Westinghouse. By the end of 1922, 70 newspapers, as well as an equal number of universities, owned radio stations.

PROGRAMMING

Early programming was primitive by today's standards. There was much scratchy recorded music (often classical), many lectures, and some news. Here is the program schedule of station WOR in Newark, New Jersey, as it appeared in the *New York Times* on May 29, 1922:

WOR Program Schedule
May 29, 1922

10:30 A.M.—"Packing the Week-End Bag," by Vanity Fair

11:30 A.M.—"Smiles," by J.E.K.

12:30 P.M.—A period of song selections from the recordings of Alma Gluck and Homer Rodeheaver

1:30 P.M.—During this period the numbers requested by our radio audience will be played

2:30 P.M.—Richter String Quartet: Beethoven Quartet, op. 18, No. IV, first and second movements, and "Andante Cantabile."

3:30 P.M.—Carl Bannwart, Superintendent of Olivet Sunday School, ex-President of the Presbyterian Union, will speak on "The Man with a Handicap."

4:30 P.M.—Ruth Dale, soprano: "The Awakening," "The Morning-Glory Song," "There Are Fairies at the Bottom of the Garden."

5:30 P.M.—A talk to Boy Scouts

5:40 P.M.—A talk on timely vegetable garden topics, by Charles H. Nissley, Extension Specialist in Vegetable Gardening from the Agricultural and Extension College at New Brunswick, N.J.

6:30 P.M.—Sky pictures for the kiddies, by Mr. Radiobug.

6:45 P.M.—Good-night stories for the children by Uncle George of The Newark Ledger.

Early broadcasters had no guidelines as to what kinds of programs to air. Early television stations imitated previous radio successes, but early radio was truly a frontier. Only a month after KDKA's broadcast, the Texas A&M University station broadcast the first college football game. A few months later KDKA broadcast the first church service, and the first radio debate on record came from WJH in Washington, D.C., on the argument that "The Daylight Saving Is an Advantage." Early radio drama consisted mainly of dramatic readings. We take sound effects for granted in radio and TV today, but the techniques had to be invented "from scratch." Thunder was created by shaking a thin sheet of metal, and the radio imitation of rain was created by rolling dried peas down a cardboard tube.

Music was the most popular type of programming on early radio, and it remains such today. Many radio pioneers believed radio would bring culture and art to the masses. Opera and classical music were quite common on 1920s radio compared to its very selective place today.

Variety and comedy shows became popular around 1922. Names such as Ed Wynn, Fibber McGee and Molly, Amos 'n' Andy, and the Gold Dust Twins were household words.

The first linking of radio stations into a "chain" (later to be known as a network) was in January of 1923 to broadcast a concert both in New York and Boston. The music was played in New York and was broadcast by WEAF to New Yorkers. But the show was also carried by long distance telephone lines to Boston's WNAC where it was aired for Bostonians.

Calvin Coolidge used a network of more than 20 radio stations to broadcast his words around the country. But these first networks were small and could reach few households compared to today's total coverage of the country by radio.

Radio did succeed in bringing music, both popular and classical, to thousands who had no access to live music. It also succeeded in creating a national interest in sports. Without mass media, sports would remain primarily of local interest. Radio (and later television) helped create national heroes out of sports stars and gave rise to the fan who knew all about nationally famous teams.

Radio soundmen of the 1920s provided audio background realism via pistol, gong, and lip microphone.

Boxing was a popular sport in the 1920s, and the heavyweight championship fight between Jack Dempsey and Georges Carpentier on July 2, 1921, became a radio event. The ringside announcer telephoned his "blow by blow" account to the radio station. The radio announcer wrote down the account and relayed the description to an audience of thousands.

Early baseball games were covered by a play-by-play announcer reading a ticker tape account of the game in a different city. The announcer would try to make the event sound live and appropriate sounds would be added to give the "game" a live quality.

Only four years after the first KDKA broadcast, Dr. Lee De Forest (inventor of the vacuum tube, the predecessor of today's transistor) announced that "radio has passed through the fad stage and has become a utility."

A typical radio dramatization of the 1920s was "The Little House Family" with Betty Garde (left) and Kenneth Daigneau (right).

Early radio sports-news casters, Graham McNamee (at the microphone) and Phillips Carlin (with glasses) broadcasting a Notre Dame-Army football game.

FINANCING RADIO

Radio was exciting and filled with potential. But how were radio stations to survive financially? How could music, sports, and talent be paid for? Entertainers agreed to perform on radio because of the publicity it generated. But as quickly as 1922, the members of the American Society of Composers, Authors and Publishers (ASCAP) demanded to be paid for the right to air their music. Stations were asked to pay annual fees from several hundred to several thousand dollars yearly. This same system of fees paid to ASCAP by radio stations and then distributed by ASCAP to its members remains in effect today.

But in 1925 radio was not as profitable a medium as it is today. A national debate raged over how to finance our radio system. Some favored the European method which was to charge a tax on every radio sold. The tax would then be turned over to radio stations by the government. Others thought radio could be supported by subscriptions or memberships. Radio pioneer David Sarnoff of the Radio Corporation of America (RCA) argued that the freedom of radio meant listeners should have to pay no fees. But who would pay the bills?

That question was answered by the discovery that businesses were willing to pay for time to advertise on radio. The first radio commercial was a long announcement by an apartment complex in New York aired on WEAF in August of 1922. The fee for the commercial was $50. The idea caught on and stations that aired advertising were called "toll stations."

Businesses agreed to sponsor specific shows. Often the corporate name was attached to the show or the performers—the Eveready Hour, The RCA Victor Hour, The Goodrich Silver Chord Orchestra or the Philco Playhouse.

REGULATIONS

The rapid growth of radio caused problems. Frequencies overlapped and some channels were not usable because of interference from competing stations. Some sort of government regulation was needed to keep radio growing in an orderly way. In 1922, Herbert Hoover was Secretary of Commerce. He called a series of Radio Conferences to act as arbitrator between conflicting interests hoping to exploit radio. Hoover played a major role in developing a radio system controlled by business yet closely watched and regulated by government.

His efforts led to the Radio Law of 1927, which created the Federal Radio Commission (FRC). In 1934 the FRC was replaced by the Federal Communications Commission (FCC) which still exists.

The Federal Communications Commission has the power to license radio stations and control many of the technical aspects (transmitter power, wavelength, antenna height, etc.) of broadcasting. The FCC has other powers, but in recent years they have been downplayed in favor of industry self-regulation.

Herbert Hoover in Washington, DC, talking over a telephone to a New York audience.

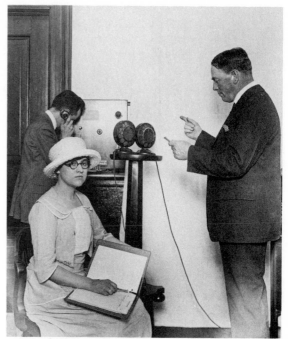

The microphones in an early broadcast studio were a far cry from the miniaturized models used today.

THE RISE OF NETWORKS

The history of radio has been one of a struggle between business interests out to make as much profit as possible, and concerned citizens and the government seeking to ensure that the airwaves are used for the public good. Business interests are firmly in control of broadcasting, but the courts and the FCC occasionally show strength.

For example, the Radio Corporation of America dominated early radio broadcasting and manufacturing. In the late 1920s the RCA network was the largest. Its name? National Broadcasting Company. Around 1927, RCA president David Sarnoff gave a cold shoulder to George Coats and Arthur Judson, two people who ran a talent agency that supplied performers to NBC. Coats and Judson formed their own network, the Columbia Broadcasting System (CBS).

In 1943, RCA operated two radio networks—the Blue network and the Red network. The struggle between the courts and business was won by the courts in this instance. The Supreme Court ruled NBC had to sell its Blue network. RCA sold the network to Edward Noble, who renamed it the American Broadcasting Company (ABC). Today NBC, CBS, and ABC dominate network radio and television. All three networks have origins in NBC and Radio Corporation of America.

Edward R. Morrow was a pioneer in radio newscasting. From a CBS station in London he broadcast the events of World War II.

NEWS

The 1920s were dominated by entertainment programming. Only with World War II did news on radio become popular. Radio commentators such as Edward R. Murrow, Dorothy Thompson, and H. V. Kaltenborn brought the war home. Network broadcasts enabled Americans to hear the sound of battle and the voices of Hitler, Mussolini, Chamberlain, and Churchill. On the home front, Franklin Roosevelt's fireside chats gave the nation a sense of leadership as it gathered around the radio.

After World War II radio news declined in importance, to be replaced by today's "rip and read" journalism. A "rip and read" newscast is so named because the announcer rips paper from the wire service teletype machine and reads it over the air. In the 1950s the "stars" of radio news joined the exodus to the exciting news medium of television.

RECORDED MUSIC

Radio station owners feared television as a new medium which would put an end to the popularity of radio. Television did change the nature of radio

programming. Much early television was simply transplanted radio; it was often the same people and content as radio but with a camera added. So what was radio left to broadcast?

The type of program (called a "format") that saved radio had its root in a 1930s program called "Make Believe Ballroom." The program contained mainly recorded music with talk or information between records. The format was inexpensive to produce and appealed to radio station owners struggling to fill air time without spending much for talent. Variations on the "Make Believe Ballroom" format evolved into today's disc jockey show and radio's almost complete dependence on recorded music.

Slowly, the disc jockey program evolved into music aimed at segments of the listening population rather than at "everyone." Some programs catered to Top-40 hits, ethnic music, "easy listening," old standards, or a balance referred to as M-O-R (middle-of-the-road). Radio became a specialized medium aimed at limited segments of the population.

Television did not put an end to radio, but it did take over the role of THE MASS MEDIA. Radio today is healthy and lively as a specialized medium.

Dick Clark, one of the most popular disc jockey's of all time, choosing a record early in his career in Philadelphia.

MEDIALAB

A Brief History of Radio

1. Talk to someone you know who remembers the early days of radio. Ask how it changed their daily activities. Ask what programs they enjoyed and if they remember how radio was replaced by television.

2. Use old newspapers, magazines, books, and other library reference aids to find an article on radio written during the 1920s. Read the article and write a brief summary. Explain how or if the author fully understood the potential for radio as a mass medium.

3. Look at the radio schedule from the *New York Times* of May 29, 1922, that appears on page 213. Compare that to the 1948 radio schedule on page 219. How do they differ? How do they differ from today's radio programs? How did radio programming influence early television?

4. Radio dramas are still available today on tape cassettes. Listen to an old radio show and write an essay arguing that old radio shows are more entertaining than many of today's television pro-

grams. Do your best on the essay even if you don't agree with the argument.

5. How would life today be different if radio had not become a mass medium? Assume that if radio were not a mass medium, there would be no television.

6. How would radio be different if we had adopted the European system of taxing the purchase of radios? Be aware that this system allows the government to control the flow of income to radio stations.

7. Explain how television helped to create the radio disc jockey.

8. Who controls radio programming—the audience, the government, radio station management, advertisers, singers and groups with the best-selling records? Support your answer.

9. Examine your local radio stations and explain how they attempt to reach certain segments of the listening audience.

This excerpt from a Standard Rate and Data Service publication shows the advertising rates of one radio station.

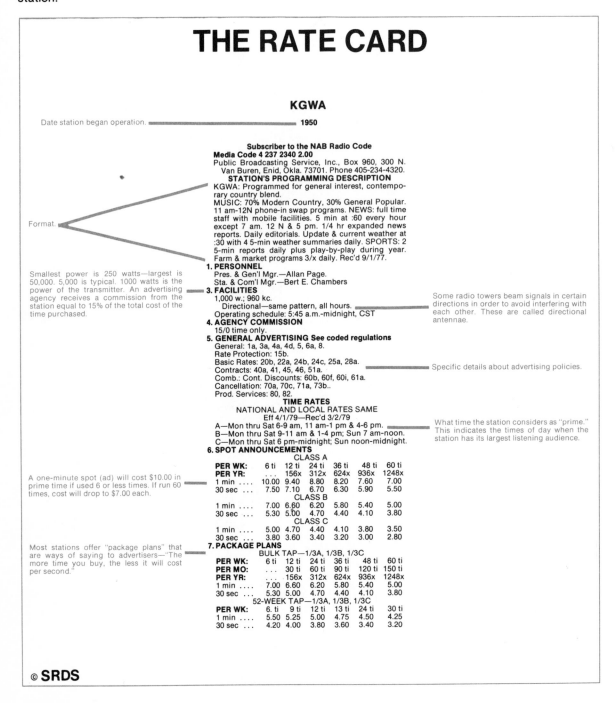

THE RATE CARD

KGWA

Date station began operation. **1950**

Subscriber to the NAB Radio Code
Media Code 4 237 2340 2.00
Public Broadcasting Service, Inc., Box 960, 300 N. Van Buren, Enid, Okla. 73701. Phone 405-234-4320.
STATION'S PROGRAMMING DESCRIPTION
KGWA: Programmed for general interest, contemporary country blend.
MUSIC: 70% Modern Country, 30% General Popular. 11 am-12N phone-in swap programs. NEWS: full time staff with mobile facilities. 5 min at :60 every hour except 7 am. 12 N & 5 pm. 1/4 hr expanded news reports. Daily editorials. Update & current weather at :30 with 4 5-min weather summaries daily. SPORTS: 2 5-min reports daily plus play-by-play during year. Farm & market programs 3/x daily. Rec'd 9/1/77.

1. PERSONNEL
Pres. & Gen'l Mgr.—Allan Page.
Sta. & Com'l Mgr.—Bert E. Chambers.
3. FACILITIES
1,000 w.; 960 kc.
   Directional—same pattern, all hours.
Operating schedule: 5:45 a.m.-midnight, CST
4. AGENCY COMMISSION
15/0 time only.
5. GENERAL ADVERTISING See coded regulations
General: 1a, 3a, 4a, 4d, 5, 6a, 8.
Rate Protection: 15b.
Basic Rates: 20b, 22a, 24b, 24c, 25a, 28a.
Contracts: 40a, 41, 45, 46, 51a.
Comb.: Cont. Discounts: 60b, 60f, 60i, 61a.
Cancellation: 70a, 70c, 71a, 73b..
Prod. Services: 80, 82.

TIME RATES
NATIONAL AND LOCAL RATES SAME
Eff 4/1/79—Rec'd 3/2/79
A—Mon thru Sat 6-9 am, 11 am-1 pm & 4-6 pm.
B—Mon thru Sat 9-11 am & 1-4 pm; Sun 7 am-noon.
C—Mon thru Sat 6 pm-midnight; Sun noon-midnight.

6. SPOT ANNOUNCEMENTS

	6 ti	12 ti	24 ti	36 ti	48 ti	60 ti
PER WK:						
PER YR:	...	156x	312x	624x	936x	1248x

CLASS A

	6 ti	12 ti	24 ti	36 ti	48 ti	60 ti
1 min	10.00	9.40	8.80	8.20	7.60	7.00
30 sec ...	7.50	7.10	6.70	6.30	5.90	5.50

CLASS B

	6 ti	12 ti	24 ti	36 ti	48 ti	60 ti
1 min	7.00	6.60	6.20	5.80	5.40	5.00
30 sec ...	5.30	5.00	4.70	4.40	4.10	3.80

CLASS C

	6 ti	12 ti	24 ti	36 ti	48 ti	60 ti
1 min	5.00	4.70	4.40	4.10	3.80	3.50
30 sec ...	3.80	3.60	3.40	3.20	3.00	2.80

7. PACKAGE PLANS
BULK TAP—1/3A, 1/3B, 1/3C

	6 ti	12 ti	24 ti	36 ti	48 ti	60 ti
PER WK:						
PER MO:	...	30 ti	60 ti	90 ti	120 ti	150 ti
PER YR:	...	156x	312x	624x	936x	1248x
1 min	7.00	6.60	6.20	5.80	5.40	5.00
30 sec ...	5.30	5.00	4.70	4.40	4.10	3.80

52-WEEK TAP—1/3A, 1/3B, 1/3C

	6. ti	9 ti	12 ti	13 ti	24 ti	30 ti
PER WK:						
1 min	5.50	5.25	5.00	4.75	4.50	4.25
30 sec ...	4.20	4.00	3.80	3.60	3.40	3.20

© **SRDS**

Format.

Smallest power is 250 watts—largest is 50,000. 5,000 is typical. 1000 watts is the power of the transmitter. An advertising agency receives a commission from the station equal to 15% of the total cost of the time purchased.

A one-minute spot (ad) will cost $10.00 in prime time if used 6 or less times. If run 60 times, cost will drop to $7.00 each.

Most stations offer "package plans" that are ways of saying to advertisers—"The more time you buy, the less it will cost per second."

Some radio towers beam signals in certain directions in order to avoid interfering with each other. These are called directional antennae.

Specific details about advertising policies.

What time the station considers as "prime." This indicates the times of day when the station has its largest listening audience.

The 1948 listing of radio programs on the next page shows the variety of programming and the great number of stations broadcasting at that time.

RADIO-TV PROGRAMS FOR TODAY

CHICAGO FREQUENCIES

WGN—720	WJJD—1160
WIND—560	WJOB—1230
WILL—580	WEDC—1240
WMAQ—670	WSBC—1240
WBBM—780	WCRW—1240
WAIT—820	WMOR—1280
WCBD—820	WJOL—1340
WENR—890	WGES—1390
WLS—890	WRMN—1410
WAAF—950	WIMS—1420
WCFL—1000	WHFC—1450
WMBI—1110	WNMP—1590

FM

WGNB—98.7	WEHS—97.9
WBEZ—91.5	WFEM—99.5
WJIZ—92.3	WFMF—100.3
WFJL—93.1	WMAQ—101.3
WAAF—93.9	WMOR—102.7
WRBI—94.3	WRGK—103.1
WENR—94.7	WEAW—105.1
WMBI—95.5	WOAK—105.9
WCHI—95.9	WKRS—106.7
WBKB—96.3	WLEY—107.1
WBBM—97.1	

MORNING

(Central Daylight Saving Time)

6:00 A.M.
WGN-Farm hour and news.
WMAQ-Phillip Hayes
WBBM-Paul Gibson
WCFL-Dawnbuster
WIND-News;Morning Watch
WJJD-Breakfast Frolic
WLS-Farm bulletin board
6:15 A.M.
WMAQ-Town and Farm
WLS-Morning Devotion
6:30 A.M.
WGN-Today on Farm
WLS-The Sage Riders
WIND-News,; Purple Sage
6:45 A.M.
WGN-Bob Siegrist
WMAQ-Alex Drier, News
WLS-Bob Lyle, news
WIND-Yawn Patrol
6:55 A.M.
WBBM-News
7:00 A.M.
WGN-Bill Evans
WBBM-World News Roundup
WCFL-News
WMAQ-Norman Ross Show
WLS-Buccaneers
WIND-News; Record shop
WJJD-News; Wake Up
WAAF-Breakfast Express
7:15 A.M
WBBM-News reports
WCFL-Morning clock
WJJD-Negro News Front
WLS-Range Riders
7:30 A.M.
WBBM-Bing Sings
WLS-Sage Riders
WJJD-News
WIND-Musical News Review
7:45 A.M.
WCFL-Bill Hamilton, News
WJJD-Wake Up, Chicago
WBBM-Jim Conway show
WLS-Bob Lyle, News
7:55 A.M.
WMAQ-News
8:00 A.M.
*WMAQ - WIEBOLTS, YOUR NEIGHBOR - Musical Variety, with June Marlowe

WGN-Robert F. Hurleigh
WCFL, WLS-Breakfast Club
WIND-News;Top Tunes
WBBM-John Harrington
WJJD-Ernie Simon
WAIT-Record Caravan
WFMF-Morning Melodies
8:15 A.M.
WGN-Two Ton Baker
WBBM-Patrick O' Riley

News Broadcasts

MORNING

6:00—WIND	9:00—WIND
6:30—WIND	9:30—WIND
6:45—W-G-N	10:00—WIND
7:15—WBBM	10:00—WCFL
7:30—WJJD	10:30—WIND
8:00—W-G-N	10:45—WLS
8:45—WMAQ	11:30—WIND
9:00—W-G-N	11:45—W-G-N

AFTERNOON

12:00—WMAQ	4:30—WIND
12:00—WAAF	4:40—WBBM
12:30—WBBM	5:00—WBBM
12:30—WIND	5:00—WMAQ
1:00—WIND	5:15—WIND
4:00—WIND	5:45—WMAQ

EVENING

6:00—WIND	10:00—WCFL
6:00—WLS	10:00—WBBM
6:15—WMAQ	10:30—W-G-N
8:00—WCFL	11:00—WMAQ
9:00—WIND	11:00—WIND
9:30—WIND	11:55—WMAQ
10:00—WENR	12:00—WIND

8:30 A.M.
WGN-Tello Test
WMAQ-Music That Sings
WBBM-Gold Coast
WIND-News, Top Tunes
WAAF-Luthern Gospel Hour
8:45 A.M.
WGN-Today's The Day
WBBM-Shopping with Mircus
WMAQ-News, Norman Barry
9:00 A.M.
WGN-Leslie Nichols, News
WMAQ-Welcome Travelers
WIND-News, A. Godfrey
WBBM-This is Bing Crosby
WCFL-Bill Evans Show
WLS-My True Story
9:15 A.M. A.M.
WGN-RECORD Relay. A full hour of recorded tunes with Holland Engle, Pierre Andre, Norm Kraft, and Bill Lansing.

WMAQ-Here's Norman Ross
WLS-Luncheon Club
WIND-News;Music by Martin
WJJD-Swing Lane; Interlude
WCFL-Marriage License Bur.
11:15 A.M.
WGN-VIRGINIA GALE with interesting and helpful suggestions to make the tasks of the homemaker easier

WBBM-Aunt Jenny
WJJD-Guess Tune; Interlude
WCFL-Personalty Time
11:25 A.M.
WLS-Carol Douglas

11:30 A.M.
WGN-The Answer Man
WAIT-Stella White
WBBM-Helen Trent
WJJD-Frankie Lane
WIND-News; Frank Sinatra
WCFL-South American Way
WLS-Martha and Helen
WNMP-Jewels of Music
WGES-Cocktail Time
11:45 A.M.
WGN-Spencer Allen; News
WBBM-Our Gal Sunday
WJJD-Marty Hogan
WCFL-Don Artisite
WIND-Como and Carle

AFTERNOON

12 NOON
WGN-Cedric Foster News
WMAQ-News
WLS-Farm World Today
WCFL-Baukhage Talking
WAAF-News Symphony
WBBM-Big Sister
WIND-News; Benny. Goodman
WJJD-Waltz Time
12:10 P.M.
WMAQ-What's New in Agriculture
12.15 P.M.
WGN-Hostess Hour
WMAQ-Food Magician
WBBM-Ma Perkins
WCFL-Music Mart
WJJD-Noon Time Quiz
WBEZ-Symphony Hour
WFJL-For Listening Pleasure
12:30 P.M.
WGN-Market Reorter
WBBM-Julian Bentley
WMAQ-Phillip Hayes
WJJD-Al Benson
WIND-News, Luncheon Music
WGES-Polish Dinner Bell
WLS-Dinner Bell
WAIT-Radio Gosip Club
12:45 P.M.
WGN-Leslie Nichols; news
WBBM-Guiding Light
2:15 P.M.
WMAQ-Road of Light
WBBM-Hilltop House
WCFL-Fred Waring
2:25 P.M.
WLS-One Man's Opinion
2:30 P.M.
WGN-Meet the Menjous
WBBM-House Party
WMAQ-Pepper Young
WCFL-News
WLS-Quick as a Flash
2:45 P.M.
WGN-Nat'l Consumer's Panel
WMAQ-Right to Happiness
WCFL-Spike Jones
3:00 P.M.
WGN-Radio Quiz
WMAQ-Backstage Wife
WBBM-Strike it Rich
WLS-Nancy Craig
WCFL-Great White Way
WOAK-The Band Stand

3:15 P.M.
WGN-Second Spring
WMAQ-Stella Dallas
WLS-Art Baker
3:30 P.M.
WGN-Linda's First Love
WMAQ-Lorenzo Jones
WIND-Record Shop
WBBM-Julian Bentley
WCFL-Hannibal Cobb
WJJD-Scoreboard
WLS-News
3:45 P.M.
WGN-Lanny Ross
WMAQ-Young Widder Brown
WBBM-Double Quiz
WJJD-Ernie Simon
WLS-Variety Music
WAIT-Footlight Favorite
4:00 P.M.
WGN-Lionel Barrymore
WLS-Bob Atcher
WMAQ-When A Girl Marries
WBBM-Paul Gibson
WCFL-Tommy Dorsey
WIND-News; Spike Jones
WFJL-Discs and Data
WOAK-Musical Matinee
WEFM-Artists Album
4:15 P.M.

WGN-MARSHALL KENT with the popular disc jocker spinning
the choice records of the day
Sponsored by Colgate Co.

WMAQ-Portia Faces Life
WIND-Harry James
WCFL-Margaret Whiting
4:30 P.M.
WGN-Bakers Spotlight
WMAQ-Just Plain Bill
WIND-News; Tommy Dorsey
WCFL-Merry Go Round
WLS-U.S. Navy Band
4:40 P.M.
WBBM-Harrington News
4:45
WGN-Singing Story
WMAQ-Front Page Farrell
WBBM-Gold Coast
WENR-Beula Karney
WIND-Travel Time
5:00 P.M.
WGN-Cisco Kid
WMAQ-George Stone; news
WBBM-Allen Jackson; news
WENR-Fun House
WIND-News; Musical Scoreboard
WJJD-News; Interlude
WCFL-Variety Time
WFMF-Melody Time
WAAF-Sincerely Yours
5:05 P.M.
WMAQ-Len O' Connor, news
5:15 P.M.
WBBM-J. Harrington, news
WCFL-Benny Goodman
WMAQ-Dave Garroway
WIND-Sports Special
WJJD-Rosemary Wayne
WAAF-From the Keyboards
5:30 P.M.
WGN-Bobby Benson
WMAQ-One Man's Family
WJJD-Race results
WCFL-Music You Like
WIND-Bert Wilson
6:45 P.M.
WGN-Fulton Lewis Jr.
WMAQ-Rich Harkness, news
WCFL-Music for men
WBBM-Edward R. Murrow
WIND-Time to Remember
WJJD-Suppertime Frolic
7:00 P.M.

WGN-RUDY VALLEE SHOW with the "vagabond lover" recalling the early days of show business and reviewing popular records.

WMAQ-Stars and Starters
WBBM-Phillip Marlowe
WIND-News; Bob Elson
WLS-The Fat Man
WCFL-Vic Barnes, news
WOAK-Hour of Songs
WEFM-Seranade Music
WNMP-Evening Concert
7:15 P.M.
WCFL-Vaughn Monroe
7:25 P.M.
WIND-Bears vs. Browns
7:30 P.M.
WGN-Xavier Cugat
WBBM-Up for Parole
WMAQ-Cloak and Dagger
WLS-This Is Your FBI
WCFL-Meet the Band
WEFM-Musical Favorites
WFJL-American Jazz Classics
WAAF-Footlight Echoes
WEAW-Concert Favorites
7:45 P.M.
WCFL-Doris Day
7:55 P.M.
WGN. WGNB-Bill Henry
8:00 P.M.
WGN-MGM Theater
WBBM-Songs for Sale
WMAQ-Dimension X
WENR-The Thin Man
WCFL-News; Novena service
WGES-Lithuanian hour
WENR-Stand By
WEFM-Evening Concert
WOAK-For Music Lovers
WRBI-Concert Music
8:30 P.M.
WMAQ-Jack Lait, Confidential
WENR-The Sheriff
WCFL-Cardinals vs. '49ers
WGES-Germanic Broadcast
WFJL-Opera Heirlooms
8:55 P.M.
WENR-Chapion Roll Call
9:00 P.M.
WGN-President Truman
WBBM-President Truman
WMAQ-President Truman
WENR-Music from Pier
WEFM-Musical Memories
WEAW-News; Holiday Paradise
9:30 P.M.
WGN-Theater of Stars
WMAQ-Sports Newsreel
WENR-The Modernaires
WBBM-Capitol Cloak Room
WIND-News; Record Spotlight
WEFM-Composers' Hour
9:45 P.M.
WMAQ-Pro and Con
WENR-Freddie Martin
10:00 P.M.
WGN-Behind the Story
WBBM-Fahey Flynn, news
WMAQ-News
WIND-President Truman
WENR-Paul Harvey
WOAK-Moonbeams
WFJL-Editor's Comment
10:15 P.M.
WGN-Chicago at Night
WMAQ-Rio Rhythms
WBBM-Weather Report
WENR-Barry Wood Show
WFJL-Evening Devotions
10:20 P.M.
WBBM-Tony Wetzel
10:30 P.M.
WGN-News
WENR-Conversation with Casey
WIND-ABC club
WGES-Rhythm Till One
WEFM-Music Guild hour
WMAQ-Big City Seranade
WFJL-Caravan of Dreams
WOAK-Great Music Moments
10:35 P.M.
WBBM-Eddie Howard
10:40 P.M.
WGN-Song Souvenir
10:45 P.M.
WGN-This Is the Story
WENR-Platter Party

---

*Indicates listing paid for by sponsor to give you more information about program

SPECIAL EVENTS

7:25 p. m.—WIND—chicago Bears vs. Cleveland Browns football game.
8:30—WCFL—Chicago Cardinals vs. San Francisco 49ers exhibition football game.
9:00—W-G-N, WMAQ, WBBM, WGN-TV, WNBQ, WBKB—President Truman discusses "The Korean Situation," On WIND at 10:00.

MEDIALAB

Radio Programming

1. A station's "format" describes the type of music it plays or the kind of programming it usually broadcasts. A "Top 40" format station programs those records currently in the "top 40" in terms of record sales. Other common formats include M-O-R (middle-of-the-road), Easy Listening, Rhythm and Blues, Country and Western, All News, Educational, Foreign Language, or Classical. Find out what format each station in your area uses.

2. After you have determined the formats of the local stations, try to determine which segment of the audience each station reaches the most. For example, a daytime-only station with "Easy Listening" music and hourly stock market reports probably is most interested in attracting people listening in offices and business people or people at home who want "relaxing" music.

3. Make a list of the products advertised during one hour on one station. Various students should choose various stations to monitor. Examine the lists and find the relationship between the products advertised, the station's format, and the intended audience.

4. The rates advertisers pay for radio time depend on the size of the audience and the time of day. Find out what rates your local stations charge for commercial time. These can be checked at the library in a book produced by Standard Rate and Data Service, which lists all the radio stations in the country with detailed information about programming and ad rates. A page from one edition of the book is shown on page 218 with an interpretation of the terms used.

5. Find out which radio station is the most popular among students. Which is the most popular among parents? Do you think that when you become a parent your listening tastes will have changed? Explain the reasoning behind your answer.

6. How does the most popular station in your area decide which records to play? To find out, you might call the station or write a letter for the entire class. If possible, invite a speaker from the radio station to talk to the class about radio programming.

7. An old radio directory is reprinted on page 219. It appeared in a daily paper in 1948. Such directories used to be printed in the daily paper just as TV schedules are today. Radio in 1948 was scheduled in a way similar to the way TV is today. Do you think television scheduling in the year 2000 might be different than it is today? Support your answer.

RADIO TODAY

After World War II, radio still resembled today's television in many ways. People listened to specific programs and radio was dominated by the three major networks. But the growth of television and the increased number of radio stations (over 3,000) changed the nature of radio.

With so many radio stations available, it was no longer possible for one station to deliver a large enough audience to make a network profitable. There were not enough advertising dollars to go around. In addition, the energies and the development dollars were being spent on the more glamorous medium of television. So radio lost network-supplied programs and became a local medium.

Local stations turned to phonograph records, disc jockeys, and "rip and read" news broadcasts to survive. Some stations tried talk shows, sports broadcasts, even all news. They needed inexpensive programs that would attract local advertisers. The formula worked and was later refined to what is sometimes called "narrowcasting." *Broadcasting* means sending out a signal to attract everyone; *narrowcasting* means carefully selecting music to attract a certain segment of the population to deliver to advertisers. A young audience is gathered by playing rock music, a somewhat older audience with middle-of-the-road programming, and the mature market with "easy listening."

In fact, the formula worked so well that the 1960s saw the greatest growth yet in radio's revenues. But no medium is immune to technical changes, even as "old" a medium as radio. The early 1960s saw a new kind of radio—FM (frequency modulation). At first FM was of interest only to hobbyists and music nuts interested in something called "hi-fi." There were very few FM sets and even fewer stations; many played only classical music. Existing AM (amplitude modulation) stations took out an FM license and broadcast the same program on both outlets.

In the mid 1960s the Federal Communications Commission decided that AM stations that owned FM outlets should not be allowed to broadcast the same signal on both stations all the time. The FCC wanted to encourage a greater diversity of programming to serve the public. So limits were placed on the amount of time an AM station could "simulcast." This ruling created a demand for a new type of programming, different from AM.

The programming void was filled by "underground rock" formats, by so-called "free-form" radio, and often by creative combinations of music, talk, interviews, and off-beat humor. Some stations narrowed their intended audience to certain sections of a large city instead of the whole metropolitan area. The programming of FM radio today is little different from AM, yet FM is threatening AM radio as much as television did in the early 1950s. FM has some technical advantages over AM.

Most radios can play FM signals in stereo; AM stereo began in the mid 1980s, but most radios still cannot take advantage of the improved sound. FM also has a higher frequency response than AM; that is, it allows a greater range of sounds to come through to the loudspeaker. FM is also better suited to large cities since its transmissions are less subject to interference from electric motors, storms, bridges, and office buildings.

These advantages, combined with sometimes more creative music formats have made FM the preferred medium for young adults. In 1978 FM passed AM in number of listeners nationwide. In 1984 a research survey found that only 17 percent of listeners would choose AM over FM if the two bands offered exactly the same programming. Only one in ten new cars with a radio lacks an AM/FM radio, and many of the portable radios worn as headphones are FM only.

So the battle for a share of the audience continues. First radio had to survive the invention of television; now AM radio has to find a way to avoid obsolescence in the face of the better sound of FM stereo.

AM stereo began in the 1980s as an effort to recapture some of the audience lost to FM. The stereo does improve AM sound; in technical terms it offers a broader bandwidth—close to that of FM. The sound is not as good as the best FM, but it is close enough to close the quality gap. So AM stations now have to offer unique programming to attract listeners who have grown up on FM.

Radio Today

1. There are two kinds of commercial radio broadcasting—AM and FM. The two represent different ways of transmitting radio waves. As recently as 15 years ago, FM was almost unknown. Only the largest cities had FM stations and few people listened to them. But today FM is the fastest-growing kind of broadcasting. In large cities there are more FM than AM stations.

Find out what FM stations operate in your area. What is the frequency of each, and what format does each use? Are there any educational FM stations in the area? Educational FM stations are usually found on the lower (or left-hand) part of the FM tuning dial.

2. Research the difference between AM and FM. What are the advantages and disadvantages of each?

3. Complete this comparison: FM radio in the 1980s is to AM radio as _____ was to radio in the 1950s. Explain your answer.

4. Take a survey to find out if AM or FM is more popular in your class.

5. Is AM stereo available locally? If so, find out if it is working to restore some of the lost audience to AM radio.

6. In your local area, which offers the greatest variety of programming, AM or FM radio?

7. A trend in television is for small UHF stations to operate in a way similar to radio stations. Some stations show music videos much of the time. Do you think such stations will pose a threat to radio? Support your answer.

8. The history of mass media shows that new technology is often seen as a threat to a particular medium. But the new medium (or the technical improvement to an old medium) often does not replace a medium so much as change it. How do you think each of these technologies will influence the future of radio?

low power UHF television
videodiscs
stereo television with large screens
AM stereo.

Chapter 9
RECORDS

MAKING RECORDS

Phonograph records and compact discs are, in a way, like film, because the music you hear on the disc never existed quite that way in reality. A record is not made by simply recording what musicians play in one sitting any more than a film is made by photographing what actors do on a stage.

TAPING

The music on today's popular phonograph records is recorded first on a master tape in a recording studio. Bits and pieces of tape are spliced together to produce the perfect performance that becomes a 45 rpm (revolutions per minute) single or a record album. Thus both films and records are created by similar processes, called *editing* in the film world and *mixing* in the recording industry.

A popular record album (one LP, or long-playing record; or one CD, or compact disc) might fill 3,000 feet of recording tape. Professional tape runs at 15 ips (inches per second)—twice the speed of the fastest home recording units and three times that of a cassette recorder. But that LP's 3,000 feet is assembled from the 30,000 or more feet originally recorded. Most of what is recorded on tape in the studio is thrown away and never reaches the final record, just as in film most of what is shot is thrown away and never appears in the print shown at local movie theaters. A feature film is a skillful blending of hundreds or thousands of pieces of film; a single hit record is usually a skillful blending of 20 or more short pieces of tape.

The person responsible for putting together the record is the producer. In film, the producer is the

person who supplies the money for the making of the film. In the record industry, the producer acts in a recording session much like a film director acts at a filming session.

In the early days of film, the public knew the names and faces of the "stars" who appeared on the screen. As the public became more sophisticated, the name of the director was often a bigger box office draw than the "star." Records are still best known for the performers—the star system thrives in the record industry today more than in film. But record audiences are slowly beginning to recognize the names of certain producers who have a following and a reputation for a particular kind of "sound."

When Carly Simon first recorded "That's the Way I've Always Heard It Should Be," the song was not an instant hit. A producer suggested the addition of a heavy but short drum passage to act as a bridge between parts of the song. Ms. Simon credits that musical idea with making the song a hit. The producer's idea gave the song a distinctive sound that helped the record stand out from the thousands

of others and stick in the listeners' minds. Most records released are commercial flops and barely earn back the money spent to produce them. Those that do succeed are the ones that are recorded by a big name star or group or that demonstrate production genius.

The producer, otherwise known as the A & R (Artist and Repertory) man, works in a glass-enclosed control room filled with recording and sound-altering equipment. He or she communicates by microphone with the performers and at the same time works with a mixing console, directing an "engineer" (who could be compared to the photographer in a film) to give more volume here, soften a tone there, vary the comparative loudness of any one instrument (bring the voice "closer" or mute the drums), overdub (so that one person can be a duet or trio or play a whole orchestra of instruments alone), provide special sound effects, or any one of hundreds of possible variations. If a dozen different record producers were to work with the same song and the same musicians, the final result would be twelve different "sounds" or versions of the song. One record company executive has said, "In the pop field, 70 percent of a record is the creation of the A & R man."

The fact that many performers want to "lip synch" their songs (mouth the words while the recording is played) for videos and guest appearances on TV attests to the importance of the producer. If these groups were to sing and play "live" for the TV camera, the results would not sound at all like the record that viewers play at home or hear on the radio. Because of the work of the producer and the recording studio, many groups are unable to play exactly what they've recorded. Live concert performances are different from the sound produced on records, although many groups bring to each concert electronic equipment equivalent to a small recording studio so they can come close to producing the same "sound." Some artists use very little production and so can match their records quite closely in a live performance, while others depend so much on production values that their music can never be performed live.

PRODUCTION

Once the producer has mixed the master tape to everyone's satisfaction, it is turned into a record. To make a record, the tape signals are fed to a recording head where the signal is converted to mechanical vibrations of the recording stylus. The vibrating stylus cuts a wavy pattern in a rotating wax-like plate called a master disc. The pattern cut is actually a picture of sound waves that can be seen with proper lighting if the record is placed under a microscope. This master plate is then used as a mold from which the records sold in stores are pressed.

This process of producing and manufacturing records has been used for only about 40 years. Compared with the long-playing record, the inventions of radio, television, and film are old-timers. In spite of the fact that the LP is a recent invention, the story of its creation is not well known.

HISTORY OF LPs

In 1944 Peter Goldmark of CBS Laboratories visited some friends who played a new recording of Brahm's Second Piano Concerto for him. Being a music lover, Goldmark was disturbed by the frequent interruptions caused by changing and turning over the six records in the album. (At that time, record albums of long pieces of music looked very much like photo albums and contained from three to fifteen separate discs.) Goldmark realized "there was no doubt in my mind that the phonograph . . . was murdering Brahms, and I felt somehow impelled to stop this killer in its shellac tracks."

In 1944 the art of sound reproduction was crude by today's standards. Goldmark resolved to improve

A collection of gramophone players from a bygone era forms a nostalgic backdrop to a conventional LP and the Compact Disc.

A Compact Disc (4.5 inches in diameter and capable of an hour's playing time), rests against a contemporary 33⅓ rpm LP.

the situation even though he admittedly knew nothing about the medium of sound recording. He set out to invent a record that could hold an entire symphony on its two sides. His success led to the multimillion-dollar record industry of today, an industry built on one person's desire to be able to listen to classical music without interruption.

The original records were made to be played at 78 rpm, but Goldmark was able to solve the technical problems that prevented slower speeds from being practical. Today's standard 33⅓ rpm speed for LPs was not chosen by scientific means but for a very practical reason: at that speed enough music could be put on a single disc to provide background music for one reel of film in a movie theater.

NEW TECHNOLOGY

The gradual improvement in the craft of sound reproduction can be clearly heard by listening to a series of records, each made a number of years later than the previous release. The original LP gave way to ''high fidelity,'' which in turn was changed to stereo, which today stands ready to give way to digital sound and laser-read compact discs.

Twelve-inch record ''albums'' will almost certainly be obsolete by the year 2001. The highest ranking

contender to replace the LP is a five-inch piece of thin vinyl called a compact disc (CD) that fits nicely in the palm of your hand. The CD can play one full hour of stereo sound per side. The player uses a laser beam to track billions of tiny reflecting pits, instead of grooves in today's LP records. The CD will never wear out, cannot be scratched, and carries with it the potential of playing video pictures along with the sound. The quality of sound is quite high and the cost is reasonable, but still more expensive than the traditional black vinyl disc.

This development in the medium of recording mirrors the history of film, painting, and photography. At first painters and photographers were content to try to imitate reality. They tried to capture in paint or on film what the eye could see, to make images ''life-like.'' But once developed, they moved beyond capturing still life and into creating a new reality. Many modern paintings and photographs resemble nothing the eye can see. A comparison of the best paintings and photographs of the first artists in these media with those of modern artists shows very clearly the change that took place. Sound reproduction is also moving into new worlds. The music played on home reproduction systems of the future may be as different from the top tunes of today as heavy metal is from Gregorian chant.

MEDIALAB

Record Making

1. Choral director Ray Conniff says, "The simple fact is that people today get a lot better sound on records than they do in live concerts." Do you agree or disagree? Why?

2. Concert pianist Glenn Gould has said that "concerts as they are now known will not outlive the 20th century." Do you agree or disagree? Why?

3. Bring to class and play some records that use overdubbing and that illustrate elaborate studio production. Contrast these with some records that reveal very little studio manipulation of the sounds.

4. In what ways are the processes of film editing and record mixing alike? How are they different?

5. Who are some of the best known record producers now? Members of the class can bring records that demonstrate various "sounds," such as the "Wall of Music" sound, the simplicity of acoustic instruments, or the complexity of synthesizers.

6. There is a trend in music today toward the more engineered and electronic sound and away from the simple, acoustic (nonelectronic) sound. Even when you attend a live concert, you usually hear electron-

ically amplified sound. Consider the idea of completely electronic music. For example, will the traditional instruments such as drum and guitar be replaced by more sophisticated electronic devices? Can computers be programmed to play electronic music? How will electronics change music in the next 100 years?

7. Play some records that illustrate completely electronic music. Do you think this will ever replace today's music? Why or why not?

8. Find different versions of the same song and explain how their production is different.

9. Prepare a report on how recorded sound will change in the next ten years.

10. Are the lyrics to today's songs important or are the "sound" and the "beat" more important? Do today's songs attempt to say important things in their lyrics? Historically, the lyrics to popular songs go through cycles of being mainly nonsense for a period of time and then slowly changing to lyrics that are very meaningful. Which phase are we in today? Bring some songs to class to prove the viewpoint you hold.

THE FUTURE OF RECORD ALBUMS

After World War II the sound quality of recordings was good enough to spark consumer interest. Stars such as Bing Crosby and Frank Sinatra appeared in films and on the radio and made records. But the recording industry became BIG business first in the 1950s and 1960s with the arrival of rock 'n' roll and culture superstars such as Elvis Presley and the Beatles. The 33⅓ rpm record album gradually replaced the 45 rpm single as the industry sales unit.

By the mid 1970s Americans spent more on rock records than on admissions to football, basketball, hockey, and baseball put together. The term *solid gold* was used to label a record that made a million dollars.

In the early 1980s the recording industry faced new competition for the entertainment dollars of the youth market—video arcades and computer games. The record boom ended. The cost of an LP rose to nine dollars or more, and listeners discovered they could make tape cassettes from the radio or from borrowed records for only two or three dollars. In 1982 record sales were actually millions of copies less than they had been back in 1973. But sales of blank cassettes had doubled.

By the mid 1980s, new stars and groups helped spur sales of records, but the medium of recorded music was sending a message. Like all other mass media, the phonograph record would react to technical advances by changing. Videotapes, music videos, the compact disc, and laser disc all threaten to either replace or change the black vinyl LP.

THE RECORD INDUSTRY

Radio station programmers play those records that are selling best around the country. But records rarely become best-sellers until they are played on the radio. The more a song is played on radio stations, the more copies it will sell—and the more it sells, the more radio stations will play it more often. Thus a hit is born.

Billboard magazine is a weekly publication for the radio and record industry. Among their services is a weekly listing of the 100 best-selling albums. Their listing looks like this:

Billboard — TOP POP ALBUMS

Compiled from a national sample of retail store, one-stop and rack sales reports.

THIS WEEK	LAST WEEK	2 WKS. AGO	WKS. ON CHART	ARTIST — LABEL & NUMBER/DISTRIBUTING LABEL (SUG. LIST PRICE)*	TITLE
1	1	1	4	USA FOR AFRICA ▲² COLUMBIA USA 40043 — *3 weeks at No. One*	WE ARE THE WORLD
2	2	2	10	PHIL COLLINS ▲ ATLANTIC 81240 (9.98) (CD)	NO JACKET REQUIRED
3	3	3	47	BRUCE SPRINGSTEEN ▲³ COLUMBIA QC 38653 (CD)	BORN IN THE U.S.A.
4	4	4	18	SOUNDTRACK ▲ MCA 5553 (8.98)	BEVERLY HILLS COP
5	5	6	24	MADONNA ▲⁴ SIRE 25157-1/WARNER BROS. (8.98) (CD)	LIKE A VIRGIN
6	6	8	12	SADE PORTRAIT BFR 39581 EPIC (CD)	DIAMOND LIFE
7	9	10	5	TOM PETTY AND THE HEARTBREAKERS MCA 5486 (8.98)	SOUTHERN ACCENTS
8	7	5	16	JOHN FOGERTY ▲ WARNER BROS. 1-25203 (8.98) (CD)	CENTERFIELD
9	10	9	27	WHAM ▲ COLUMBIA FC 39595 (CD)	MAKE IT BIG
10	8	7	48	TINA TURNER ▲³ CAPITOL ST-12330 (8.98) (CD)	PRIVATE DANCER
11	15	15	25	BRYAN ADAMS ▲ A&M SP5013 (8.98) (CD)	RECKLESS
12	12	12	13	COMMODORES MOTOWN 6124ML (8.98)	NIGHTSHIFT
13	17	26	6	THE POWER STATION CAPITOL SJ-12380 (8.98)	THE POWER STATION
14	NEW			PRINCE & THE REVOLUTION PAISLEY PARK 1-25286/WARNER BROS. (9.98) (CD)	AROUND THE WORLD IN A DAY
15	11	14	11	SOUNDTRACK GEFFEN GHS-24063/WARNER BROS. (9.98) (CD)	VISION QUEST
16	13	13	25	REO SPEEDWAGON EPIC QE39593 (CD)	WHEELS ARE TURNING
17	18	25	7	TEARS FOR FEARS MERCURY 824 300-1M1/POLYGRAM (8.98)	SONGS FROM THE BIG CHAIR
18	20	18	12	DAVID LEE ROTH ● WARNER BROS. 1-25222 (5.99)	CRAZY FROM THE HEAT
19	14	11	19	FOREIGNER ▲ ATLANTIC 81999 (9.98) (CD)	AGENT PROVOCATEUR
20	19	20	77	THE POINTER SISTERS ▲² PLANET BEL1-5410/RCA (9.98) (CD)	BREAK OUT
21	21	23	10	SOUNDTRACK A&M SP-5045 (8.98)	THE BREAKFAST CLUB
22	16	16	22	DON HENLEY ▲ GEFFEN GHS 24026/WARNER BROS. (8.98) (CD)	BUILDING THE PERFECT BEAST
23	23	28	8	DEBARGE GORDY 6123/MOTOWN (8.98) (CD)	RHYTHM OF THE NIGHT
24	25	21	11	THE FIRM ● ATLANTIC 81239 (8.98) (CD)	THE FIRM
25	26	27	6	LUTHER VANDROSS EPIC 39882	THE NIGHT I FELL IN LOVE
	22	19	50	CHICAGO ▲³ FULL MOON/WARNER BROS. 1-25060/WARNER BROS. (8.98)	17
	41	130	3	BILLY OCEAN ▲ JIVE JL 8-8213/ARISTA (8.98) (CD)	SUDDENLY
	33	33	12	RICK SPRINGFIELD RCA AJL1-5370 (9.98)	TAO
	27	30	29	ANIMOTION MERCURY 822580-1/POLYGRAM (8.98) (CD)	ANIMOTION
	29	22	31	DARYL HALL & JOHN OATES ▲² RCA AFL1-5309 (9.98) (CD)	BIG BAM BOOM
	32	22		NEW EDITION ▲ MCA 5515 (8.98)	NEW EDITION
	17	9		KOOL & THE GANG ● DE-LITE 822943-1/POLYGRAM (8.98) (CD)	EMERGENCY
	42	4		MICK JAGGER COLUMBIA 39940	SHE'S THE BOSS
	24	27		HOWARD JONES ELEKTRA 60390 (8.98)	DREAM INTO ACTION
	29	33		JULIAN LENNON ▲ ATLANTIC 80184-1 (8.98) (CD)	VALOTTE
	35	6		DIANA ROSS RCA AFL1-5009 (8.98) (CD)	SWEPT AWAY
	37	11		ERIC CLAPTON WARNER BROS./DUCK 1-25166/WARNER BROS. (8.98) (CD)	BEHIND THE SUN
	44	33		GEORGE THOROGOOD EMI-AMERICA ST-17145 (8.98)	MAVERICK
		19		SURVIVOR ● SCOTTI BROS. FZ 39578/EPIC (CD)	VITAL SIGNS
		28		AUTOGRAPH ● RCA AFL1-5423 (8.98)	SIGN IN PLEASE
		79		KENNY LOGGINS COLUMBIA FC 39174	VOX HUMANA
				LIONEL RICHIE ▲⁸ MOTOWN 6059 ML (8.98) (CD)	CAN'T SLOW DOWN
				GLENN FREY MCA 5501 (8.98)	
				THE MARY JANE GIRLS GORDY 6092GL/MOTOWN	
				MAZE FEATURING...	

THIS WEEK	LAST WEEK	2 WKS. AGO	WKS. ON CHART	ARTIST — LABEL & NUMBER/DISTRIBUTING LABEL (SUG. LIST PRICE)*	TITLE
56	71	109	4	'TIL TUESDAY EPIC BFE 39458	VOI...
57	53	50	8	SANTANA COLUMBIA FC 39527	BEYOND APP...
58	59	65	7	SOUNDTRACK MOTOWN 6128 ML (8.98)	KING
59	60	60	12	RUN-D.M.C. PROFILE PRO1205 (8.98)	BERRY GORDY'S THE LAS...
60	56	54	22	LOS LOBOS WARNER BROS. SLASH 25177-1/WARNER BROS (8.98)	KING
61	65	79	15	KLYMAXX CONSTELLATION MCA 5529 MCA (8.98)	HOW WILL THE WOLF...
62	54	46	42	THE TIME ▲ WARNER BROS. 25109-1 (8.98)	MEETING IN THE LADIES...
63	58	53	10	THE ALAN PARSONS PROJECT ARISTA AL8-8263 (8.98) (CD)	ICE CREAM C...
64	67	69	8	GO WEST CHRYSALIS FV 41495 (8.98) (CD)	VULTURE CUL...
65	51	51	8	GREG KIHN EMI-AMERICA SJ-17152 (8.98)	GO W...
66	79	91	7	WHITNEY HOUSTON ARISTA AL8-8212 (8.98)	CITIZEN K...
67	70	72	7	WHODINI ● JIVE JL-8251 ARISTA (8.98)	WHITNEY HOUST...
68	68	70	91	BILLY JOEL ▲⁴ COLUMBIA QC 38837 (CD)	ESCA...
69	64	55	23	GIUFFRIA CAMEL/MCA 5524/MCA (8.98)	AN INNOCENT MA...
70	63	62	27	ASHFORD & SIMPSON ● CAPITOL ST-12366 (8.98)	GIUFFRIA
71	92	100	4	GRAHAM PARKER & THE SHOT ELEKTRA 60388 (8.98)	SOLID
72	73	67	84	HUEY LEWIS AND THE NEWS ▲⁵ CHRYSALIS FV 41412 (CD)	STEADY NERVES
73	76	63	8	PAUL HARDCASTLE PROFILE PRO 1206 (8.98)	SPORTS
74	74	80	14	LOUDNESS ATCO 90246 (8.98)	RAIN FOREST
75	84	88	7	FIONA ATLANTIC 81242 (8.98)	THUNDER ON THE EAST
76	82	87	89	MADONNA ▲² SIRE 1-23867/WARNER BROS. (8.98) (CD)	FIONA
77	77	86	6	ANDREW LLOYD WEBBER ANGEL 38218/CAPITOL (11.98) (CD)	MADONNA
78	104	113	31	DOKKEN ELEKTRA 60376 (8.98)	REQUIEM
79	106	123	3	LIMAHL EMI-AMERICA ST-17142 (8.98)	TOOTH & NAIL
80	72	56	25	SOUNDTRACK FANTASY WAM-1791 (2LPS) (19.98)	DON'T SUPPOSE
81	83	99	4	RAVEN ATLANTIC 81241 (8.98)	AMADEUS
82	69	66	29	GENERAL PUBLIC I.R.S. SP-70046/A&M (8.98) (CD)	DON'T SUPPOSE
83	78	71	58	THE CARS ▲² ELEKTRA 60296 (8.98) (CD)	AMADEUS
84	88	68	10	VAN MORRISON MERCURY 822 895-1/POLYGRAM (8.98) (CD)	STAY HARD
85	85	75	27	PHILIP BAILEY ● COLUMBIA BFC 39542	ALL THE RAGE
86	62	52	30	SHEENA EASTON ▲ EMI-AMERICA SJ-17132 (8.98) (CD)	HEARTBEAT CITY
87	75	76	12	RAY CHARLES COLUMBIA 39415	A SENSE OF WONDER
88	81	83	10	WILTON FELDER MCA 5510 (8.98)	CHINESE WALL
89	66	64	24	DEEP PURPLE ▲ MERCURY 824003-1/POLYGRAM (8.98) (CD)	A PRIVATE HEAVEN
90	91	93	7	JOAN ARMATRADING A&M SP-5040 (8.98) (CD)	FRIENDSHIP
91	93	95	8	THE BLASTERS WARNER BROS./SLASH 25093/WARNER BROS. (8.98) (CD)	SECRETS
92	80	59		BRONSKI BEAT MCA 5538 (8.98)	PERFECT STRANGERS
93	NEW			RICK JAMES GORDY 6135GL/MOTOWN (8.98)	SECRET SECRETS
94	96	98	7	ACCEPT PORTRAIT BFR 39974/EPIC	HARD LINE
95	95	101	31	KURTIS BLOW...	THE AGE OF CONSENT
96	98			KURTIS BLOW	

MEDIALAB

The Record Industry

1. Obtain a current issue of *Billboard* (from a large newsstand or by ordering one copy from *Billboard,* One Astor Plaza, 1515 Broadway, NY, 10036, $3.50) and determine if any of the recording artists on the chart on the previous page are still listed. Why do the most popular records change so fast? The big hits of five years ago are hardly heard at all today—why not?

2. Using the most current *Billboard* list you have, go through your own record collections and check off the records you own. Would it be fair to say that if the class as a whole owns quite a few of those on the list, then its taste in music is "typical" and conforms to that of teens across the country?

3. Have each person in class go through his or her own record collection and write down the name of the record company that made the record (for example—Warner Brothers, Motown, Bell, etc.). Note how many records are owned by students and how many are from the most often listed companies. The ten largest companies account for over 75 percent of all records sold. The largest record companies are Warner Communications, CBS, RCA, Capitol, MCA, Motown, Polygram, and London Records.

4. Does the pattern of class ownership of record albums resemble the national pattern? If not, what circumstances might explain the difference?

5. If you have a favorite record next year, it will very probably be one that has been selected and ap-

proved by the handful of people who make the final decisions at the five largest record companies. If you have a favorite television program next year, it will probably be one that has been selected and approved by the handful of people who make the final decisions at the three networks. Most of the money you will spend to go to the movies next year will go to a few of the largest film companies. Do you see any problems in this arrangement? Why does this concentration exist in the media industries? Does it exist in other industries?

6. Rock 'n' roll gave birth to the record industry as BIG business. Do you see any current trend in music or entertainment that might serve to capture consumer dollars the way rock 'n' roll did in the 1950s?

7. Take a survey of buying habits in the class. How many people buy record albums and how often? How many buy blank cassettes and make recordings? How many buy music videos on tape or disc? How many spend money on video games or computers that might otherwise have gone for records?

8. Read the article on rock fans on the facing page. Then answer the following questions:

a. Why do recording stars attract such fanatical and huge followings?

b. What are the main attractions of "live" concerts?

c. What causes hysteria and mob behavior at a rock concert?

Rock fans turned away at Stadium; 1,000 riot

By Andy Knott
and Storer Rowley

AN ANGRY CROWD of about 1,000 rock fans went on a rampage Thursday night outside the Chicago Stadium, smashing car windshields, breaking windows, and injuring two policemen.

Police said the crowd, irate at being turned away from a sold-out rock concert of Earth, Wind, and Fire, tried to crash two gates at the stadium, 1800 W. Madison St., shortly after 8 p.m.

When about 40 policemen attempted to push the crowd back from gates facing Madison Street and Washington Boulevard, the mob began hurling rocks and bottles, according to Lt. Robert Reilly of the special operations group.

A HARRISON Area tactical officer, John D. Elliott, 34, was injured by flying glass when the windshield of his squad car was shattered by a brick. He was released after treatment at the University of Illinois Hospital. Police said two other squad cars were damaged.

A second policeman, not immediately identified, was bitten on the hand by a man he was arresting.

As a beefed-up force of about 150 officers drove the crowd away from the stadium, the fans broke up into gangs of 100 or more and stormed through the West Side neighborhood.

Reilly said they tried to overturn parked cars, and vandalized and looted between 100 and 150 autos in a stadium parking lot on Washington Boulevard.

POLICE SAID some of the angry fans sought temporary refuge from police in the Henry Horner public housing project on Washington Boulevard and then reemerged to attack police.

"They came out in waves, attacked, and then went back in. They came back out with bottles and bricks numerous times," said Patrolman Kenneth Fligelman of the special operations group.

Capt. William Moyer, Wood Street District watch commander, said 27 persons were arrested and would probably be charged with disorderly conduct as a result of the disturbance.

d. Many auditoriums and arenas in large cities forbid rock acts because of the problems with crowd control and damage to the building. Why do rock concert crowds have such a bad reputation?

e. What values do popular music "heroes" embody and preach by their songs and lifestyles?

f. Have you personally had any particularly good or unpleasant experiences at live concerts?

Rock, Riches and the Record Industry

In the 1960s and earlier, the dream of many teenagers was to become either a big time ball player or a movie star. In the 1980s a new dream began to occur more often. Every neighborhood has at least one group of a few high school students who play music together and call themselves a ''group'' or a band. The dream of many of these groups is to land a record contract, to become famous and tour the world living as only multimillionaire rock stars can.

No doubt some of the neighborhood groups who now play at local dances for $50 will become tomorrow's superstars. But their dreams of success in the future should be tempered with knowledge of how the record industry operates and what it takes to survive. In the following article, Allan Parachini gives a behind-the-scenes look at the world of the struggling musician versus the harsh demands of the record industry. This article was written a few years ago, but the system it describes still works today.

Rock & Riches

by Allan Parachini

Those kids are all making a bundle, right?

The houselights dim; the clamor of the crowd falls to a low buzz—low enough that the anticipatory coughing can be heard amid the hum of the PA system. In a moment the show will begin. It makes no difference what band is about to play, and it doesn't matter where. What is about to be unleashed, like a genie out of a bottle, is an IMAGE—magical, mysterious, and glamorous—one of many raised up by that energetic cultural force known as Rock, swathed in clouds of sumptuous glory, lauded in hymns of hyperbolic praise, and flattered by the proliferation of those smaller-scale imitations known as Lifestyle. This pantheon of heros and heroines has no parallel in contemporary culture, and we must go back to the early days of the silver screen—of Valentino, Pickford, and Garbo—to find anything like it. What it is is *myth,* a highly selective metaphor about life, of which both performers and their audiences, romanticized and romanticizing, are at once creators and consumers.

But myths are like Chinese boxes, one nestling inside the other on into infinity. The myth immediately inside the myth of the Rock Star is that of Untold Riches, and there is just enough truth (though not much) to it to make it an effective magnet, drawing young people to New York, Los Angeles, Nashville, or wherever else music is made and recorded to declare themselves in on a piece of the action, a slice of the fabulous take.

They arrive in Los Angeles, for instance, by battered car or bus, check into the YMCA, and hit the street. They walk up to Yucca Street, or Vine near Hollywood Boulevard, look in the Yellow Pages under "Records," and start feeding change into a payphone. Then they wait, lounging on the sidewalk outside a liquor store, having given the payphone as "a number where I can be reached," for the return call that never comes. They have a common desire—a career in the music business—and a host of very uncommon, often highly original, misconceptions about just what that business is. They are, in short, as much prisoners or victims of their myth as any Forty-niner ever was, feeding their hopes on the good news of occasional rich strikes and ignoring the multitudinous evidence of failure all around them.

The J. Geils Band, they will tell you, slaved away, first as two separate groups and then together under the Geils name, for five years in Boston barrooms before managing to land a record contract; they now average $10,000 to $15,000 a night. Black Oak Arkansas played insignificant dates throughout the South for four years waiting for what they finally got—a luscious contract with Atlantic Records. Dr. John was an obscure New Orleans studio musician for ten years before a chance hit single miraculously transformed his career in 1973. Rod Stewart, who once slept on a Spanish beach because he couldn't afford a hotel room, who used to play professional soccer to support his music habit, earns $1,000,000 annually [in 1974]. At the top, the money piles up

like winter snow in Donner Pass, and the bulldog tenacity that keeps so many musicians struggling up the lower slopes is fueled by the expectation that they too will eventually, if only they hang on, get to frolic in it. What are their chances?

Record companies sell one and one-half *billion* seven- and 12-inch discs in the United States each year. There are about 200 releases certified "gold" (meaning they sold 500,000 copies for an album, 1,000,000 copies for a single). Such figures translate very readily into Big Money, of course, and the myth has it that the musician is first in line to collect. And myth it is, for there are very few performers indeed in the most favored position.

The performer derives revenue primarily from two sources: live performances and record royalties. He may also earn something from song-publishing royalties (if he writes his own material), since there will then be royalty income from others who perform his songs and from radio stations that play them on the air as well. But before the musician realizes any income whatsoever, he must normally commit a percentage of all his earnings "up front" to a manager, unless he is clever enough to handle his own business affairs—including negotiating complicated contracts with record companies and booking agents; insuring that the provisions of those contracts are fulfilled; securing the most favorable possible terms for such seemingly incidental arrangements as production, promotion, and marketing of records, travel provisions for performance tours, and even the reservation of recording-studio time. . . .

For most musicians, a professional personal manager is an absolute necessity. Managers normally retain between 10 and 15 percent of the musician's entire gross income and can in some cases get as much as 20 or even 50 percent. Accountants (more and more indispensable the higher the sales figures get) are another accoutrement, and they get $200 to $500 a month. Such people are necessary not only to help the performer retain a reasonable part of his initial gross, but also to interpret the complex financial systems that appear to be peculiar to record companies; they are needed to make certain the musician does not, plainly and simply, get ripped off. . . .

Managers are not a race of white knights, of course. Their ranks are heavily populated by the shady and by the inept, either of whom can leave a client musician, in the manner of one of those bilked innocents in an old prize-fight movie, with no return whatever for his efforts, gold record sales or no. Selection of a good (honest, capable) manager is therefore one of the music business' biggest risks.

But to return to the question of income. Record royalties, unlike the fees paid for live performances, are established contractually between record companies and musicians for periods of between one and five years. Gross royalties are computed on a base of 90 percent of the wholesale . . . price of each record actually sold. Retail discount prices do not bear on royalties. The performer gets between 5 and 18 percent of 90 percent of retail, say (depending on the terms of his contract), and though there are several ways to compute the amount, they generally work out to about [$.50-$1.00] per album. The record producer gets a 2 or 3 percent royalty, which may in some cases be deducted from the musician's share, and the a-&-r (for "artists and repertoire") man who signed the artist to a record contract in the first place frequently gets 2 or 3 percent, normally from the record company's gross.

Under the royalty system, the *potential* for income from a record that sells well is actually not bad (more than $200,000 for a gold album, for example), and if a musician has written his own songs, he receives an additional gross of 1½ cents per song, per record, in song-publishing royalties. Normally, the manager has unobtrusively procured for himself some of the publishing proceeds; if he is honest, he has also done as much for his client. Otherwise, the naive musician may likely find that he has unknowingly signed away some or even all of the potential publishing income as part of a cash "advance" in an innocent-looking contract with a music-publishing firm or even his own record company.

Record companies have established what seems to be a

company. The consignment arrangement is a necessary one, since without it distributors and their clients would probably never gamble on a first release by an artist they had never heard of, or even on a great second release by someone who had bombed with his first. The problem with this system is that it can take at least several months, and at times as much as several years, to determine accurately the exact number of copies of a recording sold. Record companies manage this situation to their advantage, often withholding a portion of royalties against the possibility of such returns. . . .

Though it is true that there is a comfortable living to be made in music (from $50,000 to $100,000 a year) for a small number of anonymous, unglamorous studio musicians (usually older, always highly skilled), the performing musician whose name appears on records and concert billings is usually not nearly so well off. Groups in the middle area of prominence, like the Dirt Band and Poco, can, if management is competent, enjoy an upper-middle-class income. Poco's Schmit, for instance, like many other musicians, is buying his own modest home. The individual members of the Dirt Band have earned as much as $40,000 in one year—but as little as $3,000 in many others. They cannot, therefore, compute an "average" because their musical and financial fortunes have simply been too widely spread.

More frequently, the rule of the game is that of performers like Sherman Hayes. Hayes, who is thirty years old, has been playing professionally since

unique sort of company-store relationship with their artists, one that tends to cut handsomely into the income potential of royalties. First, the record companies normally try to charge back to the artist as much of the actual cost of recording and marketing a record as possible. Such costs can amount to $15,000 or $20,000 (for the most modestly produced album) to as much as $100,000 (for an over-produced spectacular). They include studio time, union pay for extra musicians, and other expenses too numerous and too unimaginable to mention—even the cost of the recording tape is levied against royalties. The record companies also charge their artists for some of the expenses of promoting and publicizing the resulting recording, including, for example, press parties and the cost (from $750 to $1,500 per month) of retaining a private publicist. A modest

tour may also be underwritten by the record company—and charged against the royalty gross; even a short introductory series of engagements in small clubs can run to as much as $50,000.

What results is in many cases an arrangement that would be bitterly familiar to any old-time Appalachian coal miner. Some recording acts owe so much of their soul to the company store that they never overcome their indebtedness; they can only watch helplessly as the royalties of their successful later records are eaten up in mid-career by early advances. Then too, determining the number of copies of a record actually sold is a task of no little difficulty. Records are distributed on consignment, meaning that unsold goods may be returned—for full credit—by individual record stores to small distributors, by small distributors to large, and large distributors to the original record

1964. He comes from a family of musicians, so he was prepared for the lean times, especially those preceding the release last fall of his first Capitol album. Sherman is married, with a three-and-a-half year old son. He owns a 1958 Chevrolet panel truck and rents a small house in Hollywood. It costs him between $600 and $800 a month to live—probably more now. He is $8,000 in debt from earlier group efforts, but Hayes, his booking agent, and his record company have faith.

He went on the road for three months last winter, playing club dates for between $150 and $500 a week. His first album, as first albums will, did not sell spectacularly. Anyway, Capitol is figuring the recording costs and their sponsorship of the tour against royalties. Hayes paid two sidemen $175 a week each on the road. He crammed his equipment (the act is acoustic and requires only one amplifier) into two trunks. There was no money for a roadie [road manager], so Hayes and his sidemen horsed the trunks all along the route. "I'm losing my___on this tour," he commented over coffee in New York one afternoon. "I don't see how anyone can be in music and not be thinking about the fact that it is a *business,*" Hayes said. "I'm just happy to be still on the label!" For people like Sherman Hayes, the lure of money is still rather farfetched, but the music is there, and for now it has to be a good part of the reward.

Musicians are, in general, people of fragile egos and are often afflicted with a profound naivete. Those who can learn to adapt to the *business* of music survive—sometimes—and a few, very few, can move beyond that to the Big Money. But, for the most part, what the uninitiated see when they look up from the orchestra or down from the balcony is an illusion. Those are not dollar signs, but just the beam of a Super Trouper spotlight reflecting off a guitar purchased through an advance against royalties. ∎

Croesus

A group's first couple of years at the threshold of the Big Time are the most critical simply because they are most often fatal. The figures below represent an attempt to estimate, by the most liberal and optimistic of standards, what a "new" group might earn that first or second year out. It should be noted, however, that this optimistic reckoning, which is based on a realistic assessment of potential, does not necessarily bear any relation to the experiences of an actual group—averages seldom do. It should be noted too that the hypothetical group Croesus, for whom these figures were run up, would be—if it existed—a lot better off than some real groups.

• Income
One album, selling 75,000 copies; royalties established at a rate to yield 42 cents per copy **$31,500**
One tour of forty-five engagements at an average fee of $1,000 per performance... **$45,000**

Total **$76,500**

• Outgo
Advance on royalties from record company at signing of contracts (spent to purchase amplifying equipment, pay union dues, settle old debts, etc.) **$5,000**
Cost of recording first album.......**19,000**
Manager's 15 percent of record royalties...**4,725**
Manager's 15 percent of booking proceeds **6,750**
Road expenses (15 percent of gross)..**11,250**
Booking agent's share of live-performance revenues at 20 percent...**9,000**
Publicity agent for six months.......**6,000**
Additional equipment expenses, normal wear and tear **5,000**

Total **$66,725**
Net income **$9,775**

Croesus is a four-member band, sharing equally in all income. The net result for each member, under this very optimistic accounting.....................................**$2,443.25**

MEDIALAB

Rock and Reality

1. What media help to spread the image of the rock star as glamorous and rich, with a wild lifestyle? Why aren't the thousands of others who make records written about as much?

2. Why is the image of the rock group presented in the mass media so glamorized and missing so much of the truth?

3. What do you think is the motivation that drives popular musicians most—the desire to make good music or the desire to make big money?

4. Make a class presentation on the realities of the record industry. The presentation can be based on library research, or based on some real-life experience.

5. Do people in other media (television, film, writing, art, etc.) need managers?

6. After reading the article, draw up a class list of "qualities needed to become a rock star." What qualities on this list are different from those needed to become a successful business leader?

7. Are any of the performers mentioned in "Rock & Riches" still popular today? What does this tell you about a career as a performer?

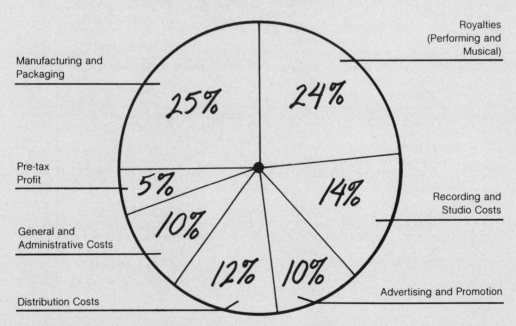

WHERE YOUR RECORD DOLLAR GOES
(Average industry figures)

- Manufacturing and Packaging — 25%
- Royalties (Performing and Musical) — 24%
- Pre-tax Profit — 5%
- Recording and Studio Costs — 14%
- General and Administrative Costs — 10%
- Distribution Costs — 12%
- Advertising and Promotion — 10%

Chapter 10
MEDIA CONTROL

The Government and Freedom of the Press

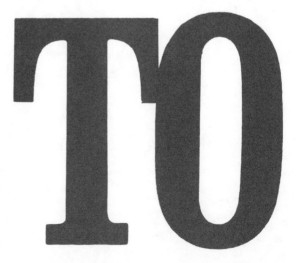

In one sentence of the Bill of Rights, you will find the most significant statement about government and the media. The First Amendment to the U.S. Constitution says: ''Congress shall make no law . . . abridging the freedom of speech, or of the press; or the right of the people peaceably to assemble. . . .''

The First Amendment does *not* say that anyone can say anything. It says simply that Congress shall make no *law* that prevents (abridges) a person's freedom to speak. One reason for the First Amendment's existence is that a democracy needs an informed electorate who can vote and make decisions. Freedom of speech and freedom of the press exist not only for the speaker or the owner of the press but also for the audience. In other words, part of freedom of speech is the right of the people to have access to a variety of viewpoints and opinions.

Freedom of speech, like any freedom, is not absolute. No society has ever existed that did not propose some kind of restrictions on the press, on free speech, and on the right of the public to have information. If a newspaper owner writes and publishes a scathing attack on someone, calling him or her ''a crook without morals and a danger to our society,'' that person could take legal action against the publisher. An attack on another person in print (or pictures or speech) that damages his or her character or reputation and is without truth is called *libel*. A person so attacked can sue the source of the libel for damages.

TO

Freedom of speech and the press exists to promote a free exchange of information and opinions. According to Thomas Jefferson, one of the framers of the Constitution, the public interest could be best served by a society in which there were numerous newspapers free to express themselves without fear of government censorship. The citizens would have to make up their own minds and would be able to do so because they were able to consider the various viewpoints on important public issues. Citizens could also use these newspapers and pamphlets to make known their own views.

But in 1787 Thomas Jefferson and the others at the Constitutional Convention could not foresee the invention of electronic media and mass broadcasting. They could not see into the future and realize that by today major cities would have a free press controlled financially by only a handful of individuals. They could not foresee that printing a newspaper would become a multimillion-dollar industry or that there would be a device such as television that gives citizens very little opportunity to "talk back."

Newspaper Freedom

Freedom of the press is a long-established tradition for newspapers in the United States and remains today a carefully guarded right. In recent years one of the "new" questions raised concerning newspaper freedom is the right of reporters to conceal their sources of information. In several cases in the late 1960s and early 1970s, reporters went to jail rather than reveal who their sources were. The reporters contended that if they were forced to reveal their sources, they would be hampered in their ability to report the news in the future. People who might talk to reporters if they could remain unknown would probably keep quiet if courts could force reporters to tell who they were. Such a law would hamper the flow of news to the people and would, in effect, be a restriction on the public's right to know. On the other hand, such a privilege might place the reporter above the law and interfere with the judicial process. Some groups advocate a "shield law" that would protect reporters from court orders to reveal their sources, and such laws do exist in some places.

A newer issue in the question of newspaper freedom concerns school papers. Students at some colleges and high schools claimed they were being denied the right to freedom of speech and a free press. School officials argued that the school newspaper was an extension of the school and could be controlled by administrators just as could course selection, rules of discipline, and other school requirements.

The Supreme Court has made it clear that the Bill of Rights is not for adults only. In 1969 the Court clarified the First Amendment rights of students in the ruling in *Tinker* vs. *Des Moines Independent School District*. The case involved three Iowa high school students, aged 13 to 16, who wore black armbands to school to protest the war in Vietnam. They were asked by school authorities to remove the armbands but refused and were suspended from school.

SERVE

The Supreme Court sided with the students and observed that wearing an armband is "symbolic speech" and is thereby protected by the First Amendment. More importantly, the Court held that students are indeed "persons" under the Constitution and have fundamental rights that school authorities must respect. *The Harvard Law Review* summarized the deeper meaning of the court decision as "the process of education in a democracy must be democratic." Schools that censor, control, and otherwise restrict the student press are, in effect, teaching the values of a system of governing that is not democratic.

A series of court cases in the early 1970s expanded the concept of freedom of the press for school papers. The general direction of these opinions is that the school must prove that such freedom of expression will lead to substantial disorder in the school or to a violation of the rights of others. Courts have never upheld the absolute right of students to publish whatever they wish in a school paper, but neither have they upheld the right of the school administration to allow students to publish only what the administration considers acceptable.

Broadcasting Freedom

Electronic broadcasting is still in its infancy. Many people alive today remember the very first radios, and the early days of television are still part of the memories of most adults. Because of their newness, radio and television have no tradition of First Amendment rights. The subject of broadcasting freedom is still very complicated and controversial.

The complications exist because the airwaves, unlike printing presses, are a limited resource. There are a limited number of television channels in each city (although the technology now exists to expand this number considerably), and even the number of radio frequencies is severely limited. In any city, the people who control the radio and TV stations could assemble easily in an average classroom. Since both TV and radio are basically one-way communication devices, great care must be taken to assure the "free exchange of information and opinions" that so concerned Thomas Jefferson. But how can the government act to ensure this free exchange without setting itself up as dictator of what people may hear and see? This is the problem that is still unsolved.

In many countries, the government owns and completely controls all radio and TV stations. In the United States, these outlets are privately owned; anyone with a few hundred thousand dollars can own a small radio station; TV stations cost more, often in the millions. If there were no central control over broadcasting, the result would be chaos. So many broadcasters would fight for the limited amount of airspace (a handful of TV channels, 97 AM frequencies, and about 120 FM channels) that stations would interfere with each other, and few people would get clear reception from any station. In the early days of radio this is precisely what did happen, as many amateurs and basement scientists set up their own radio stations. Finally, confusion grew

so great that in 1934 the Federal Communications Commission was established to regulate broadcasting.

According to U.S. law, the airwaves are "owned" by the people. They are a natural resource like air and water and cannot be bought or sold by individuals or corporations. The FCC grants licenses to qualified groups or individuals to use the airwaves for the purpose of "serving the public good." Licenses are granted for a limited number of years and are renewed if the station can prove it has indeed served the public interest. Radio and TV stations are required to ask the people in their broadcast areas for criticisms and suggestions for improvement of their programming.

The FCC controls broadcasting by deciding which of the many applicants for a radio frequency or a TV channel will be granted a license. Once the license is granted, the FCC does little to control program content.

The FCC does, however, require each radio and TV station to program time (how much time is not specified) in each of the following categories:

1. Opportunity for local expression (time for people in the local areas to express themselves on the air)
2. Development and use of local talent
3. Programs for children
4. Religious programs
5. Educational programs
6. Public affairs programs
7. Editorials (expressions of opinion) by the license holder

8. Political broadcasts
9. Agriculture programs
10. News
11. Weather and stock market reports
12. Sports
13. Programs for minority groups
14. Entertainment

Another way in which the FCC has some control over programming is through what is commonly called the "fairness doctrine." This "doctrine" (it is not a law) requires radio and TV stations to present issues of local importance and to air all the various viewpoints surrounding a controversial issue.

The "fairness doctrine" is designed to ensure that citizens are told the facts about issues of public controversy and to prevent radio and TV stations from presenting slanted news. Those opposed to the doctrine claim that it is impossible to present all viewpoints and that broadcasting stations should be allowed, as part of their own freedom of speech, to present what they consider the "correct" viewpoint. The opponents claim the doctrine allows the FCC to control programming, thus setting a dangerous precedent for government control of mass media.

Another, less controversial, government rule is called the "equal time" rule. This means that if one candidate in a political campaign receives or buys time, the station must offer other candidates the same amount of time.

Part of the idea of "fairness" includes protection against personal attack. If a station airs a discussion or a comment that attacks the honesty, integrity, or character of a person or group, the station *must*

PUBLIC

send to the person or group attacked, first, a notice of the attack along with an exact description of what was said and, second, an offer of time to respond to that attack without charge for broadcast time. For instance, if your local TV station airs a Sunday morning discussion about education in which a participant specifically attacks the students of your school as a "bunch of lazy, sloppy kids with nothing better to do than hang around street corners," then your principal or student government should be able to obtain free TV time to refute that attack.

The First Amendment to the Constitution states, "Congress shall make no law ... abridging the freedom of speech, or of the press." The Communications Act of 1934 forbids the FCC from censoring broadcasters. In spite of these general laws, broadcasting is controlled, and some of these controls appear to be censorship.

The FCC is not allowed to tell radio or TV stations which programs to carry or avoid. Hundreds of court cases have been handed down that support the "keep the government out" belief. But the FCC does control some areas of program content.

An FM station may not duplicate the programming of an AM station for more than 25 percent of its weekly air time if the town has more than 25,000 people. This rule exists to "force" owners to create a greater variety of programming.

The FCC has no clear "laws" about the broadcasting of obscenity or profanity, but the U.S. Criminal Code does. The code imposes a fine or imprisonment for material that is clearly "offensive to community standards."

The FCC does forbid "subliminal advertising." *Subliminal* means "below the level of consciousness." The most common subliminal technique is to flash one or two frames of film on a screen during a movie. The frame might say something like "Drink Fizzie." It would pass so fast that no one in the audience would be aware they had seen the message. Some psychologists believe that such a message still registers on the brain in spite of its "invisibility." Even though no evidence exists to show that so-called subliminal advertising does work, it is banned by the FCC.

The FCC also requires ads to be broadcast at the same level of sound as the surrounding program. Some TV stations have been known to turn up the volume for ads, especially those shown late at night. The practice is illegal and TV stations argue it is not done, yet many viewers report that ads are often louder than the shows.

An amendment to the 1934 Communications Act forbids radio or television advertising for cigarettes and small cigars.

Advertisers and broadcast stations themselves control the number of ads per hour and their content.

No laws exist to prevent the advertising of alcohol on television, yet broadcasters limit ads to beer and wine and do not advertise "hard" liquor such as whiskey.

GOVERNMENT CONTROL OF ADVERTISING

Advertising in the United States is not as strictly controlled by the government as it is in other countries. In some European countries the "Unfair Competition" law prohibits advertisers from making "water is wet" claims. Some laws also forbid ads that might lead to a wrong conclusion. Even "so what" claims like "margarine packed by hand" are forbidden under these laws, since packing margarine by hand gives it no extra advantage.

In Sweden the "truth-and-nothing-but-the-truth" Marketing Practices Act gives the government strict control to ensure that ads are scrupulously honest.

In the United States the federal agency charged with some degree of advertising regulation is the Federal Trade Commission (FTC). The FTC has a small staff and very little power but can take court action and order advertisers to "cease and desist" from what it considers deceptive advertising. The company simply agrees to "sin no more" and usually escapes with no other punishment. In recent years the FTC has become more strict with advertisers; it has levied fines and has even required a few advertisers to run corrective ads to make up for misleading claims made in their past advertising.

Other than broadcasting and advertising, the federal government exercises little control over the mass media. Newspaper, magazine, and book publishers are subject to U.S. laws, but there are few specific regulations or controls on what they can print.

CONTROL BY SOURCES

All mass media are controlled in some way by their sources. Newspapers can print only the news that is delivered to them or that their reporters uncover. Television programs and films are controlled by their producers and directors; magazine articles are subject to the complete control of editors, writers, and publishers. As media content passes through these hands, it is influenced by the normal human biases and perceptions.

Each medium has within it people who act as censors, although the word *censor* is rarely used. No magazine or book publisher has an official censor as an employee, yet all those who must pass judgment on the suitability of articles and photos (the "gate-keepers") act in a way as censors.

Motion picture production is subject to several levels of censorship. The scriptwriter, the director, and the producer of a film control its contents so as not to produce a film that too many people will find revolting or disgusting. Their consideration in censorship is not so much to protect the public morals as it is to maintain a good box office.

In the 1960s the motion picture industry found that parents were afraid to allow their children to go to movies because they had no way of knowing whether the film was suitable for youngsters. A voluntary rating system was established to rate films: G—acceptable to general audiences; PG—parental guidance suggested; PG-13—children under 13 should not attend; R—restricted to those over a certain age (varies locally but usually about 16-18) unless accompanied by a parent or adult; and X—for adults only. Many theaters interpret these ratings very strictly and will demand proof of age for admission to R- or X-rated films. The rating system is voluntary and does not, in itself, carry the force of law.

Some cities and counties have local censor boards which screen all films about to play in the city or county. They have the power to demand that certain scenes be eliminated or that a film be banned altogether. The power of these censor boards has decreased in recent years, especially in large cities.

Each of the three major television networks has a censor who watches commercials and programs for scenes or words that might offend viewers. Feature films are often "edited for television" to remove some of the violence, sex, or language in the original version. Local television stations also have the right to refuse network programs, although they rarely do.

The reason for television's self-censorship is that the medium is public, open to anyone who turns on a TV set, including young children. Motion pictures, books, and magazines are usually less restrictive since to gain access to them one has to pay admission or purchase a copy.

Radio stations often refuse to play songs the station director feels have double meanings, encourage drug use, are unpatriotic, or are in some way in bad taste. During listener call-in shows, many radio stations use a seven-second delay system. With such a system, callers actually speak to a tape recorder which plays their calls over the air several seconds later. This delay is introduced so the program director can "bleep" out offensive words or cut off possible libelous remarks.

ECONOMIC CONTROL

Magazines, newspapers, television, radio stations, and book publishers—all, with a few rare exceptions—share one common goal: to make money. This fact controls to some extent the content of what these media produce.

With the exception of book publishing, all these media receive most of their income from advertising. The question thus arises: does advertising in any way influence the content of mass media?

One illustration of economic influence is the true case of the Car-Puter Company's attempt to buy ads in major newspapers and magazines. Car-Puter is a company that supplies customers with a computer read-out of dealer costs on any new car they may want to buy, including options. The company also supplies the name of a local automobile dealer who, through a special arrangement will sell the customer the car for about $150 above dealer cost. The company charges the consumer $5 for this service, which is legitimate and helpful to consumers. However, when Car-Puter attempted to run a small ad, they were refused by most newspapers as well as by some magazines.

The ads were refused without a detailed explanation. The newspapers claimed they had a right to turn down any advertising—and they do. But the reason for the refusal most certainly is related to the fact that automotive ads are an important source of income for newspapers and magazines. Car-Puter Company would not be approved of by other auto advertisers.

As another example, sponsors of television programs are not likely to buy time for programs that attack business. Sponsors carefully monitor network TV shows. A group called "Stop Immorality on Television" asked major TV sponsors about their "moral stance" on the programs they sponsored. Gilette replied that "we try to see that our advertising runs in programs that are suitable for general family viewing." Eastman Kodak commented that they preview all scripts before the airing of a program: "If we find a script is offensive, we will withdraw our commercials from the program."

Although advertisers have no formal censorship power, they can exert great influence on the kinds of programs that networks will offer the viewers. A TV network would think twice before showing a documentary exposing the faults of the over-the-counter-drug industry, because so much of its advertising revenue comes from painkillers and headache remedies.

A question often asked at networks is "Will the show gain sponsors?" The importance of this question can easily limit consideration of another question: "What is in the best interests of the public?"

Newspapers and magazines vary widely in the amount of control they allow advertisers to exert. Some keep "news" and ads completely separate and will report the problems and failings of local food chains or auto dealers even though these provide the paper with thousands of dollars yearly in advertising revenue. Some newspapers, however, still have a policy of not "biting the hand that feeds them." If the health department closes or issues a warning to a local food store or restaurant, such papers will ignore the story for fear of "hurting" the advertiser's reputation. A story about a shady car dealer or home builder might go unreported if that company is a large advertiser in the newspaper.

Such control is less frequent now than it used to be, but it still exists, especially among smaller newspapers struggling to stay in business.

Record companies put pressure on radio stations to play their records. Every time a radio station plays a record, the "exposure" is as good as or better than an ad for the record. The more radio stations play any given song or record, the more it sells. Record companies can give away free records but are not supposed to give money to stations as an inducement to play the records. There have been many instances, though, of record companies slipping a little extra money ("payola") to disc jockeys to gain air time for a song. As with newspapers, this practice is less common among the largest stations and offers a greater temptation to small stations.

Control by the

Playing the ratings game is deadly

The most common kind of control over mass media is the one most often overlooked—control by the audience. If few people watch a TV show, it dies. If only a few hundred people subscribe to a city newspaper, it stops publishing. If a film is a box office flop, similar films will be less likely to receive backing.

A complicating factor in audience control or censorship of the mass media is the fact that no two people in the same mass audience experience a program or news story in exactly the same way. Each member of the audience brings along prejudices, biases, and a lifetime of experiences that shape his or her feelings and reactions to the content presented in the media.

An interesting experiment suggests exactly how important this factor is in control-by-the-audience. A special slide viewer was constructed with one hole for each eye; a person looked into it as into a pair of binoculars. In the slide viewer were two pictures, one for each eye. One slide pictured a baseball player and the other a bullfighter. First, a group of American teachers looked into the viewer and were asked what they saw. Next a group of Mexican citizens looked and reported what they saw. The results? More Americans reported "seeing" the baseball player, while more Mexicans reported "seeing" the bullfighter. The experiment points that people "see" what they have been taught to see.

Every time we look at a picture, an inkblot, a cloudy sky, a painting, a film, or a newspaper, we see those things that are most comfortable to see. We see only those things that fit in with our view of the way the world should be and filter out those things that don't seem to fit. This process of selective seeing is called *perceptual filtering.*

Each time a newscast shows a police officer struggling with a young person, the viewing audience gives the event a variety of interpretations. Some see the event as yet another example of police brutality, while others see "young punks" getting what they deserve; some see law and order at work, while others see society falling apart.

No matter how much the government or advertisers attempt to control mass media, there is no way to ensure that the audience will agree with what is presented or even "see" the same thing as the people next door.

In addition to the process of perceptual filtering, the media consumer controls the content of the media by selecting which program to watch, which magazines to subscribe to, which books or records to buy, which newspapers to read, or which radio stations to listen to. Each decision to use a mass medium can be thought of as a sort of vote approving that medium's content.

The owners of any media outlet keep a constant record of the size and type of audience they attract. The number of units sold is the main measurement for magazines, books, newspapers, records, and films. Television and radio must rely on estimates of audience numbers called "ratings."

A number of companies offer rating services to television and radio. The largest and best known is the A. C. Nielsen company—so much so that ratings are sometimes called "Nielsens." The Nielsen ratings have been accused of reflecting only the habits of those who watch a lot of television. But the networks have found the system the best available, and so the Nielsen ratings are usually the ones that determine a program's future—or lack of it.

The ratings list shown here indicates the popularity of certain shows in the mid 1980s. The first number is the rating, and the second is the "share of the market." For "Dynasty," for example, the rating was 24.9. This means that 24.9 percent of all

serious business

households with a television had "Dynasty" turned on. The 37 is a share number and means that 37 percent of all households with a TV set turned on were tuned to "Dynasty." Available research shows that "Dynasty" draws about 40 million viewers per episode.

An average rating of at least 17 is needed to keep a show alive. It would represent about 10.2 million households, or 21 million people. In other words, even a network TV show with more "consumers" than any national magazine is still in danger of being cancelled for lack of interest.

A. C. Nielsen compiles its ratings by installing devices called "audimeters" in the households of 1,200 volunteers. For their services, the volunteers receive small gifts, 50 cents a week payment, and assistance in paying for TV repairs. Inside the audimeter is a slow-moving 16mm film that records which channels are turned on during the day (though it does not show whether anyone is actually watching). These 1,200 families mail each week's film to Nielsen headquarters near Chicago, where the films are processed and fed into a computer that compiles the ratings. In addition to the audimeters, about 2,200 TV diaries are kept by volunteers and also sent each week to Nielsen.

The ratings give the audience some control over the survival of programs but none in their creation.

Here are some samples of actual Nielsen rating/shares for a week in 1985.

NIELSEN NATIONAL INDEX
PROGRAM AVERAGE RANKING

WEEK 1 (SEP 23, 1984) THRU WEEK 35 (MAY 19, 1985)
ALL REGULAR PROGRAMS IN PERIOD

RANK	PROGRAM	WEEKS	NET	DAY	TIME	DUR	AVG RTG	AVG SHARE
1	DYNASTY	29	ABC	WED	9:00	60	24.9	37
2	DALLAS	30	CBS	FRI	8:30	90	24.7	39
3	BILL COSBY SHOW	34	NBC	THU	8:00	30	24.1	38
4	FAMILY TIES	33	NBC	THU	8:30	30	21.9	33
5	60 MINUTES	35	CBS	SUN	7:00	60	21.6	35
6	A TEAM	32	NBC	TUE	8:00	60	21.4	33
7	SIMON & SIMON	30	CBS	THU	9:00	60	21.1	32
8	KNOTS LANDING	28	CBS	THU	10:00	60	20.1	33
9	FALCON CREST	29	CBS	FRI	10:00	60	19.9	34
10	MURDER, SHE WROTE	28	CBS	SUN	8:00	60	19.7	30

MEDIALAB

Media Control

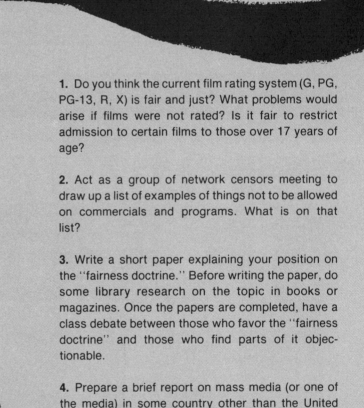

1. Do you think the current film rating system (G, PG, PG-13, R, X) is fair and just? What problems would arise if films were not rated? Is it fair to restrict admission to certain films to those over 17 years of age?

2. Act as a group of network censors meeting to draw up a list of examples of things not to be allowed on commercials and programs. What is on that list?

3. Write a short paper explaining your position on the "fairness doctrine." Before writing the paper, do some library research on the topic in books or magazines. Once the papers are completed, have a class debate between those who favor the "fairness doctrine" and those who find parts of it objectionable.

4. Prepare a brief report on mass media (or one of the media) in some country other than the United States. Compare the operation and control of the media in that country with the situation in the United States.

5. Set up small groups to go to the offices of local radio and television stations and ask to see the "public file" concerning license renewal. Report to the class on some of the file's more interesting contents.

MEDIALAB

6. The following are brief descriptions of several court cases concerned with media control. Discuss and debate each case and reach a decision of your own before looking at the court's decision at the end of the section. Each case is presented here with few details, but the basic facts come from real court cases.

a. *Scoville vs. Board of Education of Joliet Township High School*

Two students were expelled for distributing a "literary journal" on school grounds. The magazine contained an editorial critical of the school administration and urged students to disregard school rules. There is no direct evidence that the publication actually caused any disruption in the school process. The students wrote the magazine and sold 60 copies at a price of 15 cents each.

The lower court ruled that the language took the "form of immediate incitement to disregard legitimate administrative regulations necessary to the orderly maintenance of a public high school system." In other words, the magazine was a "clear and present danger" to the orderly operation of the school and so was not entitled to First Amendment protection. The students could reasonably be punished for their conduct.

The case was then taken to a court of appeals. Discuss the case and reach your own decision before looking up the appeals court decision.

MEDIALAB

b. *ACT vs. TIO*

The Television Information Office (TIO) is an organization that acts as a public relations arm for the television industry. It prepares TV spots, printed reports, and other services designed to enhance the image of television. One of its TV spots (made by TIO and offered free to TV stations to use as public service announcements) pointed out the benefits of TV programming for children. Many stations around the country used the spot.

Action for Children's Television (ACT), a group concerned with improving children's programming and often critical of the television industry, requested that the FCC, under the fairness doctrine, order stations that carried the TIO ads also to carry a counter-ad pointing out that children's television is "unimaginative, inartistic, commercial-ridden, and harmful to children." The FCC, rather than a court, made the ruling on this case. What do you think?

Decisions: In *Scoville* vs. *Joliet Board of Education,* the Court of Appeals found that the expulsion of the students was unjustified and constituted an invasion of their First and Fourteenth Amendment rights.

In *ACT* vs. *TIO,* the FCC denied the argument of Action for Children's Television and emphasized that the fairness doctrine required an overall balance on issues and that ACT had not proved the spots created an imbalance.

7. Why do you think liquor advertising is limited on television? Remember that a glass of beer or wine contains about the same amount of alcohol as a mixed drink. Could you propose a better approach to the control of advertising for alcoholic beverages?

8. Cigarette advertising is not permitted on television but can appear in newspapers and magazines. Would you favor cigarette advertising as (a) allowed anywhere to protect freedom of speech, or (b) forbidden everywhere since it is a drug and a social menace.

9. Here are typical comments from a network censor about an old NBC series called "High Chaparral": "Victims of homicide are to be shown with their eyes closed and not positioned grotesquely." "In the montage of the warring Indians being hunted down and shot, take care that this is not overdone so that it becomes a brutal thing; nor should we see Buck [one of the characters] grinning fiercely just before the killing. This would give him the aspect of a sadist." "As the kid is shot and he starts to fall, please avoid sensationalizing the fall as he goes tumbling down the rocks. It will be unacceptable to see the kid bouncing from rock to rock in his fall." "As Maria cradles the dying Ramon in her arms, avoid showing the knife protruding from Ramon's chest."

Do you think these observations are valid or do the observations tend to make the violence that does appear more unreal and therefore more harmful than if it were presented in a realistic way? Support your answer.

Chapter 11

MEDIA AND OUR IMAGE OF THE WORLD

STEREOTYPE

Each person has a mental picture of what the "world out there" is like. For centuries, this picture was shaped by personal experience and education. These two factors are still present in shaping mental pictures, but there is a third force that assumes an ever increasing importance. Today, the mass media play a major role in teaching people what the world is like.

By pushing aside the limitations of experience and schooling, mass media have created a nation of people who have opinions on just about every subject and mental pictures of places never visited, people never encountered, and events experienced only as tiny images on a television screen. News and entertainment media distribute so much information about the world that many educators claim schools are no longer the main source of learning for most people. Mass media have taken over the role of forming our mental image of the world.

Our mental "map" or picture of the world is in some areas quite detailed and well developed. But sometimes our picture of the world "out there" is only a rough sketch with few details. Human psychology seems to demand that the sketch be filled in with details. Once the outline is formed, we use what we are taught by our parents, schools, and mass media to fill in the details. Often what we are taught, though, is stereotype.

A stereotype is an oversimplified idea of something, based on limited experience. For example, for four years, between the ages of 6 and 10, Henry lived in a neighborhood where there was one French family on the block. This particular family was unable to keep a neat house or yard, and people in the neighborhood talked about those "sloppy Frenchies." From this limited experience, Henry generalized that people from France were generally sloppier and dirtier than Americans. Henry never went to France, never met many other French people, and did little reading. When he married and had children, he still made remarks about "sloppy Frenchies." Henry's children also grew up believing that people from France were dirty and sloppy.

The application to an entire group of the qualities of a limited sample of that group is a stereotype. In themselves, stereotypes are a convenient mental device. They help us deal with the vast amount of reality that can never be known in detail. The problem is that most stereotypes contain only a kernel of truth and so are dangerous if taken to be the whole truth.

Stereotypes give people a feeling of security, a feeling that something complex is understood. They provide the illusion that we know our way around in what otherwise would be unknown territory. When the stereotypes we hold (and everyone believes *some* stereotypes) are attacked or challenged, we view this as a personal attack and often actively defend our stereotypes.

Clearly, stereotypes are not limited to the prejudiced or bigoted, to racial categories, or to the unschooled. Many stereotypes are strengthened by the mass media, although at other times they are the same media that replace a commonly held stereotype with a fuller picture. Because of the power of mass media, some stereotypes are rather commonly accepted as the full truth.

Television, for example, often shows "cardboard characters"—people whose personalities are not developed in the plot. These cardboard characters—such as the jolly fat man, the dumb secretary, or the hard-boiled cop—are easily recognized by viewers and can be used for laughs or instant plot development. The constant repetition of such characters tends to condition viewers to expect fat people to be jolly and secretaries dumb or cops hard-boiled. People who belong to often-stereotyped groups find it difficult to overcome media-created expectations.

Even criminals are stereotyped by television and other media. A professor of communications at Queen's College in New York and seven assistants monitored one week of prime-time TV and found that

Jean Stapleton and Carrol O'Connor played the media-created stereotyped characters of Edith and Archie Bunker in the television series "All in the Family."

criminals on TV were 85 percent male, 78 percent between the ages of 20 and 50, and 90 percent white. The picture of the criminal presented by television is that of a white-collar, middle class person. On TV much crime is committed to cover up for other crimes. In reality, however, 35 percent of those arrested are under 20, and 30 percent are nonwhite.

On television, murder, assault, and armed robbery are the most common crimes. In reality, quiet burglaries, clever larcenies, unspectacular auto thefts, and drunkenness are the most common. Video detectives solved 90 percent of their cases. In reality, the figure is considerably lower. On TV only 7 percent of violence occurs between relatives. In reality this accounts for 25 to 30 percent of inter-personal violence.

Groups that are often stereotyped include the following:

Scandinavians	People over 65
Poles	Housewives
Women	Intellectuals
Texans	Construction workers
Italians	Professional athletes
French	Straight-A students
Blacks	"Jocks"
Mexicans	Wealthy persons
Artists	Librarians
"Freaks"	Radicals/Conservatives/
"Straights"	Liberals
People on welfare	Professors
Jews	Scientists
Teenagers	Overweight people

Sometimes the mass media do replace stereotypes with a fuller picture of a group of people. Stereotypes are easy and familiar, however, and the media will continue to use them as long as audiences accept them.

MEDIALAB

Media and Stereotypes

1. Are stereotypes always bad? Are they always partially wrong? What use do stereotypes have?

2. Why do stereotypes exist?

3. Find examples of some of the stereotyped qualities of as many of the groups on the list as you (as a class) can. Add to the list other stereotyped groups. A good way to fill in the details about a stereotyped group is to brainstorm each group, starting with the statement, "Most (*name of stereotyped group*) are presented as. . . ."

4. Find examples of stereotypes in any mass medium and bring them to class.

5. As a research project select one group you believe has been stereotyped. Describe the stereotype and bring evidence of its falseness. For example, you might believe that the stereotype of people on welfare being lazy loafers is unfair. As proof you could bring reliable statistics showing that only 1 percent of those on welfare are able-bodied men—most are disabled, or elderly, or women with dependent children.

6. Find someone in the class who can tell of a stereotype that he or she has recently learned is not true.

7. Find examples of "cardboard characters" on TV. Explain why you think they are not realistic.

8. How do cartoons use stereotypes for humorous effect?

9. Assume you are the "National Minister of Stereotypes" in a country where all mass media are government-controlled. You have access to whatever media you desire. Devise a media campaign to create a stereotype of a certain group you want to elevate to positions of power. For your campaign to be most effective, the citizens of your country should remain unaware of it, yet become completely convinced of the truth of the stereotype you are creating.

10. Find some group of which you are a member that is the target of occasional stereotyped comments. Refute those stereotypes.

11. Pick some group that is frequently stereotyped on TV (e.g., women, teenagers, fathers, criminals). Conduct a study similar to the one described in the chapter dealing with criminals on television. Watch as much prime-time TV as you can for a week or longer and note each time a member of the group appears in any way on a show or ad. Take notes on how the person is presented. Combine your notes and present your own report titled "How Television Stereotypes *(name of group)*." Your report should be specific.

12. The study of the television image of criminals mentioned in this chapter pointed out some unrealities. Do you think these could have an effect on people's attitudes towards crime or law enforcement?

RUMOR AND DISTORTION

Rumors are stories that grow as they go. Rumors fall somewhere between the extremes of gossip and news. Rumors and stereotypes are distant cousins. Both contain some truth combined with a large and often dangerous amount of nontruth. Both can lead people to irrational action, both are often accepted as truth, and both can be created, intensified, or lessened by the mass media.

Rumors often start out as truth. A psychologist once "planted" a rumor in the cafeteria of an Air Force base by asking, "Is it true they are building a tunnel big enough to move B-52's to town?" A half day later the planted question came back to him as a statement: "They are building a tunnel to move B-52's to town." Notice the differences: The original question came back as a statement, without the "Is-it-true?" at the beginning. Added to the statement was the "fact" that a tunnel was being built to move B-52's, whereas the original question merely referred to a tunnel "big enough" to move B-52's. The distortions introduced are typical of those that convert fact to rumor.

True stories are distorted in three main ways in becoming rumors—sharpening, leveling, and assimilation. *Sharpening* refers to the tendency for items in the original story to become more dramatic. A "weapon" becomes a "loaded gun." A "large octopus" becomes a "sea monster."

Leveling refers to the fact that as the story is repeated, details drop out rapidly at first and then level off to a simple, easily repeatable version.

Assimilation refers to the tendency for stories to be repeated in terms familiar to the person telling the story. A rumor that starts about an event in a European cafe might end up being told in the U.S. as happening in a drive-in restaurant.

Rumors usually serve some kind of emotional need. One researcher has coded rumors into three basic varieties: (a) pipe dreams, expressing wishful thinking; (b) bogie rumors, arising from fears and worries; and (c) wedge-driving, dividing groups and destroying loyalties.

Pipe-dream rumors seem the least frequent. A common example of a bogie rumor is the sighting of a flying saucer—a report often verified by numerous people. The wedge-driving rumor is particularly popular in politics. During the 1972 presidential campaign, a New Hampshire newspaper attacked Sen. Edmund Muskie for supposedly making an insulting remark about the French-Canadians in the state, calling them "Canucks." The only evidence the paper had was a letter from someone who said he had heard the remark. Though his letter was later discovered to be a fake planted by the opposition, the incident harmed Muskie's standing with French-Canadian voters in the primary election.

Writer Norman Mailer has coined the term *factoid* to describe rumors that have no existence except that they appear in print or in another medium. In spite of their lack of truth, people repeat them as if they were facts. *Pseudo-facts* might be another appropriate term.

A pseudo-fact can cause harm. In 1883, the Brooklyn Bridge had been open only six days when tragedy struck. Even though thousands of people had walked safely across the bridge, rumor had spread that it was unsafe and would collapse. Someone screamed while walking across the bridge, and panic followed as the cry spread, "The bridge is falling." Forty people were injured and 12 were trampled to death as a result of panic caused by rumor.

Mass media have the ability to cause a rumor to sweep the nation. In 1938 a famous radio broadcast of the drama *War of the Worlds* set off a nationwide rumor that invaders from outer space had landed in New Jersey, causing a small panic.

Since mass media can spread facts quickly, they usually tend to control rather than inflame rumors. For instance, during urban rioting, TV and radio have both provided "rumor control centers," reassuring viewers and listeners that disturbances were only in certain areas, that fires were under control, that the trouble was not spreading, and so on.

One exception to this tendency serves to illustrate the power of the media and people's belief in television. On the "Tonight" show, Johnny Carson said on national television, "You know what else is disappearing from the supermarket shelves? Toilet paper. There's an acute shortage of toilet paper in the United States."

By noon the next day supermarkets all over the country were faced with a stampede of people buying from 5 to 25 extra rolls. The kind of toilet paper that was in short supply was not the kind sold in stores, but government issue toilet paper bought only in large lots by bids. Carson had made the point clear that his comment was not a news report, but only a humorous speculation. But because of leveling, sharpening, and assimilation, within four days there was a real shortage of the better quality supermarket paper because people were hoarding.

Officials of the Scott Paper Company assured the public to "stay calm. There just isn't any shortage." By the middle of January supermarket shelves were full again, thus assuring shoppers there was no shortage. One TV star watched by millions can start a national spree of toilet-paper buying. One wonders in what other ways the remarks of widely watched TV personalities can influence what people do and think.

MEDIALAB

Rumor and Distortion

1. As a class experiment, conduct a study in the process of rumor creation. One person looks at a picture and describes it to another. The second person, who does *not* see the picture, repeats the description he has heard to a third person. The third person repeats the description to a fourth and so on, until a sixth person has received the verbal picture description. The first and last picture descriptions should be tape-recorded for study. Compare the first description with the final to see what differences there are. Are any of the differences explainable as leveling, sharpening, or assimilation? The best kind of picture to use is one from a newspaper or magazine that shows several people doing something.

2. What are some interesting rumors you've heard recently? Note: gossip is more personal (about someone in the school, for example) than rumor.

3. Find out if your local government has a "rumor control" center. If so, find out what it does and perhaps invite someone from the center to talk to the class.

4. If there were no mass media do you think there would be more rumors or fewer? Why? How do mass media serve in time of crisis or disaster to cause or prevent panic and rumors?

INFLUENCE ON LANGUAGE AND THOUGHT

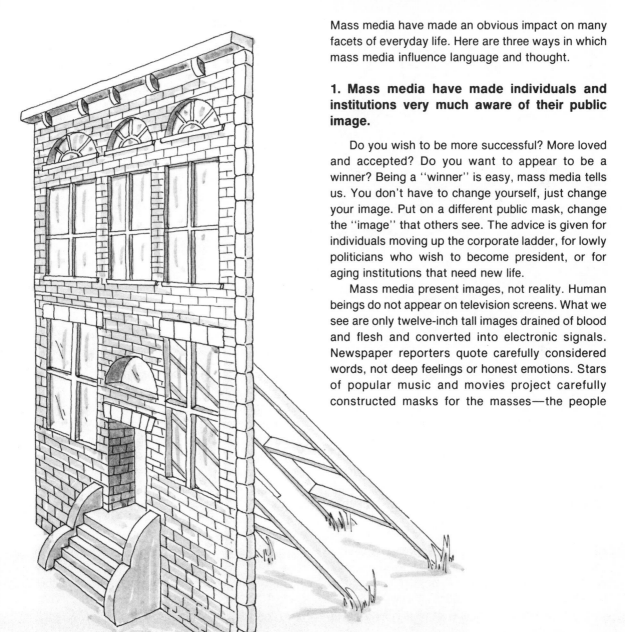

Mass media have made an obvious impact on many facets of everyday life. Here are three ways in which mass media influence language and thought.

1. Mass media have made individuals and institutions very much aware of their public image.

Do you wish to be more successful? More loved and accepted? Do you want to appear to be a winner? Being a "winner" is easy, mass media tells us. You don't have to change yourself, just change your image. Put on a different public mask, change the "image" that others see. The advice is given for individuals moving up the corporate ladder, for lowly politicians who wish to become president, or for aging institutions that need new life.

Mass media present images, not reality. Human beings do not appear on television screens. What we see are only twelve-inch tall images drained of blood and flesh and converted into electronic signals. Newspaper reporters quote carefully considered words, not deep feelings or honest emotions. Stars of popular music and movies project carefully constructed masks for the masses—the people

behind the masks are far less important. The image counts.

Politicians and other public figures, who survive on the basis of their images, often make statements carefully designed to offend no one. Politicians have always been known for their ability to appear to be all things to all people, but only since mass media have threatened to make every statement public knowledge have they truly mastered the art of public evasion.

Before press conferences, television news coverage and mass circulation newsweeklies, what a candidate for office might say to a crowd one day could easily be changed the next, and only the closest observers would notice. Today, however, mass media act as a reminder of what the politician said yesterday or even last year. Such a "public memory" can be embarrassing. Instead of keeping candidates "honest," media memory seems to keep them vague. The safest way to speak, many politicians believe, is to phrase statements so they can be interpreted in a variety of ways—all favorable to the listener. Too much of such intentional vagueness, however, can cause the public to see the image of a "spineless" or "wishy washy" candidate.

Politicians and spokespersons for corporations are not alone in their concern for how the public will interpret their words. Professional organizations in many fields encourage their members to choose words carefully so as to create a "favorable public image." Janitors have become maintenance engineers, garbage collectors are sanitation workers, and undertakers are funeral directors.

A professional organization concerned with the public image of dentists gave them the following list of words to help them speak their way to a better image:

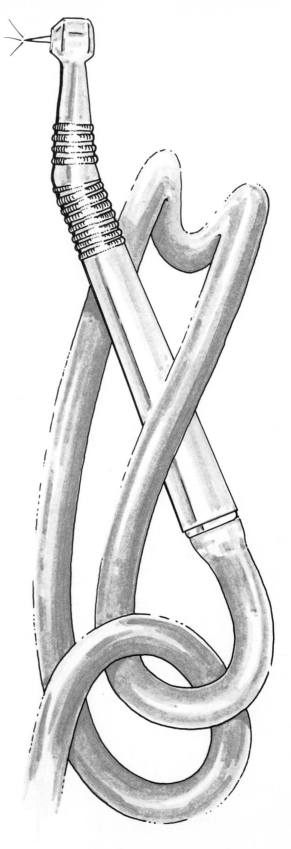

Do Say	Don't Say
Reception room	Waiting room
Treatment room	Operatory
Consultation room	Private
Case discussion	Case presentation
Necessary x-rays	Full-mouth series
Diagnostic models	Study models
Complete dentistry	Rehabilitation
Treatment or dentistry	Work
Considerable (or small amount of) decay	Cavities, areas or surfaces
Restoration	Filling
Sedative dressing or medicinal restoration	Temporary filling
Removal	Extraction
Follow-up visit or preventive program	Recall
Prepare the tooth	Grind the tooth
Partial denture	Partials
Primary or foundation teeth	Baby teeth
My assistant	My girl
Fee	Bill
How did you plan	Would you like
Take care of	Pay for
Payment arrangements	Financial arrangements
Agreement	Contract or note
Investment	Cost
Did you want to take care of this by cash or check?	That will be ten dollars.
Three twenty-seven	Three hundred twenty-seven
I recommend	I suggest
The doctor recommends	Doctor would like
Bookkeeper's allowance	Discount
Professional courtesy	Professional discount
Thorough examination	Checkup
Mrs. Scott, Doctor is ready to see you now.	Would you like to come in?
Uncomplicated	Simple
Dr. Adams is with a patient right now. This is Ann, Doctor's secretary. How may I help you?	Who's calling please? Doctor is busy. May I help you?
Do you prefer mornings or afternoons?	When would you like to come in?
Doctor's schedule is filled for today. However, she can see you . . .	She's all booked up. She can't see you until . . .

Even teachers (or is it educators?) have tried to use words to influence the way they are viewed by parents. Consider the following helpful hints given to the teachers of a school in New York for talking to parents and writing comments on report cards:

FOR PARENT INTERVIEWS AND REPORT CARDS

Harsh Expression (Avoid)	Euphemism
1. Does all right if pushed	Accomplishes tasks when interest is stimulated
2. Too free with fists	Resorts to physical means of winning his point or attracting attention.
3. Lies (Dishonest)	Shows difficulty in distinguishing between imaginary and factual material.
4. Cheats	Needs help in learning to adhere to rules and standards of fair play.
5. Steals	Needs help in learning to respect the property rights of others.
6. Noisy	Needs to develop quieter habits of communication
7. Lazy	Needs ample supervision in order to work well
8. Is a bully	Has qualities of leadership but needs help in learning to use them democratically
9. Associates with "gangs"	Seems to feel secure only in group situations; needs to develop a sense of independence.
10. Disliked by other children	Needs help in learning to form lasting friendships

REPORT CARD

	1	2	3	4	5	6
CHEATS			✔			
LIES					✔	
STEALS		✔				
NOISY					✔	
LAZY				✔		
OTHER						

2. Advertising has used some of our most important and meaningful words so many thousands of times that the words may have lost some meaning.

Consider words like:

love	alive
freedom	excitement

Sometimes these words are used by advertisers to hint that the product will somehow create freedom, love, or aliveness. The ads often imply that if you use this brand, you will experience freedom; if you apply that brand, you will feel more alive. Such "hints" or indirect appeals can be attractive to people who fear they are not loved or who frequently feel bored or trapped. Love, freedom, and a sense of aliveness are all very difficult and fragile states of being. They are goals that require struggle and often great effort and even pain.

If we repeatedly hear phrases such as "Fizzle soda tastes like love," or "Love is giving a gift of a fine watch," or "Virginia is for lovers," or "Au Revoir perfume is love in a bottle," doesn't the word *love* mean less when used to express a genuine feeling?

If *freedom* is riding a motorcycle on a dirt hill on a Saturday afternoon, or driving a certain kind of car, or having a no-wax floor, or wearing a certain brand of jeans, then isn't the personal struggle for true freedom somehow made less important?

If being *alive* is drinking a cola, having a second car, or being able to eat caviar while riding a yacht, then doesn't the word *alive* mean less?

Advertising influences words much like inflation influences the dollar. The constant application of words like *love, freedom,* and *aliveness* to everyday products make these words "worth less." Today's dollar buys less than the dollar of ten years ago; similarly, today's *love* means less than the *love* of ten years ago.

3. Mass media presents models of language for our imitation.

Students in English classes examine grammar, usage, and examples of correct English. However, a few dozen homework assignments, an occasional test, or even a six-week crash course in grammar are tiny efforts in comparison to the thousands of media messages we see and hear every day. Each media message can be considered an example of acceptable grammar and language use. Media users simply spend far more money to present examples of language than does any school system.

Many, perhaps most, of the language messages sent through mass media use language correctly and creatively. Ad writers, speech writers, and news writers are educated people who know more about the correct use of language than most people.

Many of the slogans, catch phrases, and jingles find their way into the everyday speech of millions. The expressions and speech mannerisms of popular television entertainers or advertisements are repeated perhaps millions of times a day by those who formed the original audience. Often our idea of a clever phrase is a copy of one we heard on television the night before.

On some occasions, media "teach" incorrect grammar. Some advertisers seem to feel that the audience they want to reach finds incorrect grammar the normal way of communicating. So to "speak their language," the advertiser will intentionally use incorrect grammar. One cola manufacturer advertised "What's good enough for other folks ain't good enough for me." They knew *ain't* is not proper in print but probably felt that potential cola drinkers would find the word the most appropriate. Perhaps they thought "What's good enough for other folks isn't good enough for me" would sound awkward. The cola advertiser may have said, "What's good enough for the masses is good enough for our ads."

The non-word *gonna* sometimes appears in print ads and the word *got* is often used incorrectly. The hair conditioner slogan "You're gonna swear you got more hair" illustrates both. The phrase in proper construction is "You're going to swear you have more hair."

Got is a perfectly acceptable word. It is part of the present perfect "have got." A beer claims, "If you've got the time, we've got the beer." A fast food chain claims, "We've got the best darned burger in the whole wide world." These are examples of the correct use of *got.* But a car manufacturer who uses the simple phrase "you got it" isn't making a clear statement or one that is grammatically correct. The ad headline, "what you want, it's got" would be more correctly written as "it has what you want."

Grammatical errors are relatively easy to find in advertising and in the speech of people on talk shows. Do such mass examples of poor language use have any influence on the way we speak or write? Do the thousands of examples of correct language and grammar do more to improve our language? Perhaps media have little if any effect on our language. What do you think?

Media and Language

1. Find examples in newspapers and magazines of politicians using language to create a favorable public image.

2. Do mass media help "keep politicians honest" in any way? Support your answer.

3. Give examples of actions people take, words they use, products they buy, and places they go that are chosen to help further their favorable image.

4. Find an example of a public statement given to mass media by some government agency that uses language to create a favorable image.

5. Analyze a press conference (on tape or film) or speech by a candidate for public office. Examine that person's use of language.

6. Examine the "say/don't say" list for dentists. Discuss why a particular phrase appears in the "don't say" column. Would you feel differently about treatment from a dentist who used all the "don't say" phrases than you would from one who used all the correct words and phrases?

7. Has mass media in any way presented the dentist unfairly, thus making dentists very concerned about their public image? Explain your answer.

8. If you were a teacher, would you say "your child cheats" or "your child needs to learn the rules and standards of fair play"? Why?

9. Do you agree that advertising "cheapens" certain words? Provide examples that support your answer.

10. Find examples of ads that use important words in a trivial way.

11. In what way does advertising act as a kind of "dictionary of everyday life?"

12. Find examples of current ads that use incorrect grammar. Are the ads using words that way on purpose, or are they simply mistakes?

13. Is the overall effect of media to improve our use of language or to make correctness less likely? Support your answer.

14. Are the three ways in which media influence our language and thought statements of fact or opinion? Prove your answer.

Chapter 12
NEW MEDIA & FUTURECASTING

THE VIDEOTAPE REVOLUTION

Most revolutionary changes in media are not totally new inventions that sweep the world. Instead, they are changes in already existing media. The recording of visual images began with the use of film and remains that way today, although many improvements have been made over the first crude films. The medium of film had no challengers to its supremacy until the recent invention of videotape (VT). Videotape raises the possibility that film will go the way of horse-drawn buggies, the stagecoach, and high-button shoes. Perhaps going to theaters to see a film will be replaced by watching the same ''film'' (made either with film or videotape) on a wall-sized home TV screen.

Currently both film and VT are used extensively on television, but feature-length movies are still made with film rather than VT. More and more TV commercials use VT rather than film as do some new TV series. In order to understand the advantages and differences of VT and film, a comparison is necessary.

A Comparison of Film and Videotape

FILM	VIDEOTAPE
Images can be seen when film is held up to the light (film is transparent).	Videotape all looks alike, whether blank or filled with images (tape is opaque).
Needs to be developed by a long, complicated, and expensive process that takes days or weeks.	Can be seen immediately after shooting on a TV monitor.
Inexpensive super-8 cameras and projectors make it possible for anyone to purchase and make films. All necessary equipment can be purchased for $350 or less.	Videotape cameras, monitors, and connecting hardware are expensive.
Film can be used once and only once and is not erasable.	Videotape can be reused hundreds of times but also can be accidentally erased.
One hour of color 16mm sound film is $200; one hour of sound super-8 is about $160.	Two hours of reusable videotape on a cassette costs only around $10.
Sound is an expensive and complicated option.	Sound is automatically part of every videotape.
Can be shown easily to a large audience on a huge screen.	Screen size is limited to the size of the TV monitor. The ability to project a large picture exists but is very expensive.
Copies of films can be made at film laboratories at low cost.	Videotapes can be copied with two recorders, just like audiotapes.
Easy to cut and edit. A viewer and editing equipment for super-8 film costs under $100.	Since the images cannot be seen with the eye, videotape is difficult to edit. Good equipment for editing tape costs many thousands of dollars.
Does not have a practical fast-forward or fast-reverse speed in the projector.	Tape can be fast-forwarded or reversed quickly and easily.
There is no "standard" film size: 16mm, super-8, and 35mm all require different projectors. But a film made in any one format anywhere in the world can be shown on any projector of the same format.	Various sizes of videotape (¼ inch, ½ inch, 1 inch) are not compatible, and all require different recorders and playback units to use. International compatibility is weak.
Clear, sharp image.	Clear, sharp image. A greater sense of "presence" than with film.
Many special effects require complicated and expensive laboratory work.	Special effects require special equipment (e.g., a special effects generator or multiple cameras and a switching board) but can be observed as they are being done and can be played back instantly and redone if desired.

MEDIALAB

Film vs. Video

1. Judging from the information you just read, what are the advantages of film over VT? What are the advantages of VT over film?

2. While watching commercial television, you may be able to tell the difference between material that is filmed and material that is on videotape. How would you describe that difference? However, you will not be able to tell VT from a ''live'' broadcast.

3. Are most commercials on VT or film? Most weekly programs? Do you have any idea why this is true? What about soap operas?

4. Make an educated speculation on the future of film and VT. Will film become obsolete? Will film improve so it is superior to VT in some way? In what different areas will each method be used?

5. What impact will the lowering of prices of VT equipment have on film?

6. Try an experiment in class: film and tape the same scene or bit of action. Watch both the VT and film versions together and discuss the differences.

Cable Television

Of all the communication devices studied in this book, cable television might turn out to be the most important and the one that most changes your life.

Cable TV began about 35 years ago as a simple solution to a problem in rural areas. In mountainous areas far from TV stations, an enterprising business-person would construct a huge master antenna on a mountaintop to capture TV signals from stations 100 or more miles away. People in the area paid a fee to have their own set wired by a cable to the master antenna. People thus had good TV reception without the expense of an elaborate rooftop antenna. Any signal fed into the antenna could be relayed easily through the cables to the system's subscribers.

The next step in the development of cable TV was the realization that since everyone was hooked up by wire, it would be relatively easy and inexpensive to set up a small TV studio and feed original programs into the antenna. Some stations set up an automatic revolving camera that scanned a clock and a weather forecast and sent this service to subscribers on an otherwise unused channel.

From isolated rural areas, cable TV moved to the large cities. There, the problem of TV reception becomes difficult because signals ricochet off tall buildings and airplanes, causing "ghosts" on home TV receivers. With TV sets connected directly to a tall master antenna, such problems were eliminated; so cable TV moved to some cities. A few cable systems offered subscribers additional channels brought in from nearby cities as an added service.

The cables used to connect the TV antenna to the set can transmit hundreds, some say thousands, of channels of information. Cable TV opens the possibility of more TV channels than are now possible with broadcast television. The combination of this larger multichannel potential, plus the perfect picture fed into every set could lead to cable television replacing broadcast television. If this does happen, cable TV, like the telephone lines, would become a service provided for a monthly fee.

The greatest potential of cable television is that it offers a huge number of channels to everyone. With current television programming, millions of viewers are needed to make a program a lasting success. If "only" a few hundred thousand people are interested enough to watch, the program dies. This leaves many interests unsatisfied. With cable TV, a local chess tournament that might attract only 2,000 viewers could easily be shown, as could the city council meeting, the stock market ticker, a wire service video teletype machine, and similar programs

for other special interest groups. In addition, the Federal Communications Commission has required each cable operator to provide a channel for ordinary citizens to express their viewpoints—a public access channel. The cable operator is also charged with providing assistance with VT equipment to interested parties who wish to make a tape to be used on the public access channel.

The most revolutionary aspect of cable television is that it can easily function as a two-way communication system. Since each house is connected by a cable, messages can be sent back to the central sending station. Just as with telephone wires, the video cable can carry video or audio messages in both directions. Two-way cable TV is technically possible now; no new inventions need be perfected in order for the "wired city" to exist.

Robert Galvin, board chairman of Motorola, has claimed that the acceptance of two-way cable will do away with the need for standard broadcasting, and that a date should be set for closing down all ordinary TV stations. Two-way cable TV could easily become as common and essential as a telephone in the not-too-distant future.

With two-way cable and the necessary coding and message-sending "boxes," subscribers could gain access to their savings and checking accounts to pay bills via TV; they could take part in school or special education classes from home; they could shop, vote, or express opinions on important public issues, or even call up research information from the local library computer.

Most of the cable systems now in existence in the United States are still one-way systems. But FCC regulations require two-way capacity in all newly constructed systems.

Comparison ol
Over-The-Ai

Over-The-Air

Quality of signal varies with location of set and with weather.

Number of channels available is limited. Even a large city such as Chicago has only ten channels.

Currently reaches about 95 percent of all families.

Requires a TV set and sometimes a rooftop antenna.

Free. No monthly bills.

One-way system.

Needs many viewers to interest advertisers.

Few individuals can obtain TV time to state their opinions.

Cable

Consistent high quality of transmission for everyone.

Over 50 channels available including commercial networks.

Currently reaches 70 percent of all households with TV sets.

Requires that the house be wired to the cable operator. The hook-up charge ranges from nothing to $100.

Those wired to the system pay an average monthly fee of $5–$100.

Has the potential of two-way communication.

Needs far fewer viewers than over-the-air transmission to be economically workable.

Each cable franchise will be required to have at least one channel for citizen access.

Cable TV with Transmission

One possible far-reaching effect of cable television is to make movie theaters a thing of the past. Attendance at films declined enormously with the invention of television. More people went to films more often in 1940 than they do today. To attend a movie requires an auto or bus trip somewhere, a $2.00–$5.00 admission fee, maybe parking or babysitting costs, perhaps standing in line and putting up with a noisy crowd, and tolerating overcooled or overheated movie houses and over-priced popcorn and candy, not to mention finding a seat only to have a 6 foot 8 inch basketball player sit in front of you.

All these problems vanish when first-run feature films are offered through cable television systems. A few systems have already experimented with offering subscribers first-run films for an additional fee. In Sarasota, Florida, a cable company called Theater-Vision offered first-run films at $2 per movie. Three different films were shown on even days, three on odd days—each played several times during the day on one of the three channels. A subscriber paid only once for each movie by inserting a coded ticket in a box connected to the TV set.

MEDIALAB

Cable Viewing

1. Find out what sort of cable systems exist in your area. If none exist currently, do some research to find out what applications for cable "franchises" exist. Who has made the applications and what have they promised?

2. If a cable TV system with 50 channels started operation tomorrow, what sort of programs would you like to see carried? Remember that the ideas would have to be inexpensive to produce (to put a camera in a city council room is easy, but to produce a weekly filmed TV show is much too expensive for such an operation).

3. If cable TV were offered tomorrow, would you subscribe? If cable TV already does exist in your area, find out what factors influence people's decisions about whether or not to subscribe.

4. Do you think first-run movies on TV would bring about the end of movie theaters? Would the public acceptance of cable TV change your opinion?

5. Prepare a report on two-way cable television as it exists today. Be sure to find out about the QUBE system.

6. Brainstorm as a class for possible uses of two-way cable television.

7. How might cable television change television as we know it today?

8. Many predictions of the future turn out to be little more than wishful thinking. Do you think two-way cable TV is a significant social invention or merely a fad?

9. Could two-way cable in any way change schooling?

10. Two-way radio has never made a major impact on society. Amateur radio is for hobbyists, and citizen's band is used more for companionship than for important communication that would allow people to work or shop at home. Why should two-way video be any more important?

YOUR NEW INFORMATION UTILITY

A home computer terminal is not a mass medium by itself. But if it allows a home to access a news service, a library, stock market quotes, and airline and hotel reservations, it becomes part of an information utility. The following article describes ways in which a home computer terminal can be used as an information utility. Some of the uses have become more common in the several years since the article was written. Other uses are still very much in the future. Computer technology is changing rapidly. A few years from now, new types of computers and new uses for them may have emerged.

THE HOME COMPUTER TERMINAL

by Hollis Vail

Today, more and more homes have computers. How will they be used? It is possible for a home computer to become a true "information utility."

John, when are you going to finish with the terminal? I need to send some messages."

"Just a bit, Mom. I have to have this paper for school tomorrow and the speller's been acting up."

"No wonder! If you learned to spell some of the words yourself, the computer wouldn't have so much trouble. Spelling "physical" f-i-s-i-k-a-l! No wonder you have trouble!"

"Well, they ought to spell it fisikal. That's how it sounds."

Susan Young wondered if they should buy John his own terminal. He had his own phone and television. So why not? Then a terminal would be available when she wanted it. Except, of course, when her husband Bill was playing games on it. That *really* tied it up.

The terminal Susan is thinking about looks like a television with a typewriter keyboard in front. It also has a place for the phone so that the terminal can be connected to a computer some distance away.

When connected, the terminal is used like a typewriter except that the typed words appear on the screen. Also, the computer writes on the screen as it responds to Susan or whoever is using the terminal. John was doing this when he commanded the computer to check his spelling. The computer checked each

word against its word dictionary and then played out the possibles until John selected one. In the case of "fisikal," the computer had the same problem we have when we do not know the first two or three letters of a word and its sound misleads us.

Many Services Available Today
The home of Bill and Susan Young is located a few years in the future, but only a very few years. Already thousands of American families have discovered the possibilities of a terminal in the home for phone and cable TV services. They also are pioneering, for the "information utilities" are in their infancy. Many of the potential services are available today. But today's users must also live with the growing pains of the industry.

Let us go forward again to Bill, Susan, and son John. Susan wanted to send some messages.

This can be done today. It is one of the better developed services of these utilities. The main difference between what Susan could do and today is the number of people she could reach. When terminals become as common as phones or televisions, then almost anyone will be on a system and thus able to receive and send messages. Today, of course, the number of possible "addresses" is much smaller.

Sending a message via a terminal is simple. Susan first tells the computer she wants the SEND MAIL service by typing SEND MAIL. The computer connects her to its program for sending and receiving messages and writes "To:" on the screen and waits for Susan to enter the "address" (similar to a phone number) of each person she wants the message to go to. Then the computer asks for a subject line. Next, it asks for the text.

When she finishes the message, Susan types a SEND command and the message is sent to the people on the "To:" line.

The message is not actually sent, as one would send a letter. Instead, the computer assigns a unique electronic mailbox to each person using the service. Susan's message is stored in each person's mailbox, where it waits until they come on line and ask for their mail.

Today such messages can be sent to and from over 300 cities in the United States and Canada and between many cities elsewhere in the world as well, just by dialing a local phone number. This number connects the user to a long-distance network that specializes in carrying messages between terminals and computers. Thus, Susan can send a message from her home in Richmond, Virginia, to a friend in Seattle, Washington, as easily (and as inexpensively) as to a friend across town. Also, the computer involved may be in some other city such as Silver Spring, Maryland.

At the end of the day, Bill "signs on" (establishes electronic contact with the computer). Bill has a portfolio of stocks that he follows, so he tells the computer to search for the stocks in his portfolio. Susan and Bill have invested in a printer that is coupled to their terminal, so Bill has the quotes printed out in "hard" copy [paper copy].

Bill then asks for information on a number of companies that he thinks might be promising investments. The computer shifts to another data bank and prints out financial and other information on these companies. Bill then leaves a message for his broker.

Next, Bill posts the checks he wrote that day. In posting, he notes whether they are tax deductible and assigns them to various family accounts. He also directs the computer to generate "checks" for bills that came in that day and "posts" these checks. The computer then comes back saying:

"You have a balance of $302.37 in your savings/checking account."

At this point, Susan calls out, "Don't sign off, Bill. I have something I want to do."

"How long will you be? A group of us were going to get on tonight to play poker in about 20 minutes."

"I'll be done by then. I just want to plan the dinner we are having Friday."

Planning a Dinner Menu

Soon Susan sits down and types in MENU. The computer delves into its memory bank and locates a program called MENU. This program then tells the computer to look up Susan's cooking profile, which contains information about Susan's cooking preferences and information on her common guests. In this case, the profile tells the computer that Susan has a microwave oven, a slow cooker, a food processor, and the other usual kitchen appliances. It includes a listing of the dishes she has chosen for menus during the past year and indicates that she likes to experiment with new dishes, but only when entertaining old friends.

"Who are your guests?" the computer asks.

Susan types in the names of her guests. The computer matches the names with prior guest lists and, where they

match, notes the preferences and diet restrictions that Susan had previously entered for each guest. Since new guests are on Susan's list, the computer asks Susan to provide what she knows about the new guests' preferences.

The computer is now ready to help Susan work out a dinner menu. In its memory are the recipes for over 5,000 dishes. It also holds information on how to cook exotic foods. A built-in clock/calendar enables the computer to keep track of changing seasons, so it knows what is likely to be available in Susan's market. It can even estimate the amount of a dish needed to feed heavy, moderate, or light eaters— and project the approximate cost of each dish. So the dialogue begins:

COMPUTER: Quick, slow cooking, or prepared?
SUSAN: Quick, slow cooking.
C: Fish, chicken, beef, or meatless?
S: Chicken, meatless.
C: American or other?
S: General.
C: Familiar?
S: Yes.
C: Expense?
S: Moderate.
C: Your files show you have cooked the following dishes two or more times during the last year: Chicken Tarragon, Chicken Kiev, Quick spaghetti with soup and bacon, Quiche Lorraine.
S: Can Chicken Kiev be cooked in the microwave?
C: Yes. . . .

The Information Utility: An Infant Industry

This scenario of a day in the life of the Youngs could include many other uses of the information utility. John could use it to study subjects such as math, history, and geography. Bill could use it to enhance his management skills through the use of

simulation games. The family could store many documents and records in the computer's magnetic memory file. The possibilities exceed today's imagination, for the information utility is definitely in its early infancy. And, as with any infant industry, its future can take many courses. Some of today's pioneers may go broke while others prosper. The information utility concept is certainly not without its risks and problems. . . .

So far, the information utilities have been piggybacking on existing computer centers and telecommunications networks to gain the national and international user base they need. They also have priced their services to encourage their subscribers to use the cheaper, off-peak time periods (evenings and weekends). The day may come, though, when these utilities will be so big that they will have to use more than the spare capacity of existing computer centers and telecommunications networks and will develop new ones of their own. . . .

Access to data banks is one of the key services offered by information utilities. As these services expand, the number, size, and variety of data banks they offer will sharply increase. Encyclopedic services such as the New York Times Information Bank and topical services such as the UPI news stories will coexist with reservation banks (make your airline reservations at home), cookbooks, entertainment calendars, catalogs (shopping by computer), and personal data banks. Today, however, there is little consistency in the procedures for using and searching such data banks.

An almost untouched area is that of interactive services. The education field has done some good work in developing interactive program instructions. Such instructions go beyond simply posing problems or questions and making different responses according to the student's answers. Interactive programs can develop a profile for each student that "judges" his or her individual strengths and weaknesses and offers instructions keyed to each unique profile. Also, such programs enable students to ask for and get special information or extra practice. A great part of the computer's future lies in the development of interactive programs. Just as Susan used the computer to help her deal with the many variables of planning a dinner party, many other programs are needed that can respond appropriately to the unique requirements of each individual using the system.

Planning a Vacation

One instance might be planning a vacation. There are thousands of vacation options, most of which we never think of. Have you, for instance, considered a flight in a glider over the Arizona mountains?

In interacting with Bill and Susan, the computer might start by asking for information that will set firm limits within which the vacation must occur. How much money can they spend? How many days do they have available? Do they prefer an active or leisurely pace? Scenery or night life? Will they drive their own car? Will they stay in motels or campgrounds? Etc.

Once the parameters are set, the computer can stimulate Bill's

and Susan's imaginations. Gliding? White-water rafting? Seeing glass being made and cut? Finding and polishing rocks? Exploring the "buried" cities in Central America? Participating in a scientific expedition?

As Bill and Susan narrow their vacation options, the computer helps them keep track of comparative figures on cost and time. And, once they make their decision, the computer can arrange for a reservation and obtain travel material. It could also remind them to stop the newspaper delivery and arrange for having the lawn mowed while they are gone.

As the information utilities address and resolve the problems facing them and the number of their subscribers increases, other changes will probably take place, changes in society itself.

Work Life, Home Life May Merge

For example, work life and home life may merge. Susan is active in an association that supports the expansion of pocket parks throughout the United States and Canada. These parks are small plots of ground in urban areas that provide opportunities for open air meals and relaxation, play space for children, scenic locales for artists, and self-cycling ecological environments. Susan's professional responsibilities include preparing and editing a newsletter and maintaining a data bank on the many types of ecological environments created in these parks.

Park association members from all over the United States and Canada send Susan mes-

sages on pocket park activities in their locales. Susan reads through these messages and selects those worthy of mentioning in the newsletter or adding to the data bank. She also uses the information utility for conducting "written" interviews and to gather background on the items for the newsletter and data bank.

Finally, using the utility's text editor, Susan composes her newsletter and sets up the data bank items. She then transmits the newsletter to the association headquarters in Washington, D.C. They, in turn, edit the newsletter in final form and transmit it to a printer located in Phoenix, Arizona.

The association that Susan belongs to has had to radically alter its structure as its members began to subscribe to the information utility. At one time, Susan's involvement would have been limited to a local chapter. Now the activities of the association are dispersed across the membership regardless of where the individual members live. Soon, the newsletter will not actually be printed. Members will receive it through their computer terminals.

Bill and Susan have also become the customers of businesses that saw opportunities in the growing number of information utility subscribers. A major news service recognized that people who moved around wanted to maintain contact with hometown events. Which high schools won last night's games? Did the city council decide to buy the old Henry estate? So the news service contracted with city newspapers for access to the files they maintain on local news.

The Youngs had recently moved from Denver to Richmond and John wanted to keep tabs on his old high school. Susan, incidentally, continued her newsletter activity when the family moved, since it did not matter where she lived as far as this activity was concerned.

The entertainment world, too, was interested in the information utility since it provided an inexpensive way for theaters, restaurants, and other entertainment spots throughout the country to advertise their special features and events to potential visitors from distant places. Thus, subscribers planning a trip could learn in advance about plays, concerts, shows, or local celebrations and could often make advance reservations.

Banks, too, quickly got into the act—offering people like Bill and Susan direct access from their homes and offices to their personal checking and savings accounts. Now, Bill and Susan could know at any moment which checks had cleared and which were still outstanding. They could pay bills through the bank, and the bank would even answer financial questions and provide income tax service.

Soon, mail-order houses across the country were taking orders via the information utility and accepting payment directly through the same utility.

Hotels and motels also began to provide terminals, first in special "information centers," later in every room, so Bill and Susan never needed to be far away from their records, their data bases, their mail, or contact with their bank. Nor could John get far away from school, for he could always sit down wherever he was and study his lessons.

This scenario hardly begins to suggest the potential uses of information utilities. Strong evidence suggests that terminals will someday contain their own computer capabilities and memory storage. Some will come stocked with prepackaged programs for those who do not want to learn how to program computers. Others will be programmable so that those who use them can develop programs "hand tailored" to their special needs. Competition among information utility companies is just starting. Who knows where this will lead the industry? It certainly will lead to diversity as competing utilities explore and nurture more and more potential service opportunities. It also could mean some very different subscribing patterns. For example, the giant telecommunications companies might absorb these new small information utility firms and emerge as a unified information and computer supplier that connects people to many specialized services.

Whatever the future direction of information utilities, the likelihood is high that the 1990s will see computer terminals added to the list of essential household items. Today's school-aged children will grow up using these computer-based services as routinely and as easily as their parents now use libraries, checking accounts, credit cards, and other "modern" devices. ■

MEDIALAB

Transforming the Household of Tomorrow

1. The article says "many of the services are available today." Find out more about what is available today. Select one of the following reports or activities:

a. Use a personal computer to demonstrate an "information utility" such as The Source, Compuserve, Dialog, or a local bulletin board service.

b. Explain an information utility such as one of those mentioned above. Explain what information it offers, how to use it, how much it costs, and what you need to take advantage of its services.

c. If a local public library offers any kind of computerized information search, explain its operation to the class.

d. Explain any of the electronic mail systems that currently exist. What are they good for? How can they be used and what do they cost?

2. How might life change if every household had a computer terminal wired to a central computer?

3. Argue that this piece of futuristic writing is off the mark. Show that the services explained are either already available in other forms or are not in great demand.

4. Do you think the fact that an information utility user should be skilled in typing is a problem? How could the problem be solved?

5. An information utility could prepare a personalized newspaper every morning. The computer would select only those news items it "thinks" would interest you. Of course, you have already told the computer your interests. While you make the morning orange juice, the printer attached to your terminal makes up your own personal "Daily News."

Is this idea practical for the future? Why or why not?

6. Where are terminals that are attached to a central computer used now? Much of what the article describes already exists, but not in the house. List terminal installations that you could use today. For example, remote teller machines at banks and airline reservation computers available through a travel agent or a phone call.

THINGS TO COME

Predicting the future is dangerous; it's so easy to be so wrong. The following article appeared in *Modern Mechanix* in May, 1938. Fifty years later our newspapers are still printed much the way they were in 1938. But this lesson from the past serves as a warning to our current predictions about the electronic home of the future.

YOUR NEWSPAPER BY RADIO!

This 1938 article enthusiastically announces a new system of receiving a newspaper through the radio. Do you think this system could still become popular?

A private newspaper with any spot in your home as the press room, the world's best editors and reporters on your staff, and the radio as your copy boy—this is not the dream of Jules Verne—but an actual accomplishment, available today to anyone in the United States owning an ordinary radio receiver.

No thundering press will deafen you when your paper is printed, but instead, equipment contained in a small, attractive box, will silently print your "latest edition" while you sleep, completing it in time for reading at breakfast.

Facsimile transmitters and printers have been announced by two manufacturers, Finch Telecommunications Laboratories, Inc., of New York City, and RCA Victor, of Camden, N. J.

Predicted to be in widespread use within the year, many large broadcast stations have started tests with the system, and actual broadcasts on a definite schedule will be an accomplished fact as soon as these tests are completed. Of great significance is the fact that the Federal Communications Commission has granted the broadcasters permission to operate the facsimile equipment on the regular broadcast frequencies. Translated into actual use, this means that when the householder is through listening to his favorite station, he merely turns a switch which will, at the correct time, again turn on the radio for reception of the same station, but this time instead of sounds emitting from the loudspeaker, an up-to-the-minute newspaper will unfold.

At present one of the largest eastern broadcast stations, WOR, is supplying this type of transmission, though not yet on a regular schedule. It is being done both on the regular broadcast channels as well as on the ultra-short waves. Plans are under way for regular service of facsimile transmissions early this spring.

Among other stations that have received F.C.C. permission to make facsimile broadcasts are WGN, Chicago; KSD, St. Louis; WHO, Des Moines; WGH, Norfolk, Va., WHK, Cleveland; KSTP, St. Paul; KMJ, Fresno, and KFPK, Sacramento.

The facsimile recorder will be sold at a price no higher than the average good broadcast receiver. When production is increased the price is expected to be reduced to that of the average medium priced midget receiver. With the exception of the recorder, no special equipment is required except the broadcast receiver itself.

This new medium of entertainment and education is not to be confused with television, differing most widely from it in that its operation produces a tangible newspaper on which appears the printed word, photographs, drawings, sketches, and even advertisements. As the newspaper is produced, it can be removed from the machine and preserved if desired, differing from the conventional type only in size.

Briefly, the operation of the transmitter and recorder is as follows: The copy to be transmitted—whether it is pictures, news flashes, line drawings or comic strips—involves no special printing or preparation because the material itself can be inserted directly into the transmitter. An electric bulb, throwing a spot of light, moves back and forth across the copy to be transmitted. This action is similar to that of the human eye as it sweeps from left to right across a line of type. In its movement across the copy, the spot of light is reflected back into a light-sensitive photo-electric cell. When the scanning light strikes the white portions of the copy, it returns a full reflection to the light-sensitive cell. When it strikes a black area, no light is reflected, while for the shaded areas, a corresponding reflection is obtained.

Because of the action of intermittent light at the cell, these reflections are changed into electrical energy or impulses. At the receiver or recorder, these impulses operate a stylus sweeping in synchronism with the scanning light at the transmitter.

MEDIALAB

1. This 1938 magazine article is typical of thousands of glowing articles and press releases predicting wonderful benefits just around the corner from a new invention. The article predicts the newspaper-by-radio system will be "in wide-spread use within the year." Almost 50 years later, the system still is not in operation. Why doesn't this wonderful new invention exist in millions of homes today?

2. The popular press often reports on new technology more with the eye of a cheerleader than of a critical evaluator. Find examples of current articles that predict marvelous benefits from a new invention. Evaluate the device with a critical eye.

Evaluate the new invention from an economic viewpoint by asking these questions: Would production of the invention cost so many millions of dollars that only the largest corporations could afford to experiment with it? Can the invention make a profit for its producers? Who would be most threatened by the invention? Would there be a great demand for the invention or would it be little more than a toy for the rich?

3. In what way might interactive television supply much the same services promised by newspaper-by-radio?

4. Are there any devices in operation today whereby printed copies of news or other material are transmitted by (a) broadcasting, or (b) telephone wires?

5. Read the description of how the newspaper-by-radio invention works. Does it sound a bit like any existing device? Is the description complete or are some very important parts left out?

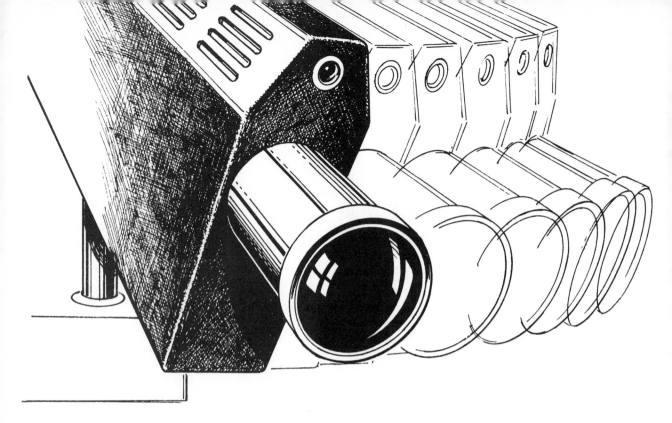

Cameras, Computers, and Control

Much discussion of new technology involves considerations of its benefits to humans. However, there is another side to new technology—its potential to limit freedom, to allow control of the masses by the few.

For example, if two-way television becomes a standard part of every household, records can be kept on what people watch, what items they order by television, how they vote or register opinions on questions presented for polling, where they travel, and what subjects interest them.

If crime or shoplifting is a problem in a specific area, it is tempting to "patrol" the area with a television camera. Many stores and banks use cameras to prevent shoplifting and robbery. A few cities use television cameras mounted on city streets and connected to a police station to remote-patrol high crime areas. Many public buildings and corporate headquarters are "protected" by scores of television cameras monitored by a guard. These camera systems free us from fear of harm. On the other hand, some degree of freedom is sacrificed. When we walk these TV-patrolled streets or enter television guarded buildings, we are aware that any unconventional act of dress or behavior might be marked and recorded. Are we willing to trade feeling safe because someone is watching for feeling we must conform to some standards because someone is watching?

The computer is another example of a communication device that can be misused as a means of people control.

There are now about over 3 million people in America who, at one time or another, had a driver's license revoked or suspended; their names and offense records are stored in a national computer file at the Department of Transportation. There are over 10 million names in the U.S. Civil Service Commission "security file," used to determine "suitability involving loyalty and subversive activity." The Secret Service has a computer file of thousands of activist critics of American policy.

Through computer hook-ups police departments exchange records ranging from criminal convictions to the names of children who have been arrested (and not necessarily convicted) for truancy or disturbing the peace.

Some people fear that computerized recordkeeping will lead to a society in which there is little privacy. An attorney for a Maryland couple explained that "in the computer age, when you get a black mark on your record, you're dead." The couple learned about computer data banks after their "new" Ford blew up.

The couple refused to pay the balance of their installment loan to Ford Motor Credit when the firm and the Ford dealer were unresponsive to their complaints. Ford Credit said that the condition of the car was not the firm's concern, warned them that legal action to collect the debt would be noted by their local credit bureau. The debt was settled by a partial payment of $600, a figure acceptable to both the couple and Ford Credit Company. Months later the couple found they were unable to obtain credit to purchase items on the installment plan and were unable to obtain a mortgage to buy a house.

They discovered that the credit company had informed the local credit bureau of a "repossession." The couple sued Ford for $1.25 million. They won their case and were awarded $150,000 in damages.

Control Data's CYBER 203 is designed for improved processing performance and faster data transfer.

MEDIALAB

Cameras, Computers, and Privacy

1. What experiences have you had with being "watched" by remote control cameras? How did you feel? Did you act differently?

2. In novels such as *1984* and *Brave New World*, computers and surveillance devices are used to safeguard society, but only at the expense of individual freedoms. Do you see any conflict between personal freedom and the use of new technology to protect citizens from crime?

3. Your school very likely uses computers to assist in its recordkeeping task. What records are kept on students, for how long, and who has the right to inspect these records?

4. Do you think the couple in the example of the car that blew up received justice?

5. The details in both of the following "debate situations" are based on accurate descriptions of actual systems currently in operation. Debate the pros and cons of each system and decide each by taking a class vote.

DEBATE SITUATION NUMBER ONE

You are on a committee to decide upon the installation of surveillance cameras in the school. The proposal is to install cameras to monitor students in classrooms, the cafeteria, and in hallways. The reason for the system is to limit the student misbehavior and vandalism that have plagued the school in recent months.

The cameras would be mounted in corners near the ceiling and would take one still picture every thirty seconds. The cameras would be soundproof so the clicking would not be heard. Note that the cameras use super-8 film, they are not video cameras that broadcast a picture to a monitor. The cameras cost around $300 each, and the film has to be changed approximately every five days.

The school administration has assured students that "We're not interested in spying on students who are conducting themselves in a manner normal for their age level." They assure you that the film will be processed and looked at only when "incidents" occur that require establishing responsibility.

DEBATE SITUATION NUMBER TWO

The city council has just suggested that an experimental type of protection system be installed in your neighborhood subject to the approval of those who live in the neighborhood.

Every home would be wired for two-way TV, including a fire detector, emergency call alarm, and a burglar alarm for security purposes. Each television set has buttons on it to alert the police of a fire, burglary, or other emergency. Pushing one of the buttons lights a light at police headquarters. The on-duty TV patrol person then turns on the TV camera inside the house and looks to see what is wrong and sends the necessary help.

The police believe this system would strongly discourage thefts (your neighborhood has expressed a fear of theft in recent months) and would definitely save lives. Health emergencies would receive almost immediate assistance, and burglaries and fires could be reported even when the family is not home.

The only possible abuse of this system is that a curious video patrol person could turn on the TV cameras at any time and those in the house might not know they were being watched. The police chief has assured citizens that such abuses would never happen.

OTHER MEDIA INNOVATIONS

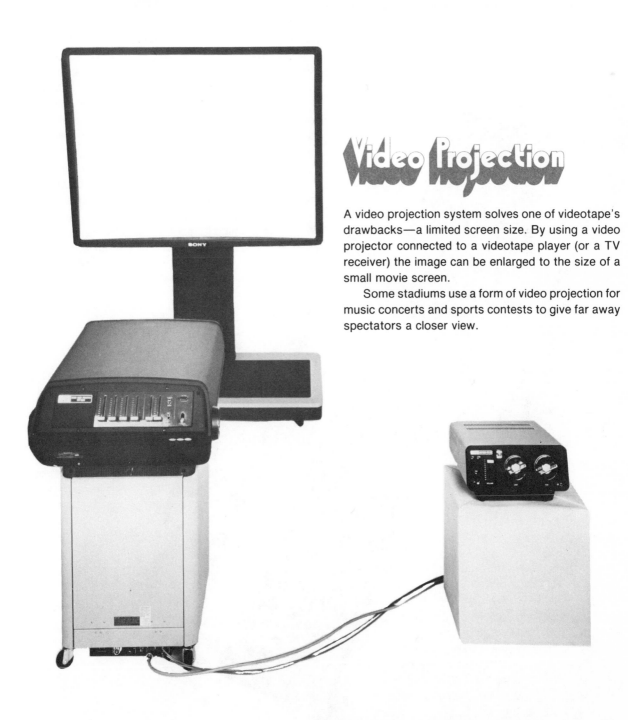

Video Projection

A video projection system solves one of videotape's drawbacks—a limited screen size. By using a video projector connected to a videotape player (or a TV receiver) the image can be enlarged to the size of a small movie screen.

Some stadiums use a form of video projection for music concerts and sports contests to give far away spectators a closer view.

VARIABLE SPEECH CONTROL

The human ear is a mechanism far superior to the rather clumsy tongue and mouth. If only people could talk as fast as others can listen. You can easily listen to speech at 500 words per minute, but no one can talk at that speed with the possible exception of a few talented auctioneers. If people could talk twice as fast, then we could do our listening in half the time.

Variable Speech Control (VSC) is an invention that will allow a tape recording to be played back two or three times faster and still be easily intelligible. VSC already exists and may be part of some tape recorders. The VSC unit is smaller than a sugar cube and is wired into a tape recorder. With the VSC-equipped recorder comes a small hand unit (like the remote control devices with TV sets) connected by a wire to the recorder and containing a control which enables the listener to vary the speed of *any* recording from 100 to 500 words per minute. The VSC unit compresses speech, seemingly eliminating unnecessary pauses and shortening long vowel sounds while at the same time doing away with the usual "Donald Duck effect" which normally makes speeded up tapes unintelligible.

With VSC, a lecture delivered in one hour can be listened to in as little as 20 or 30 minutes. If you miss a class, you could have a friend tape the class and then listen to the 50-minute tape in only 20 minutes. With some practice it might be possible to learn to listen at speeds up to five, six, or ten times that of normal speech. *Hamlet* in 15 minutes? A one-hour lecture in ten minutes? Perhaps.

HOLOGRAPHY

Holographic film looks like a piece of clear plastic about the size of this page. But if that piece of plastic is held up so that a laser beam can pass through it after first going through a special lens, the plastic reveals an amazing sight.

Appearing on the plastic is an utterly realistic three-dimensional picture—say, for example, of a child's alphabet block. Looking down into the picture, you can see the top "A" of the block. As you move your head around, you can see the other sides of the block, even the back and bottom. Holography may well be the most important addition to photography and film since color. Holography (the word translates roughly from the Greek meaning "the whole picture") is not a dream of the future; it exists now.

To add to the aura of magic, that piece of plastic could be removed from the ruby-red laser light and cut into one-inch squares. When each tiny square is put into the light, the entire picture remains intact.

Holographs can be made so real that a viewer can walk around an image and be convinced it is real. If a holograph is made of a scene that includes a magnifying glass, viewers will see a magnifying glass that actually works. As viewers move their heads, whatever appears behind the magnifying glass will be enlarged.

Making holographs is still an expensive and highly specialized process. But if holography can be made practical for film and television, movies in the future might be projected all around the audience instead of on a two-dimensional screen.

PICTUREPHONE

A picturephone is a combination of two familiar communication devices—the telephone and television. When combined, the two make person-to-person communication possible visually as well as audially. The picturephone service already exists in some large cities, but its cost currently limits its value to businesses.

VIDEO DISC PLAYBACK SYSTEMS

The problem with television is that the people must sit and keep their eyes glued on a screen; the average American family hasn't time for it. Therefore, the showmen are convinced that for this reason, if for no other, television will never be a serious competitor of broadcasting.

—New York Times
March 19, 1939

The videodisc player is attached to an ordinary television receiver much like a videotape player. A special videodisc is inserted in the player and the program can be seen and heard on the television set. Videodisc is a cross between a phonograph player and a videocassette player. Unlike a videocassette system, the owner cannot copy any programs from television.

Videodisc holds the promise of programs sold in record stores or supermarkets (or even bound into magazines on thin plastic sheets) that will cost as little as $10 for a full length movie.

The *New York Times* reporter who decided that people do not have time for television underestimated the attraction of moving images on a screen. Videodisc and other soon-to-arrive improvements in television suggest that in the future the television might be the most important invention in existence.

The Latest in Media Technology

Here are some innovations in media technology that could become either the next information revolution or just another failed fad:

MDS—Microwave delivered pay TV. A microwave relay station on a tower or tall building delivers movies to the TV sets of subscribers with the proper decoding equipment.

VCR—Videocassette recorders were introduced in 1975. In 1983 alone, four million units were sold. This means that about eight million homes in the U.S. own a VCR—still a minority, but a growing one.

CAMCORDER—Introduced in 1983, this is not really a new invention so much as it is a new package for an older invention—a video camera. The device is a one-piece video camera and recorder. Camcorders could mean the end of super-8 film as a means of making "home movies."

TVRO—TV Receive Only earth stations. These dish-shaped antennae allow individuals to pluck television programs from the stars. The receiving stations can pick up programs intended primarily for the use of TV stations and cable systems. These TVRO systems still cost a few thousand dollars at least but are gaining popularity especially in remote areas.

VIDEOTEXT—A system whereby a television set becomes a means of two-way communication. Viewers at home can access a computer which displays screens of information on the television. The system is seen as opening the way to electronic shopping, banking, mail, news, and other services. Notice that this invention is a refinement of the device described in the *Modern Mechanix* article from 1938 that appears on page 293.

STEREO—Stereo sound has been around for quite a while in phonograph records, tapes, and FM radio. But the late 1980s will see stereo become the normal means of reception for AM radio and television.

UHF—UHF stands for ultra high frequency—TV channels 14 through 83. These channels have room for many more stations, especially low power transmitters serving a very limited area. The potential for UHF is great enough that it could change the nature of television. UHF could make television a source of new programming and add the dimension of TV as a local medium instead of one that is purely national. UHF could, in many ways, become radio with pictures.

PC—PC stands for personal computer. In the early 1980s sales of microcomputers grew and those in the industry saw a computer in every household. But a "secret" of the early boom in PCs was that many of the computers sat in closets, unused. People found them too difficult to use.

At first, the PC was seen as a time-saving way to balance checkbooks, keep track of recipes, and organize tax receipts. But users quickly found that file cabinets and even shoe boxes worked just as well. The computer required typing skills, great patience, and lots of entering data.

Media history shows that new media are often seen first as ways of increasing culture and education. Early apostles of radio, film, and television preached the uplifting potential of these new inventions. Computers, too, were seen as highly educational, and they do play a role in education. But, like other media, their success depended on entertainment. Without computer games the "computer revolution" would have been left in the dust of other media.

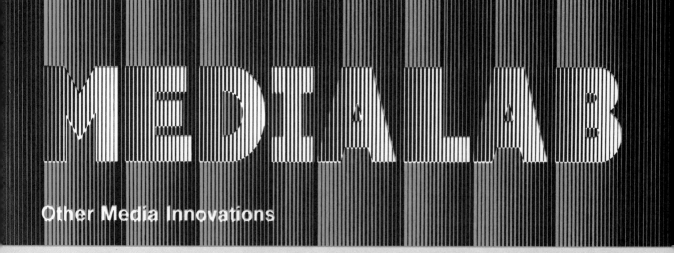

MEDIA LAB

Other Media Innovations

1. Large-screen television is increasing in popularity. Some movie theaters are experimenting with large-screen TVs to replace traditional methods of film projection. If a feature film could be fed by satellites to movie theaters, the distribution system would be greatly simplified. Currently films are duplicated at a great expense and these heavy packages are shipped around the country to movie houses.

Do you think large-screen television will influence movie theaters? Will projection TV become the norm and future houses have a media room instead of a living room? Support your answers.

2. Discuss the possible benefits of variable speech control. How could you use it to save time?

3. Holography is a technology still in its infancy. Imagine holographic television. How would it change viewing habits and programming?

4. The picturephone has been around for at least a decade now but has never caught on. Part of the reason is expense and technical limitations. Can you think of other reasons why a picturephone might never replace our voice-only telephone system?

5. Videodiscs are convenient and more compact than videocassettes. A videodisc player can access a single image on the disc rather quickly. When coupled with a microcomputer to access images, the videodisc becomes a powerful means of learning.

Discuss how the combination of a computer and a videodisc could change learning and entertainment.

6. Cable television has often been assumed to be the "wave of the future" for television. But consider that sending impulses through wires is old technology. Newer technology involves sending impulses through the air. What are the disadvantages of cable?

7. Consider cable as a delivery system for television images. What technological advances could render cable obsolete? Be sure to consider TVRO in your answer.

8. Will personal computers in the year 2000 be as common as calculators and radios today? Argue both sides of the question—computers as essential tools and as a fad whose real value is limited to businesses.

In attempting to predict what the communication media of the future will be like, there are few certainties. Perhaps the only sure thing is that tomorrow's media will be as different from today's as today's are from those of the nineteenth century. You will one day tell stories to your grandchildren of the old days of broadcast television, of the days when you first operated a computer, and of the time when pictures were projected in only two dimensions. The grandparent of the year 2020 might well recall the quaint custom of going to something called movie theaters, the old-time stereo FM radio, the plastic disc phonograph records, and the days when even large cities had no more than a half a dozen television channels.

Predicting or speculating about the future is more than a mere exercise of imagination. To the unprepared, the future arrives as a shock; to the prepared, the future arrives as a logical extension of the present. To speculate about how the communications media will develop is to take some part in that development. To have considered what is desirable in human communication is to be able to make a value judgment about what the future of media should be.

The Future of the Movies

An 1877 prediction of global radio was considerably easier to make than a 1924 prediction of what the young invention of film would be like in the year 2024. But in 1924 the man most qualified to make such a prediction was David Wark Griffith, an early Amer-

ican film director often considered the "father of American cinema." Back in 1924 D. W. Griffith looked into his educated crystal ball marked 2024 (100 years later), and this is what he saw.

THE MOVIES
100 YEARS FROM NOW

by David Wark Griffith

In 1924 an important film director predicted the future of films. How many of his predictions have already come true?

In the year 2024 the most important single thing which the cinema will have helped in a large way to accomplish will be that of eliminating from the face of the civilized world all armed conflict. Pictures will be the most powerful factor in bringing about this condition. With the use of the universal language of moving pictures the true meaning of the brotherhood of man will have been established throughout the earth. For example, the Englishman will have learned that the soul of the Japanese is, essentially, the same as his own. The Frenchman will realize that the American's ideals are his ideals. All men are created equal.

. . . You will walk into your favorite film theatre and see your actors appearing in twice the size you see them now, because the screens will be twice

as large, and the film itself twice as large also. With these enlargements, "close-ups" will be almost eliminated, since it will be relatively easy to picture facial expression along with the full figure of the performer. It will always be necessary to picture the face in pictures. It is the face which reflects the soul of a man.

Our "close-ups," or "inserts," as I call them, are sometimes cumbersome and disconcerting. I invented them, but I have tried not to overuse them, as many have done. It is a mechanical trick, and is of little credit to anyone.

We shall say there are now five elaborate first-run picture theatres on one New York street, Broadway. In 2024 there will be at least forty. Cities of 1,000 will average at least six. Cities of 20,000 and thereabout will have over a hundred. By virtue of its

great advantage in scope, the motion picture will be fitted to tell certain stories as no other medium can. But I must add that the glory of the spoken or written word in the intimate and poetic drama can never be excelled by any form of expression.

In the year 2024 our directors of the better order will be men graduated from schools, academies, and colleges carrying in their curriculum courses in motion-picture direction. Our actors and actresses will be artists graduated from schools and colleges either devoted exclusively to the teaching and study of motion-picture acting or carrying highly specialized courses in acting before the camera. This is inevitable.

It really seems to me a bit humorous now to realize how narrow a place in our everyday life the film is playing, despite the great rise in attendance in the last few years. One hundred years hence, I believe, the airplane passenger lines will operate motion-picture shows on regular schedule between New York and Chicago and between New York and London. Trains, which will be traveling twice or three times as fast as they do now, will have film theatres on board. Almost every home of good taste will have its private projection room where miniatures, perhaps, of the greater films will be shown to the family, and, of course, families will make their albums in motion pictures instead of in tintypes and "stills." Steamships will boast of first runs, which will be brought to them in mid-ocean by the airplanes, and I may add that almost all subjects in our schools will be taught largely with the use of picture play and the educational animated picture.

By the time these things come to pass, there will be no such thing as a flicker in your film. Your characters and objects in pictures will come upon the screen (which by then may not even be white, and certainly may not be square, or look anything like what it does now), and they will appear to the onlookers precisely as these persons and objects appear in real life. That much-discussed "depth" in pictures, which no one as yet has been able to employ successfully, will long since have been discovered and adopted. The moving canvas will not appear flat, but if a character moves before a fireplace you will recognize the distance as between the character and the fireplace. Likewise, in landscapes, you will feel the proper sense of distance. Your mountain peaks will not appear to rise one on top of the other,

D. W. Griffith

but will appear exactly as if you stood and looked at them. Of course these are merely details that will require long and intense study and experiment, but they will come. In other words, from the standpoint of naturalness, motion pictures one hundred years from now will be so nearly like the living person or the existing object pictured that you will be unable, sitting in your orchestra seat, to determine whether they are pictures of the real thing.

By a perfection of the studio lighting system, film will be smooth before the eye as if it were a stationary lighted picture. By that time the studios will have changed greatly, and instead of actors being forced to work before great blinding lights, which now at times register 117

degrees of heat, we shall have "cold" lights. We are experimenting in these already. Our studios will be great spreading institutions, as large as many of the cities surrounding New York. I think that one hundred years from now there will be no concentrated motion-picture production such as our Hollywood of today. Films will be made in various cities, most of which will be located near to New York.

Now let us prepare for a small-sized shock. One hundred years from today it will cost perhaps twice as much as it costs today to see the really first-class cinema. It is perfectly proper that it should. Time, effort, energy, and preparation put into pictures at that time will have advanced greatly. I am just honest enough to say that I do not at the moment understand how more time, effort, energy, and preparation could have been put into my own pictures; but, then, for the average large picture play this will hold true. The average supposedly high-class film play in 2024 will be on view at not less than $5 a seat.

In looking into the crystal I have seen many things which I have not touched upon here. Perhaps they would be too tedious to bring out and discuss. But of one thing I may place myself on record plainly and without qualification. The motion picture is a child that has been given life in our generation. As it grows older it will develop marvelously. We poor souls can scarcely visualize or dream of its possibilities. We ought to be kind with it in its youth, so that in its maturity it may look back upon its childhood without regrets. ∎

MEDIALAB

Predicting the Future

1. Griffith predicted that film will contribute to international understanding. Has it done so, or has it increased misunderstanding between peoples?

2. What prediction did Griffith make that turned out correct? Which were incorrect?

3. Look into your own crystal ball and write a brief essay in which you predict any one of the following:

"The Movies 100 Years from Now"

"Television 100 Years from Now"

"The Electronic Home of the Future"

"Radio and Records in 100 Years"

"The Newspaper in 100 Years"

4. Read the two announcements at the bottom of this page. Do you think either of the two fictional "news items of the future" might come true? Why or why not?

5. Read the two advertisements on the following pages. In what way do they resemble ads for "new" inventions today? Why do radios cost less today than they did in the first six decades of the twentieth century?

6. Read and report on one magazine article about mass media in the future.

7. What new inventions related to television are now making their way into the average household? Why is television changing more than radio or movies?

8. In what ways are computers becoming a communication device useful in the home?

9. Read the following announcements again. What do you think of the idea that a knowledge of filmmaking is essential for survival in contemporary society? Would you want to watch a full-length film in 12 minutes? How important are films in your life?

(AP)—New York. Speed Viewing, Inc., announced today that it is expanding its services to 50 major population areas. Speed Viewing claims that schools have not properly taught students how to watch cinema. Their course helps young and old alike to increase their viewing speed. Special projectors with adjustable speeds are used as practice aids. Some students, the institute claims, are able to view such classics as *War and Peace* and *Woodstock* in twelve minutes with full retention.

(AP)—Washington. The U.S. Office of Education announced today that 8 percent of the population is still unable to make films. In fact many of these ill-cinemates cannot distinguish between a zoom and a cut. It also announced that funds are being made available so that adults can take remedial filmmaking at night school. The office reminded Americans that such a basic skill as filmmaking is utterly essential for survival in contemporary society.

The Magnavox Reproducer and the Magnavox Power Amplifier

"These two devices have revolutionized Radio"

MAGNAVOX Radio equipment takes the feeble sound vibrations produced by your receiving set and builds them up into full, round tones in exact accordance with the original broadcasted speech or music.

The development of the Magnavox is one of Radio's spectacular achievements.

Magnavox R3 Reproducer and 2 stage Power Amplifier, as illustrated . . $90.00

R2 Magnavox Reproducer with 18-inch curved horn: the utmost in amplifying power; requires only ⅙ of an ampere for field . $60.00

R3 Magnavox Reproducer with 14-inch curved horn: ideal for homes, etc. $35.00

Model C Magnavox Power Amplifier insures getting the largest possible power input for your Magnavox Reproducer . . 2 stage $55.00 3 stage 75.00

Magnavox Products can be had from good dealers everywhere. Write for new booklet.

THE MAGNAVOX CO. Oakland, Cal. New York: 370 Seventh Ave.

MAGNAVOX Radio The Reproducer Supreme

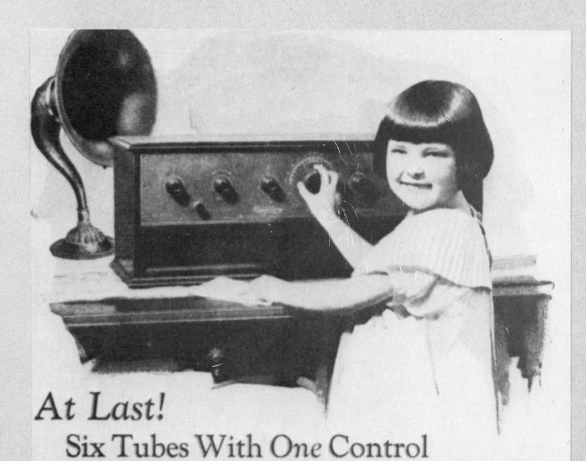

At Last!
Six Tubes With One Control

NOTHING like it has been seen or heard before. Thermiodyne embodies an entirely new principle of radio reception—so simplified and so certain that a child can tune in six to ten stations a minute. If it's in the air Thermiodyne will get it.

Calibrations are in wave lengths, just as listed in the daily press. There is nothing to remember, no figuring to do, no fuss or bother. Select the station wanted, turn arrow to position—the station clicks in at once.

It comes in at the same point always, no matter where the set may be—all other stations are shut out completely—and each signal is loud, clear and wholly free from distortion. Local stations and distant stations cannot interfere.

Tubes, batteries or loud speaker of any kind may be used. Mounted on Bakelite panel and enclosed in handsome mahogany cabinet. Unconditionally guaranteed.

Write for descriptive folder containing the whole wonderful story of Thermiodyne. Ask your dealer to demonstrate Thermiodyne against any set he has, regardless of cost.

Price $140

Without Accessories

DEALERS and JOBBERS

Write for full particulars regarding franchise for selling the most remarkable receiving set on the market. A few territories are still available, but act quickly.

THERMIODYNE RADIO CORPORATION   PLATTSBURGH, N. Y.

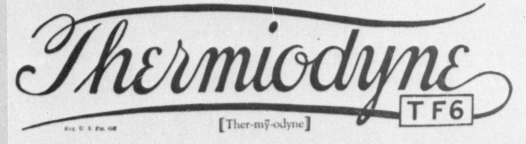

[Ther-mȳ-odyne]

TF6

INDEX

ACKNOWLEDGMENTS

Readings

"The Allure of Daytime Television Drama," reprinted with permission of *Popular Psychology*, 1972, pp 37–41. "TV Violence *IS* Harmful," by Jesse L. Steinfeld, reprinted with permission from the April 1973 *Reader's Digest*. Copyright 1973 by the Reader's Digest Assn., Inc. "Why Do Two Networks Refuse to Run This Commercial?" Reproduced with permission, © Mobil Oil Corporation. "In Defense of Television," and "Some Questions to Ask Yourself About Your Own TV Watching" by Peggy Charren and Martin W. Sandler, from *Changing Channels* © 1983, Addison-Wesley, Reading Massachusetts, pp 2, 3, 5, 6, 152 & 153. Reprinted with permission. "Of Directors, Magic, and Waterfalls of Salad Dressing," from *The Best Thing on TV—Commercials* by Jonathan Price. Copyright © 1978. Reprinted with permission of Viking Penguin Inc., New York. "Keeping the Customer Satisfied," by Richard Corliss. Copyright 1984 Time Inc. All rights reserved. Reprinted by permission from *Time*. "Summer Movies," by Michael Healy. Reprinted with permission of *The Denver Post*. "The Technique of the Gag Cartoonist," from *The Fourth Estate: An Informal Appraisal of the News and Opinion Media* copyright © 1971 by John L. Hulteng and Roy Paul Nelson. By permission of Harper & Row Publishers, Inc. "What Comics Can Teach You About Movies," by Steve Gerber, reprinted from *SUPER-8 FILMAKER*, vol 2, No. 5, 145 East 45th Street, New York 10017. "How to Manage TV News," by Joe Saltzman, full professor and chairman of the Journalism Department at USC. "The Accident, A Cross Media Study." From pp 7–17 in *the News Business* by John Chancellor and Walter Mears. By permission of Harper & Row Publishers, Inc. From *More Language That Needs Watching* by Theodore M. Bernstein. Copyright © 1962 by Theodore M. Bernstein. Reprinted by permission of the author and Atheneum Publishers. From 1985 *Writer's Market* copyright 1984 by Writer's Digest Books. "Rock & Riches," by Allan Parachini. Copyright © 1974 Ziff-Davis Publishing Company, reprinted by permission of *Stereo Review Magazine*. "The Home Computer Terminal," by Hollis Vail, from *The Futurist*, December 1980. Published with permission of the World Future Society, 4916 St. Elmo Avenue, Washington, DC 20014.

Illustrations

A. C. Nielsen: 21; Advertising Age: 206–207; AP/Wide World Photos: 52, 177, 216, 226–227, 260, 267; Apple Computer: 287; Archive Pictures, Inc.: iii, 72–73; AT & T Corporate Archives: 302; The Bettmann Archive Inc.: 213–214, 261, 307; Billboard Publications, Inc.: 232; *Boston Evening Transcript* reproduction courtesy of the Library of Congress: 49; Brian Seed © 1985 Click/Chicago: ii, 196–197; Brown Brothers: 215; CBS Entertainment Press Information: 8, 13; *Chicago Tribune* Media Services: 24, 26, 114–117, 140; *Chicago Tribune*: 80, 175; Control Data: 297; Johnson & Shiromani: 30; LASERPHOTO: ii–iii, 156, 260; *Mad Magazine*: 20; Marvel Comics Group: 126, 128–130; Milt & Joan Mann: iii, vi–vii; Movie Still Archive: 263; National Aeronautics and Space Administration: 134–135, 261, 276–277; *New Yorker* Magazine: 2–3; Nikon Inc.: 205; North American Philips Corporation: 229, 230; Panavision—photography by Frank and Ron Bez: 100; United Press International Inc.: 182; various drawings: Vernon McKissack.

NTC LANGUAGE ARTS BOOKS

Business Communication
Business Communication Today!
Thomas & Fryar
Handbook for Business Writing,
Baugh, Fryar & Thomas

Essential Skills
The Book of Forms for Everyday
Living, *Rogers*
Building Real Life English Skills,
Starkey & Penn
English Survival Series, *Maggs*
Essential Life Skills Series
Everyday Consumer English,
Kleinman & Weissman

Genre Literature
Another Tomorrow: A Science Fiction
Anthology, *Hollister*
The Detective Story, *Schwartz*
The Short Story & You, *Simmons &
Stern*
You and Science Fiction, *Hollister*

Journalism
Getting Started in Journalism,
Harkrider
Journalism Today! *Ferguson & Patten*

Language, Writing and Composition
An Anthology for Young Writers,
Meredith
The Art of Composition, *Meredith*
Lively Writing, *Schrank*
Look, Think & Write, *Leavitt & Sohn*
Writing in Action, *Meredith*
Writing by Doing, *Sohn & Enger*

Media
Photography in Focus, *Jacobs &
Kokrda*
Television Production Today! *Kirkham*
Understanding Mass Media, *Schrank*
Understanding the Film, *Johnson &
Bone*

Mythology
Mythology and You, *Rosenberg &
Baker*
Welcome to Ancient Greece, *Millard*
Welcome to Ancient Rome, *Millard*
World Mythology, *Rosenberg*

Reading
Reading by Doing, *Simmons & Palmer*

Speech
The Basics of Speech, *Galvin, Cooper
& Gordon*
Contemporary Speech, *HopKins &
Whitaker*
Creative Speaking, *Buys, et al.*
Creative Speaking Series
Dynamics of Speech, *Myers &
Herndon*
Getting Started in Public Speaking,
Prentice & Payne
Listening by Doing, *Galvin*
Literature Alive! *Gamble & Gamble*
Person to Person, *Galvin & Book*
Public Speaking Today! *Prentice &
Payne*
Speaking by Doing, *Buys, Sills & Beck*

Theatre
The Book of Cuttings for Acting &
Directing, *Cassady*
The Book of Scenes for Acting
Practice, *Cassady*
The Dynamics of Acting, *Snyder &
Drumsta*
An Introduction to Theatre and Drama,
Cassady & Cassady
Play Production Today! *Beck, et al.*

For a current catalog and information about our complete line
of language arts books, write:
National Textbook Company,
a division of NTC Publishing Group
4255 West Touhy Avenue
Lincolnwood (Chicago), Illinois 60646-1975 U.S.A.